ANTIQUE COMBS & PURSES

by Evelyn Haertig

Gallery Graphics Press

Antique Combs and Purses

Editor: R. A. McCormack
Design Director: Paul Pfanner
       Pfanner + Catheron + Brown Design Inc.
Production: Anne Peyton
Typography: Alphabet Type
Printing: Times Printers Sdn. Bhd.

ISBN 0-943294-002
Library of Congress card number 81-90128

Printed in Singapore

Produced by The Newport Press, 1920 East Warner Ave., Santa Ana, California 92705 for the publishers, Gallery Graphics Press, Carmel, California.

Private collections photographed by Milton Haertig.

CONTENTS

A sapphire bodkin for the hair.
Or sparkling facet diamonds there;
Then turquoise, ruby, emrauld rings,
For fingers: and such pretty things,
As diamond pendants for the ears,
Must needs be had, or two pearl pears,
Pearl necklace, large and oriental,
And diamond, and of amber pale.

EVELYN.. A Voyage to Maryland. 1690.

PREFACE AND ACKNOWLEDGEMENTS

Following a quarter of a century spent in secondary teaching and antique collecting, I retired to become an active dealer in antiques. Somehow my interest in American brilliant cut glass, which I had avidly pursued for many years, waned, and was replaced by an equally passionate interest in combs and purses. Much to my distress I found there was virtually no scholarly material on either topic nor has any book been devoted entirely to purses, and only one privately printed and privately distributed nearly sixty years ago, deals with combs.

There are a surprising number of comb and purse collectors for whom there exists no information, no readily available resource, no pictorial reference by which their collections may be dated, compared and fully appreciated. Though a few books on the development of costume give them passing reference and museums world wide host at least nominal collections, no comprehensive text exists, to my knowledge, exclusively dealing with combs or purses. This is the first volume which attempts, therefore, to cover the origin and development of combs and purses for the antique dealer, collector, historian, designer, museum, and the reader who, for whatever reason, wishes to learn more about these useful and decorative articles of apparel. Four years in the writing, it has been an unbelievably expensive undertaking.

Hopefully it will enlighten, assist in categorizing and identifying objects in a collection and provide pictorial evidence of both rare and easily obtainable specimens. There are more of the latter by far, for rare and costly museum pieces are generally unobtainable to the average collector.

Grateful acknowledgement is made to the many friends, collectors, show devotees, antique dealers, historical societies, and museums whose encouragement and enthusiasm, willingness to share their collections and expertise have made this book possible.

I am indebted to Louise Doyle for allowing me to use the work of her father, the late Bernard W. Doyle, to Mrs. Alice Sawyer for her encouragement and sharing her marvelous collection of combs with me and others; to Mrs. Evelyn Hachey and John Graves of the Leominster and Clinton Historical Societies for allowing me such free access to their treasures and extending kindnesses beyond expectation; to Mrs. Gerri Levine for counsel and research assistance; to Augenstein King for so many gifts; to Kikki Smith a special thank you; to all of these people and museums who so kindly lent their collections and extended aid and comfort…a heartfelt thank you. I sincerely hope the book will meet your expectations in some measure and that it will aid researchers after me to add to the body of knowledge on the fascinating subjects of combs and purses.

Evelyn Haertig
Carmel, California
1982

ANTIQUE SECTION I
COMBS

FRONTISPIECE. Beautifully executed in tortoise shell, this commemorative comb is by the Harris Co. of Clinton, Massachusetts. The pony express and train symbolize a century of progress, 1776-1876.

CHAPTER 1
ANTIQUITY IN COMBS

Regardless of whether one lives in a primitive or sophisticated society, is young or old, rich or poor, educated or illiterate, religious or agnostic, traditional in life style or oblivious to the social mores of the group within which he lives, regardless of race or political persuasion or any of the many factors which divide humanity, he will own and use the oldest known accessory of dress, the comb. Combs are worthy of study as objects of art and as historical artifacts.

Anthropologists conjecture that the first comb was not a comb at all but the fingers of the human hand which originally disentangled, smoothed, and helped cleanse the locks of prehistoric man. This theory was formally advanced in 1927, by Professor J. Rendell Harris of Cambridge University, in a lecture entitled, ''The Comb in Human History'', in which he theorized that the prevalence of the five and ten tooth combs evolved from the human hand. Lending credence to this theory are two curious combs which can be found in the Chesters Museum, Cilurnum, England, which have been authenticated by the British Museum as having come from a region near the ruins of an ancient Roman Wall in Northern England. These decorated bone combs are in the form of a hand and wrist approximately six inches in length. Each hand contains ten fingers; the wrist and arm portions are so elongated they leave no doubt that they are indeed shaped as hands.

The desire to improve on the hand brought about a more efficient, rigid, useful implement probably first formed of wood or the bones of fishes. During the Stone Age, (10-15,000 B.C.) combs of bone and ivory were formed, using stone implements, into crude

Drawing of ancient comb found in Roman ruins in England. "Hand" has 10 fingers.

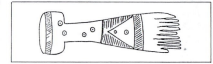

animal, bird and fish shapes atop long teeth. These combs have endured due to the nature of the material, whereas most of those carved of wood have deteriorated or crumbled completely, though fragments may be viewed at major museums throughout the world. In the United States the Metropolitan Museum in New York has unrivaled collections in their Egyptian, Greek and Roman galleries.

With the advent of metals in the Bronze, Iron, and Brass Ages (4,000-1,000 B.C.) combs could be cast, though few ancient combs of these materials have survived. Tools made from these metals such as knives, saws, drills, chisels, and the like enabled man to work with harder materials notably horn, ivory, bone, baleen, walrus, alabaster, onyx, tortoise shell, hardwoods such as ebony, fruitwoods, boxwood and even such exotic materials as slate, iron, tin, and lead. Delicate inlays were also made possible, and as machines as we know them did not exist prior to the mid 18th century, all were accomplished by hand artistry.

At the outset combs should properly be divided into two classifications: the straight, utilitarian or dressing comb, and the decorative comb, which in addition to securing the hair in place acts as an ornament and has come to be defined as a jewel when enriched with precious and semi-precious stones and constructed of rare and costly metals. Considering man's penchant for personal adornment it is probable that the decorative comb or hair ornament was used long before the Egyptians dominated the ancient world, but in order to serve the best interest of the modern collector, the scope of this work will concentrate on the European, Asian, North American and African cultures (as it pertains to ancient Egypt).

Combs found in Egyptian tombs dating from 4,000–2,500 B.C. are both wooden and ivory, the wooden ones being very modern in appearance much like the small pocket comb carried today having 16–23 medium spaced teeth, rounded ends, and simple line drawings above the teeth as a form of decoration. The

attached to the base of the case by a pin. Compared to a modern comb, it is only 3/4 of an inch shorter, with a pyramid shaped bridge.

The Etruscans were an interesting people who are something of an enigma to historians. They appear to have been of Asian pre-Roman stock and had a highly developed culture which was modified by their trade with Greece. Their simple ivory combs had such charming bird designs that they were imitated during the Byzantine Era, (9th century A.D.) though the latter comb is approximately twice the size and is somewhat more elaborate.

Two fine examples of Consecration Combs, so called because they were used during the consecration of bishops and at other devotional acts of the higher clergy, are found at [*Plate 4, Fig. 4*] and [*Plate 4, Fig. 5*]. Both are of ivory and beautifully carved though *Figure 4* appears quite mundane in composition. It was called the Comb of St. Hildegard from the 6th century A.D. and was in the possession of the last Abbess of the Nunnery at Elbigen, Rudesheim, Germany, until 1803. It was seen and sketched by Hefner-Alteneck when in the possession of her heirs, but its present whereabouts is unknown.

The comb of St. Herbert is from the 9th century A.D. and is in the Public Museum at Cologne, Ger-

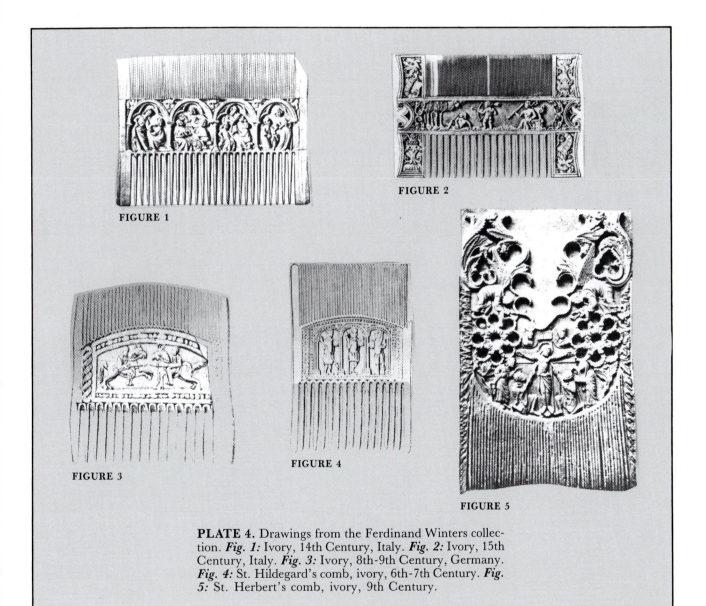

FIGURE 1

FIGURE 2

FIGURE 3

FIGURE 4

FIGURE 5

PLATE 4. Drawings from the Ferdinand Winters collection. *Fig. 1:* Ivory, 14th Century, Italy. *Fig. 2:* Ivory, 15th Century, Italy. *Fig. 3:* Ivory, 8th-9th Century, Germany. *Fig. 4:* St. Hildegard's comb, ivory, 6th-7th Century. *Fig. 5:* St. Herbert's comb, ivory, 9th Century.

FIGURE 1

PLATE 5. *Fig. 1.* Late 18th Century
Russian Holmogor, ivory *(courtesy The
Walters Art Gallery, Baltimore, Maryland).*
Fig. 2: 12th Century Siculo-Arabic,
ivory *(ibid Fig. 1).*

FIGURE 2

many. It too is ivory and is a significant comb of large dimensions, being 6 × 4-1/2 inches. It shows the influence of the beautiful rose which later becomes inseparable from the Renaissance and the Gothic church motifs in particular. The crucified Christ is shown among the angels and sacred figures.

Two 17th century ivory combs 5-1/4 × 2-3/4 inches have teeth of uniform spacing, the teeth are wide and flat rather than pointed. Each of the three adjacent teeth is a short step longer and sharply pointed. Across the top of the bridge are some fanciful profiles of a warrior with some type of armour, a beaded headdress, long stylized curly hair, gripping a nasty looking, wavy edged broadsword. Two of the creatures have curved beaks and feathered necks, the other two look like overfed, openmouthed dogs, although I am sure they are mythical creatures of some sort; perhaps a lion such as is shown with a well modeled body and a most unlionlike head. It is the Russian or Norse words which are curious and are probably associated with a saga of bold warriors. [*Plate 5, Fig. 1*] Although the double Siculo-Arabic comb which follows was carved in the 12th century, note the incised dog. He has the proportions and alert stance of any dog drawn yesterday, cartoon style. The

encircled birds are easily recognizable also, as the art closely follows that of the Western world [*Plate 5, Fig. 2*].

FROM THE 9TH century throughout the Middle Ages combs continued to be decorated as were other art forms, by such sacred motifs as the adoration of the Virgin, the crucifixion, monks toiling in vineyards, various religious rites and the martyrdom of the saints. Worldly motifs ranged from battle scenes, panoramas of love and adoration, courtiers dancing in long stately lines, mythical beasts and birds, peasants frolicking in courtyards and figures so imperfectly rendered it is impossible to tell what the action represents. In each instance, profane or sacred, there is an attempt to tell a story significant to both the comb maker and the user relative to their day and age. Defective as these combs may be, they give an accurate picture of the events considered worthy of recall and record.

Occasionally a comb was fitted with a ring and worn about the neck, indicating its value as a bit of decoration and utility, but for the most part they continued to be made along traditional lines, neither the size nor shape varying greatly. Double sided combs were popular on the European continent, though single sided combs were made as well. Oriental combs

PLATE 6. 13th Century etching by Ritter Van Turm, "Of a noble lady as she stands in front of her mirror preening herself and how she saw the Devil in the mirror showing his behind." The sins of pride and vanity were favorite subjects of etchers in the Middle Ages, intended to keep the womenfolk meek and virtuous, paying less attention to their appearance.

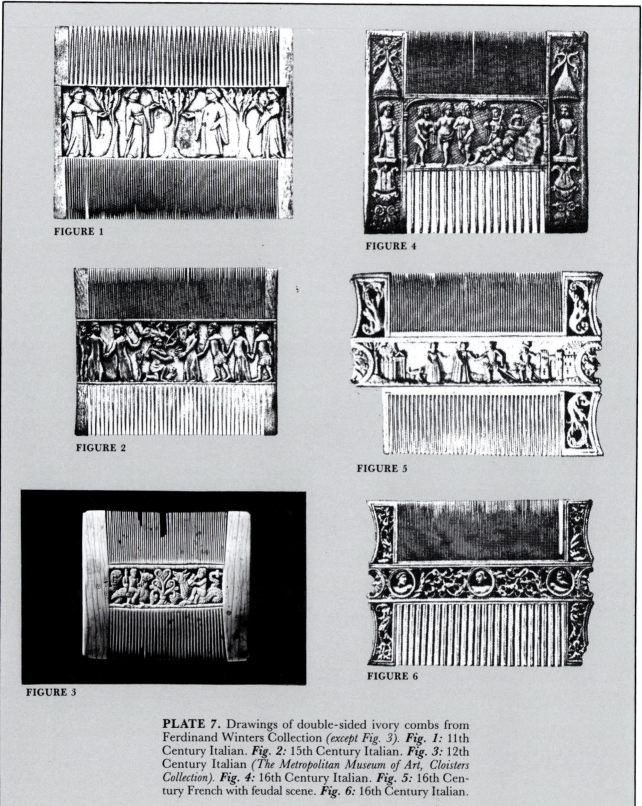

FIGURE 1

FIGURE 2

FIGURE 3

FIGURE 4

FIGURE 5

FIGURE 6

PLATE 7. Drawings of double-sided ivory combs from Ferdinand Winters Collection *(except Fig. 3)*. ***Fig. 1:*** 11th Century Italian. ***Fig. 2:*** 15th Century Italian. ***Fig. 3:*** 12th Century Italian *(The Metropolitan Museum of Art, Cloisters Collection)*. ***Fig. 4:*** 16th Century Italian. ***Fig. 5:*** 16th Century French with feudal scene. ***Fig. 6:*** 16th Century Italian.

appear to have been single sided from the 14th century onward.

The finer teeth of the double sided comb were used for removing lice, vermin, small particles of dirt, twigs or straw from the hair, and the coarser teeth for actually separating the strands of hair in preparation for some form of coiffure. It should be borne in mind the standards of cleanliness which are practiced today were unknown until approximately the last 50 years. The daily or bi-weekly shampoo was probably only accomplished in six month intervals and not at all in the winter months, as it was thought to jeopardize the health to bathe. Even royalty slept on the rudest of rope beds on which a straw mattress of sorts was placed, which contained all manner of insects. A noteable exception to unkempt hair and lack of body cleanliness were the Viking tribes, whose long blond tresses were carefully groomed and were considered the most valuable masculine attribute a warrior could display. There are many tales of the inordinate care that they gave the hair and from them conquered people learned the art of hair care. The ancient Greeks and Romans had been famous for their baths—as was

PLATE 8. 5th Century B.C. solid gold Scythian comb and close-up showing detail *(Hermitage Museum, U.S.S.R.)*.

15

the Turkish Empire—but during the Dark Ages such refinements were abandoned in an unstable and coarse feudal society.

Wooden Viking combs measuring approximately 3 inches, which contain one row of medium fine teeth only, have been found in Scotland dating from the 9th century. One such comb has a rudimental design on an arched bridge, and another fits neatly into a bone case with matching design.

IN ANY EXAMINATION of dressing combs three celebrated combs deserve attention for their beauty, extraordinary workmanship and novelty, if for no other reasons. The first, the most valuable comb in existence, was discovered in the ancient royal tombs at Solokha, now in the Hermitage Museum, Leningrad, U.S.S.R. [*Plate 8*] Dating from the fifth century, B.C., it is credited to Greek goldsmiths commissioned by Scythian royal command and is of pure gold. The Scythians were a nomadic ancient people famed for their savagery. They lived in the steppes of the Black Sea and the Sea of Aral, and though Iranian in stock, they were influenced to a high degree by the Greek civilization which was then flourishing. Their warlike nature is reflected in the design of the comb depicting two infantrymen and a mounted cavalryman, engaged in battle; a wounded horse lies in the background. The clothing, hairstyles, and weapons reveal them as barbarians, a name attributed by the Greeks to those whose culture was foreign to their own.

The Greek historian Herodotus noted the Scythians believed in life after death and it is because of this belief that the comb was found. The Scythians buried their leader, killing and entombing with him his favorite horses, wife, servants, and household effects. The tomb was filled forming an embankment as high as possible. This tomb when unearthed contained five horses and their trappings; at a lower level, the king and a young slave, the keeper of the horses and a royal cup bearer. Around the corpses were vessels holding the food and drink which they considered necessary in the new world. Near the head of the ruler was a comb 4-7/8 inches high, 4 inches long, and 1/4 inch thick, made of pure gold weighing 10-3/8 ounces. At today's gold value the comb would be worth over $4,000!

The figures were soldered lightly to the bridge of the comb which is separated from the teeth by five reclining lions, all superbly detailed and executed. One author doubts this comb belonged to a woman because of the masculine subject matter being inappropriate as an ornament. I believe him wrong on both counts, as the comb is not an ornament at all, and why did it have to belong to a woman? It is clearly a utility comb used by both sexes and the size is quite compatible with similar combs of this era, though the decoration and the material place it in a category unique unto itself. Even had the comb been intended for a lady's use, male craftsmen used ornamentation symbolic to a whole people such as fierce animals, mythical beasts, wrestling matches, battles, insects and reptiles, all with precious little regard for the potential feminine user.

BY SHEER COINCIDENCE the remaining combs are of Russian origin but their novelty and sentimentality are immediately recognized. Made of mammoth ivory in the 18th century, [*Plate 13*] it is the most romantic comb of them all, and a puzzling one at that. When deciphered from the Russian the message reads, ''I present it to him whom I love.'' Was this a comb commissioned by a nobleman to be given to a lover, relative, spouse or a dear friend? It is possible the love referred to is not romantic but filial or the deep friendship felt by one person for another.

Ivory obtained from the extinct wooly mammoth in all probability was expensive and it is unlikely the carver would have made it for his personal use. It may be the carefully balanced, beautifully executed message will forever remain a mystery.

The second ivory comb [*Plate 12, Fig. 1*] leaves no doubt as to its owner or date; there is, however, some controversy over the country of origin. Walters Art Gallery, to whom the comb belongs, believes it to be Russian though it cannot be verified. Mr. Walters purchased the comb at Trondjheim, Norway, in 1900. The dispute centers around the double eagle and crown motif which depicts the eagle grasping a sword in one claw and a sceptre in the other. The crown could well be the Romanov crown. The symbols in the lower left and right corners appear to have some religious significance. Some feel the comb is not Russian, as the name Michael Bauer is in Roman letters rather than in the Russian Cyrillic alphabet used in Russia from the 6th century onward.

A similar comb is attributed to Vierlanden (Germany), circa at least 19th century, probably 18th. It is made of ivory and the shape is identical to the Russian comb. It is the shape which is intriguing, as these are the only specimens known to have coarse, fine and medium teeth on a single comb. The shape is pleasing and the adroitness of the carver, as well as his resourcefulness, make it a most remarkable piece. The background or field between the triad is filled with the same overall coiling of leaves and tendrils as shown in the Bauer comb. Two cherubs support a crown canopying a large wreathed heart, but there is no name or date to help establish its source.

THE ANCIENT NEAR Eastern cultures of Egypt, Babylonia, Persia, and Assyria wore symbolic false

PLATE 9. "Portrait of a Lady," Franco-Flemish *(National Gallery of Art, Washington, D.C.)*.

FIGURE 1

FIGURE 2

PLATE 10. Fifteenth Century Italian noblewomen. *Fig. 1:* Simonetta Vespucci by Sandro Botticelli. Pearls are entwined in braided and coiled hair bound in velvet ribbon. Feather ornaments are supported by holder atop head. *(Stadelsches Kunstinstitut, Franfurt Au Main.)* *Fig. 2:* "Madonna" by Fra Filippo Lippi del Carmine *(1406-1469).* Typical 15th Century garb, with ethereal, gossamer-like headdress trimmed with pearls. Graduated "V" of pearls on forehead is symbolic rather than practical. *(Musee Conde, Chantilly.)* *Fig. 3:* Another portrait of Simonetta Vespucci, this by Piero di Cosimo. Elaborate coiffeur contains small jewels and pearls, with strands of pearls running over and under stiff braids. A red velvet cap is worn beneath the braids. Typical 15th Century hair ornamentation. *(Uffizi, Florence.)* *Fig. 4:* Beatrice Sforza by Alessandro Araldi. Gold hairnet is interspersed with jewels. Diadem of emeralds maintains the cap securely, and a pendant of pearl, emerald and ruby is suspended over the ear. Portrait has a very photographic quality *(ibid Fig. 3).*

beards and elaborate woolen wigs over shaved heads. The bright red, blue and green wigs protected the head from the brutal desert sun while strange as it seems, the evaporating perspiration actually lowered the body temperature.

In the 15th century B.C. Egyptian queens are known to have worn a hoodlike headdress of pure beaten gold inset with glass and gemstones. Felt crowns, feathers, ostrich plumes, linen braids were also owned by both sexes of the ruling classes.

Ivory, bone, gold hairpins and tiaras were probably first widely used by the ancient Greeks in the 2nd century B.C. to contain their natural hàir styles, which were worn in flat curls to the back of the head, in braids, coils and other upswept arrangements.

Greek and Roman dress consisted of a simple rectangle of cloth, usually linen or fine white wool, as wide as from the wearer's shoulders to the floor and pinned at the shoulders, variously called a palla, himation, or casula. The excess portion was often folded over the head forming a hood. The custom of thus covering the head, especially among women, continued in one form or another throughout the 11th century A.D. The wearing of combs, pins and other

FIGURE 3

FIGURE 4

ornamentation was therefore superfluous and many odd headcoverings including the hennin, barbette, wimple, heuke, crespine and baldric were worn for the next three centuries. These headcoverings survive even to the present day in certain habits worn by Roman Catholic nuns. They so concealed the hair that only unmarried girls were seen in public with exposed tresses.

The 15th century may be considered the dividing line between the Dark Ages and the Renaissance in Europe, and Italy under the De Medici, Este, Montefeltro, Gonza, and Malatesta families led the way. Costumes were rich and elegant in accordance with the sumptuous life style the rulers of the city states had managed to achieve by fair means or foul. The practice of shaving the forehead was adopted by the women of these dominions, as the royal houses of Valois, Tudor, and Burbon, were afflicted with hair so scant that one Spanish queen was virtually bald and Elizabeth I a century later lost much of her hair during a severe illness. It is a truism that absolute monarchs ruled absolutely and when they established a fashion it was slavishly followed. Better to shave the forehead than lose the whole head it was wisely

reasoned. The practice of shaving the forehead to match the royal lack of hair is clearly shown in the painting at *Plate 9.*

Originally credited to the Italian painter Pisanello (1410-40), the National Gallery of Art, Washington, D.C., now believes *Portrait of a Lady* to be of the 15th century Franco-Flemish School. Note the sharply detailed hair pins and the hair drawn forward into a sort of horn, a hair style popular in Italy but less so in other countries. Why this shaving of the head was considered an enhancement to beauty seems to rest more on the royal prerogative than on taste, it would appear.

Milia Davenport in her monumental, *The Book of Costume* (Page 244, Vol. I., 1979 Edition) tells us that ''The hair, clipped high on the neck, in service to the European idea of hairlessness, is otherwise shown and handled in a specifically Italian way. Instead of being enclosed in the conventional jewelled, reticulated net, it (the hair) is drawn forward, and bound around in a coronet arrangement with the ends looped back and ending in a little lock. . . . The decorative use of simple pins will also be noted in XVc. Flemish costume. The stuffed roundlet which

PLATE 11. Portrait of Elizabeth, Countess of Southampton, by an unknown artist. The Countess was a maid of honor to Elizabeth I. She is shown holding an inscribed ivory comb. *(From "English Domestic Needlework" by Therele Hughes.)*

FIGURE 1

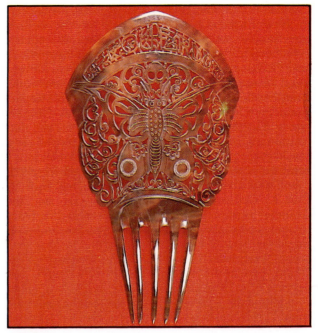

FIGURE 2

PLATE 14. *Fig. 1:* Tortoise comb, Ch'ing dynasty, 18th Century *(Metropolitan Museum of Art, bequest of Edward G. Kennedy)*. *Fig. 2:* 19th Century Chinese tortoise comb with ivory inserts *(Collection of Kathe Kilot)*.

PLATE 15. Chinese ivory comb *(Collection of Elizabeth Anne Buzzell)*. *Figs. 2 & 3:* 19th Century Chinese tortoise comb and shipping box *(author's collection)*.

FIGURE 1   FIGURE 2   FIGURE 3

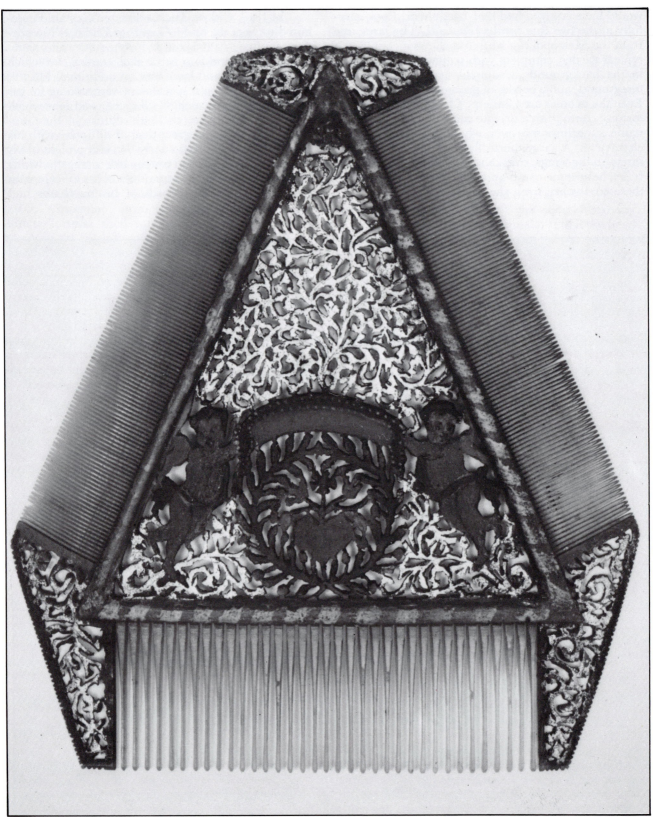

FIGURE 2

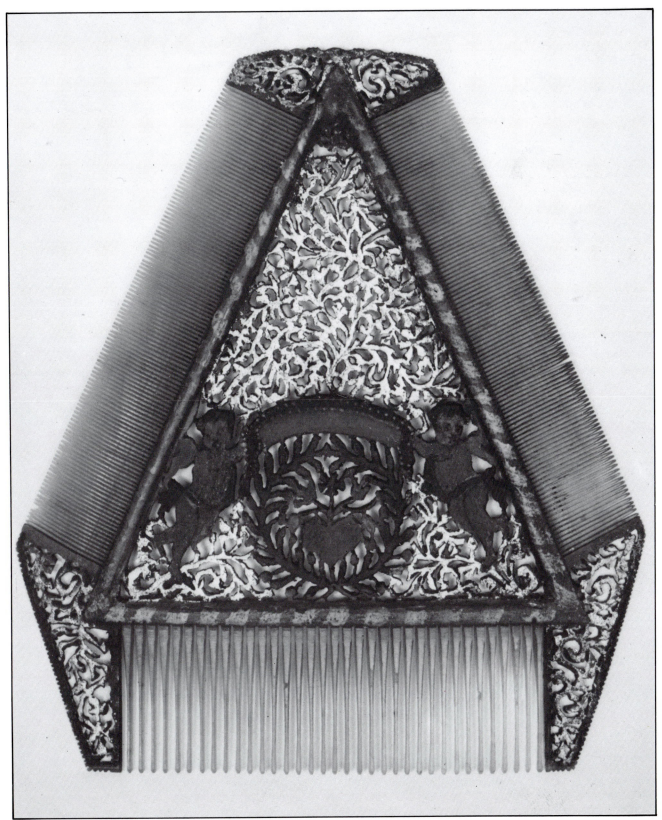

FIGURE 2

would have enjoyed had they used them. Look carefully at the two fine combs [*Plate 14*]. The large one from the Metropolitan Museum shows a couple in a typical garden complete with willow tree, a pagoda in the background, a sampan approaching in the foreground, and a border of peonies, buds and leaves. Even the peonies are Chinese. The smaller high back tortoise comb from a private collection has a word or name superimposed over what looks like Chinese characters. A large butterfly with mother-of-pearl insets on the wings, eyes, and body is center featured. It is a handsome comb and very impressive. Both of these combs are from the early 1800's.

In 1819, Gideon Tucker directed Captain Benjamin Shreve of the brig ''Governor Endicott'' to purchase for him, ''some blue and white stone china plates with gilt edge and four turtle shell combs'' for which he paid $34.00 and later sent an additional $16.00. Other Salem business speculators were anxious for the usual exotic items such as silks, tea, and fans which were imported during the 19th century by the thousands. Shreve had a great deal of difficulty with his ship and during a particularly bad storm eight of his crew of 19 were washed overboard, a tragedy which haunted Shreve for the remainder of his life. Captain Shreve kept careful records of his purchases and

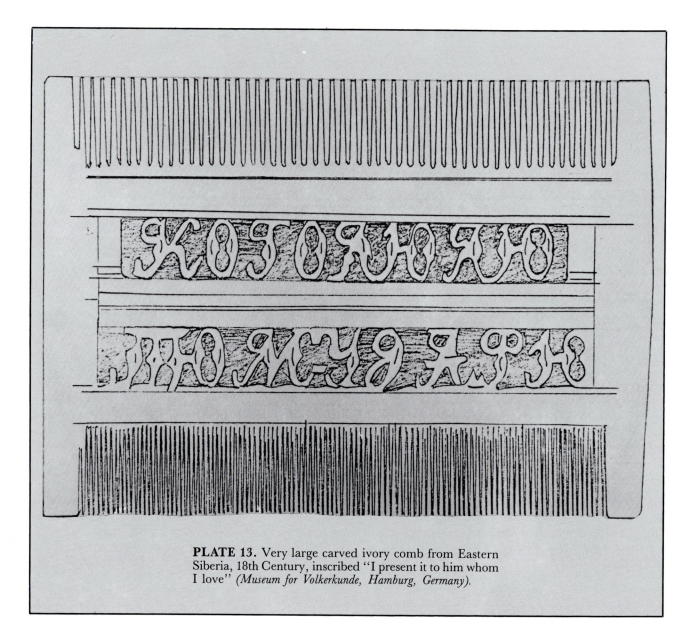

PLATE 13. Very large carved ivory comb from Eastern Siberia, 18th Century, inscribed ''I present it to him whom I love'' *(Museum for Volkerkunde, Hamburg, Germany).*

FIGURE 1

PLATE 12. Triangular ivory comb inscribed Michael Bauer and dated 1778, perhaps Russian *(The Walters Art Gallery, Baltimore)*. *Fig. 2:* Another triangular comb, this painted and gilded, from the 18th Century and thought to be a marriage comb *(Gewerke Museum, Bremen, Germany)*.

is set on the hair is in the twisted Italian form; its decoration in an eyelet-studded, rather than a reticulated pattern.''

The hair pins more closely resemble what are called ''horseshoe'' pins by stained glass craftsmen, rather than a true hair pin as they have only one shaft and an enlarged, flat head and are merely woven through some strands of the hair holding it in place.

Noble Italian ladies from the 15th century are shown on *Plate 10* illustrating several hair arrangements then popular among the ruling class. [*Fig. 1*] Sandro Botticelli's portrait of Simonetta Vespucci shows pearls entwined in braided and coiled hair bound with velvet ribbon. A feathered ornament is held in a container atop her head.

Fra Filippo Lippi del Carmine (1406-1469) presents his madonna (in actual fact she was his beautiful mistress named Lucrecia Buti) in typical 15th century garb with an ethereal gossamer-like headdress and halo, trimmed with pearls and a graduated V of symbolic pearls above the forehead.

Simonetta Vespucci must have been a rugged individual for she is never portrayed in the conventional garb worn by her contemporaries, though *Fig. 3* does show her with the shaved forehead just mentioned. She is seen by Piero di Cosimo (Musée Condé, Chantilly.) wearing an extremely elaborate coiffeur containing small jewels and pearls, while strands of pearls run under and over the stiff braids, beneath which is a rose velvet cap. The lady appears to have been fond of intricate and costly headdress.

[*Fig. 4*] Alessandro Araldi's portrait of Beatrice Sforza—first wife of the Duke of Urbino—shows a reticuled cap or hairnet of gold, interspersed with jewels and a diadem of emeralds which maintain the cap securely. Over the ear are an enormous pearl, emerald, and ruby suspended from the cap. Note the almost photographic quality of the painting style.

A century later in England the Countess of Southampton poses in her bedroom in rich embroidered dress; her ruff and finery showing in the background. Her forehead appears to have been shaved and she is holding her large ivory comb rather awkwardly, almost backward [*Plate 11*].

For the next three centuries (16th-19th) hoods, veils, wigs, caps, huge hats, ribbons, kerchiefs, nets, berets, turbans, bonnets were alternately stylish then discarded. Extreme styles such as the hennin, baldric, barberre, etc., were not revived, however.

In the American colonies wealthy men wore wigs which were generally restrained and simple but the ladies wore their own hair augmented by wiglets, curls, frizzes, switches and other false hair. The huge wigs worn at the French court in the closing years of the XVIII century were not adopted in America.

Natural hair styles required combs, pins, and decorations which American artisans prior to the American Revolution were able to supply in simple, rude styles but the finer tortoise and horn examples came from Europe. Those superb tortoise and ivory specimens which arrived from as unlikely a place as ancient China, constitute a fascinating story in itself.

China, once known as the ''Celestial Empire,'' after mistreatment by Portuguese merchants in the 1600's, had cut itself off from outside influences. Emperor Ch'ien Lung wrote to George III of England, in 1700, ''We possess all things. I set no value on objects strange or ingenious, and I have no use for your country's manufactures. This then is my answer to your request to appoint a representative at my court.''

There was established, however, on one street separated from the city itself, a port of trade at Canton where captains of foreign vessels might exchange goods with a few Chinese merchants. Both the Boston traders and the Chinese knew a good thing when they saw it and by 1780 a mutually profitable trade was in full swing. The Bostonians manufactured boots, shoes, rum, ginseng, cotton, quicksilver, etc., which they carried on sailing vessels to California and Oregon where some items were bartered for sea otter skins, hides, and tallow. The skins, finer than mink and warmer than sable, were highly prized by the Chinese, who learned in short order what the American market demanded, and they produced these goods for export only, making them to order virtually on the spot. What did the Americans want? The greatest demand, which could not be met elsewhere, was for tea; after all, they were, for the most part, transplanted Englishmen, and tea was a staple drink they had become accustomed to. Next to tea were the luxuries with which the wealthy merchant class (including the sea captains) adorned themselves and their mansions: hand painted wallpapers, silks, bronzes, rugs, porcelains, jade and ivory carvings, teak furniture, screens, spices *and* tortoise shell combs. Incidentally, the tortoise was taken from the South Sea Isles and Fiji to China, along with sandalwood, mother-of-pearl, pearls, and birds' nests. The Chinese were delighted. Many a ship's crew got their comeuppance, for the fierce Fijis slew and ate them whenever they got the chance. Considering the perils of the sea, pirates, cannibals, scurvy, the lengthy voyages, (up to 3 years at sea), fatigue, foul weather, being considered ''foreign devils'' by their reluctant hosts, it is nothing short of amazing any trade was possible at all.

THOUGH EXPORT GOODS were made to order they reflected the customs, manners, and appearance of the Chinese, so many of those combs which are so magnificently carved depict scenes which the Chinese

PLATE 16. A beautiful Chinese empress from the 19th Century is pictured wearing a Phoenix headdress. Close-up shows a typical example, in solid gold mesh. *(Courtesy National Gallery of Art, Washington, D.C.)*

HERODOTUS DESCRIBES THE bird though he confesses, ''I have not seen it myself except in a picture. Part of his plumage is gold-coloured, and part crimson; and he is for the most part very much like an eagle in outline and bulk.'' When its very existence was questioned in the 17th century, a wit named Alexander Ross is said to have retorted, ''His instinct teaches him to keep out of the way of the tyrant of the creation, man, for if he were to be got at, some wealthy glutton would surely devour him, though there were no more in the world.'' Symbolically, the dragon and phoenix bird appear on early combs and purses.

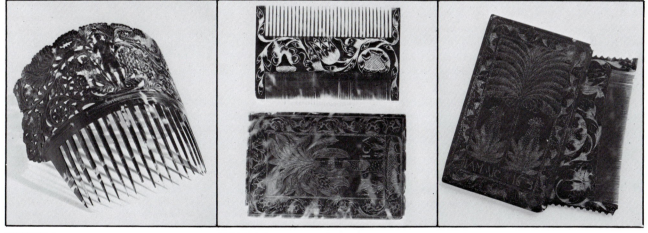

FIGURE 1   **FIGURE 2**   **FIGURE 3**

PLATE 17. Three tortoise shell combs from the Francis du Pont Winterthur Museum. *Fig. 1:* Carved by Alfred Willard, Boston, Massachusetts between 1820-1840. *Figs. 2 & 3:* Cased tortoise shell combs from Jamaica, c. 1673-1683.

CHAPTER 2

COMB MANUFACTURE IN THE UNITED STATES

Comb making in America developed in part at least from three oddly related factors; the harsh New England winter, the release of a mercenary Hessian following the British defeat in the American Revolution, and the loss of the British market for imported combs.

During the long winter months which prohibited working the land, farmers turned to comb making as a means of supplementing their incomes. There was a steady demand for combs of both the decorative and utilitarian types and the Revolution created a vacuum which had to be filled. Enter the enterprising Yankee who ultimately overtook the market by creating a superior product at a lower price, though the Europeans continued to manufacture and export fine combs to the United States for nearly a century.

It must be kept in mind that all women, without exception wore their hair long. Such styles required numerous pins, combs and ornaments, and a great deal of time and attention was lavished on the maintenance and embellishment of these tresses. Men of the upper classes wore wigs and long hair was fashionable for most men, so the comb was an essential toilet article for everyone regardless of sex or social station.

It is difficult for us for whom the comb is such a commonplace thing to imagine a time when the lowly comb was so highly prized that it was specifically mentioned in estate settlements and was considered so valuable that we read, "In 1653 Captain Edward Hull, a pirate, robbed a trading station at Block Island owned by one Captain Kempo Sebarda, and among other goods stole one hundred of Combs, 2 lbs. 10 shillings." And in 1666, Nicholas Vanden, a servant who ran away from his master, Robert Cross, of Ipswich, was accused of "breaken open a cheast steelin' a come cost 12 pence money."

These early combs were invariably made of three materials; horn, tortoise shell, or ivory, and they were often works of art intended to last several lifetimes, and they did!

As the domestic manufacture of ivory combs was limited due to the exotic nature of the material and the difficulties in working ivory, it is best to examine the two remaining natural substances in detail, returning later to consider ivory.

Most authorities credit Enoch Noyes of West Newbury, Massachusetts, as the founder of the comb industry in the United States, although Doyle in his book, *Comb Making in America* (Perry Walton, Boston, 1926), mentions a certain Captain Robert Cook of Needham, Massachusetts, as a "horn breaker and comb maker" a few years prior to 1759 when it is thought Noyes cut his first horn comb in that town.

Little is known about Cook's comb making, but he was a captain of the Colonial militia and served his town and country in many political capacities such as selectman for a number of years, a treasurer for for thirteen, and representative to the General Court for three terms. It is not surprising that such an active public life left him little time to engage in the less profitable comb making occupation.

Noyes, however, devoted his full energies to making combs which he sold to the townspeople. He was joined in his efforts by a former Hessian soldier named Willian Cleland who had brought his comb making tools with him from Germany, as it was the custom of the mercenaries to carry the tools of their trade with them in the hope of making "a little money on the side." Cleland taught Noyes how to make more sophisticated combs than those which he had cut with a pen knife and hatchet. Both men ultimately used a variety of hand tools with great skill in their basement shop.

Of the various kinds of animal horns available to Noyes and other comb makers, it was found that steer horn was the most suitable. Readily and cheaply obtained, least brittle and thinner than other horn such as buffalo, oxen, antelope, deer, etc., it was more easily shaped and clarified. Originally, comb makers purchased cow and steer horns from neighboring farmers and later obtained them from the slaughter

houses and tanneries centered in nearby Worcester.

Early comb making was a cottage industry and processing horn before the advent of labor saving machinery was an odoriferous, laborious, time consuming task for both the comb maker and his long-suffering wife and family, for not only did the horn and pith smell, but the stench from the boiling oil in which the horn was steeped for days, softening in the household fireplace, must have been nauseating. Imagine the inconvenience as well, when this fireplace was the sole means of cooking and heating the home.

Initially whale oil was used for this softening process, but when it became too expensive comb makers turned to mineral oil and later to parafin. Hot water baths were frequently substituted for any of the above when its cost in turn became excessive.

OVER THE YEARS machinery was invented which reduced the amount of hand labor involved in comb making, but in Noyes' time the following steps were used to produce raw horn combs. After the raw horns were softened by boiling, they were charred in the fireplace blaze and placed between two heavy flat stones or irons, and left to cool. The stones were replaced by a crude press made of a large log 4–5 feet long, hewn flat on two sides. Near the middle was a square hole into which were inserted several hot iron plates placed side-by-side. The boiled horns were forced between the iron plates and a wooden wedge was driven in at one end with a heavy mallet. This press continued to be used until 1824 when it was replaced by more sophisticated machinery.

Prior to 1812, when Moses Emery obtained a patent for a ''horn splitting comb stamp twinning

PLATE 17-A. The invention of the ''twinning machine'' made it possible to produce two combs in one operation, with the teeth of one comb formed as the opposing teeth of the second were sheared from the horn blank.

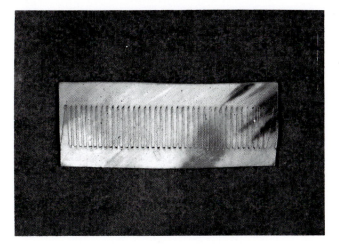

machine,'' the teeth of each comb had to be hand sawn from the solid stock. The twinning machine was a great improvement as two combs could be made in one operation; the teeth of one comb were automatically formed when those of the opposing comb were sheared. A fine example of a set of combs thus produced is shown courtesy of Mercer Museum, Doylestown, Pennsylvania, which museum contains the finest collection of comb making tools in the United States. If the end tooth is closely observed it is easier to see how clever the process was.

The base of the old twinning machine contained a cast iron stove approximately 18 inches long, 12 inches wide, and 6 inches deep, with a front opening and an outdoor vent to the rear where a charcoal fire warmed the machine. Atop the stove was a sliding plate called a drag and an iron frame, which held a gang of cutters of the proper shape and size to cut the required teeth. Originally hand power was achieved by a shaft with a balance wheel, a wooden handle on its rim. In the center of the shaft was a crude cam which worked a sliding rod forcing down each tooth cutter in its turn. The feed was applied by a ratchet and a latch which forced the drag along bit-by-bit. Thus the cut teeth bisected the blank which when separated made two straight combs ready to finish.

About 1826, David Noyes, a descendant of Enoch Noyes, invented an improved tooth cutting machine which could produce 48–60 straight or utility combs an hour with handpower, and 600–700 per hour by the time steam power had arrived in 1844.

About 1805 (there is a difference of opinion as to dates here), there was a demand for fancier combs and the process of clarifying horn was begun. The process of preparing the stock was essentially the same as for raw horn, except that once the horn was sufficiently softened it was opened with tongs and put between the irons of the screw press, which by 1818 had replaced the wedge press, the screw tightened and the horn left to cool. When it was thoroughly cold, it was removed, trimmed and split on one side and was then ready to clarify by soaking in cold water, then hot water and oil, and when well softened and hot, it was placed between hot irons and recompressed. If the horn was merely to be straightened, the irons were not heated. When the process was complete the horn was clarified, semi-transparent, and ready to make into combs.

The principle of the screw press continued to be used as long as horn was pressed by hand. Later it was replaced by a large cog-wheel and lever, and still later by hydraulics and steam, which kept the stock in a pliable condition.

Many hand tools were used to reduce the stock to uniform thickness such as the guillotine and shave which removed flaws and wrinkles. The surface was

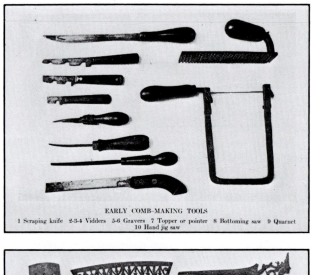

EARLY COMB-MAKING TOOLS

1 Scraping knife 2-3-4 Vidders 5-6 Gravers 7 Topper or pointer 8 Bottoming saw 9 Quarnet
10 Hand jig saw

EARLY COMB-MAKING TOOLS

1-2-3-4-5 Comb patterns 6 Vidder 7-8-9 Engravers' tools

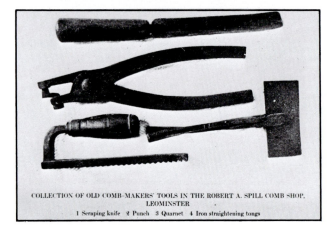

COLLECTION OF OLD COMB-MAKERS' TOOLS IN THE ROBERT A. SPILL COMB SHOP,
LEOMINSTER

1 Scraping knife 2 Punch 3 Quarnet 4 Iron straightening tongs

PLATE 17-B. Collection of old comb making tools as shown in the Robert A. Spill Comb Shop in Leominster, Massachusetts.

smoothed by use of the quarnet, the topper and pointer to point the teeth which had been cut square; the grail rounded off and finished the teeth. Engraving tools were used for decoration such as the quiller which cut a bead before embossing the bridge with metal dies. Finally the bottoming saw rounded and sharpened the spaces between the teeth.

Combs were shaped after softening and the rough blanks were cut by bending them around a wooden block or mandrel and tying them in place for several hours. Once shaped, hand drawn patterns were traced onto tissue paper, glued to the surface of the shell or horn and cut with a fine hand-guided jig saw no more than 1/12 of an inch wide.

AFTER THE TEETH had been rounded and in other respects brought to the proper form with suitable tools, the combs were polished. Bernard Doyle writing in *Comb Making in America* tells us, ''Rubbing and polishing are performed on balls or wheels usually made of old woolen carpet cut into circular pieces about 18 inches in diameter with a hole in the center of each piece large enough for a spindle to pass through. A sufficient number of these pieces of carpet together with about the same number of smaller circular pieces placed alternately as filling are clamped between two flanges on a spindle to make a ''ball'' from four to six inches thick. The ends of the spindles are pointed and run in the ends of hard wood plugs held by iron plug holders or double iron plug holders on a wooden frame. The method of making and using these balls remains unchanged. The operator holds the work on the upper side of the revolving ball while the under edge runs through a mixture of hard coal ashes and water. Pumice stone or fine sand is sometimes used, but hard coal ashes sifted fine are generally preferred. Rubbing tongs are sometimes used to hold the work while rubbing, but generally the operator prefers to use his hands. After the combs have been rubbed they are polished in much the same manner on balls made like rubbing balls except they consist of cotton cloth. One half of the ball is coated with rotten stone and oil, the other half left clean, the comb which is to be polished is first held on the coated and then on the uncoated side. An upright board, fastened to the floor in front of the ball, protects the operator from the dust from the ball. After being polished and rubbed the combs are ready for shipment.'' This is assuming that the comb is not to be colored.

Preferred colors varied from time-to-time in both horn and tortoise shell, so oxblood red stain was stylish at one time and various brown shades another. Some horn combs were solidly colored, others were treated to create a tortoise shell effect and so skillful were the results that it is difficult for the novice to detect one

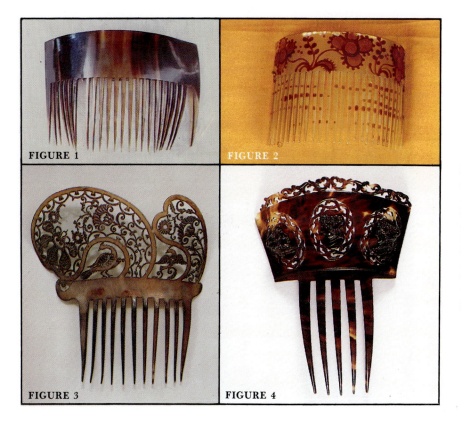

FIGURE 1

FIGURE 2

FIGURE 3

FIGURE 4

PLATE 18. *Fig. 1:* Rare old American horn comb *(author's collection).* *Fig. 2:* Decorated horn comb *(Leominster Historical Society, Leominster, Massachusetts).* *Fig. 3:* Carved raw horn comb, 19th Century European *(The Metropolitan Museum of Art, gift of Mrs. Ridgely Hunt in memory of William Cruger Pell).* *Fig. 4:* Carved tortoise shell with cameos, 19th Century European *(ibid Fig. 1).*

material from the other. Care was taken to select horn stock which contained little of the natural black color (see the twinned comb for a good example of this color). Various chemicals were used in an effort to render the horn white before dyeing it, especially chloride of lead, but most authorities agree, with little success.

The combs to be colored were first immersed in a mixture of nitric acid in hot water, which gave them an amber color. Next they were washed in cold water and spotted or streaked with a mixture of lime, saleratus and red lead. This solution remained on about half an hour, was washed off with cold water, and the comb was then dried and polished. Streaking was done from the top of the comb to the bottom in a diagonal which ran from left to right, and is the most obvious imitation of the two processes.

Abraham Rees, writing in 1819, tells us, "Tortoise shell combs are much esteemed; and there are methods of staining horn, so as to imitate it, of which the following is one: The horn to be dyed is first to be pressed into a flat form, and then done over with a paste, made of two parts of quick-lime and one of litharge, brought into a proper consistence with soap ley. This paste must be put over all the parts of the horn, except such as are proper to be left transparent, to give it a nearer resemblance to tortoise shell. The

horn must remain in this state till the paste be quite dry, when it is to be brushed off. It requires taste and judgment so to dispose the paste, as to form a variety of transparent parts, of different magnitudes and figures, to look like nature. Some parts should also be semi-transparent, which may be effected by mixing whiting with a part of the paste. By this means, spots of a reddish brown will be produced, so as greatly to increase the beauty of the work. Horn thus dyed is manufactured into combs, and these *are frequently sold for real tortoise shell.''* If those who were accustomed to purchasing these materials could not tell the difference, it is not surprising we are unable to do so 200 years later.

MOST OF THESE old horn combs are not very attractive and have virtually disappeared from the market as well. Sadly, they have not been considered of any particular value and have been discarded. The really old specimens will have very sharply pointed, fragile, 3 inch long teeth, the square spacing between the teeth indicating they were hand carved; and a plain bridge about 2 inches deep. They are much lighter in weight than celluloid, and probably will not be in mint condition, much like the comb [*Plate 18, Fig. 1*] which was found in an ancient jumbled-up shop of odds and ends near Sebago Lake, Maine. Though missing teeth

and sadly neglected, it is a genuine, old, American comb and deserves an honored place among combs. If you should find its like, buy a real piece of American history, as they are soon going to be unobtainable at any price anywhere, if they have not already vanished.

Blanche Bates, an early American actress who starred in "The Girl of the Golden West" melodrama, wore the now unusual hand painted comb [*Plate 18, Fig. 2*]. Combs of clarified horn were crudely painted with the same chemicals which were used to color the combs so the range of colors available was restricted to mahogany red, brown, ochre, tan, and other brownish tones. The florals did not exceed the artistic abilities of the comb maker, his workers, or possibly members of his family. They are reminiscent of the work done by the Pennsylvania Dutch, rather childishly gay. They must have been a welcome note among the prim and proper clothing worn by early 19th century women.

Though these combs measured as much as 8-1/2 inches wide, they were worn in pairs or as many as their owners could cram on their heads. It was not unusual for a woman to have her portrait painted wearing as many as three or four at one time. How fortunate we are to have just such a painting from Fruitlands Museum in Harvard, Massachusetts, located on the panoramic and pastorally beautiful site selected by Bronson Alcott (father of the illustrious Louisa May, author of *Little Women*, etc.), for his short lived utopian community.

Ruth and Samuel Shute, folk art painters working between 1827–1836 in the New England states, traveled from town to town painting portraits for a living. The May 24, 1834 *Plattsburg Republican* announced: "Portrate Painting . . . Mrs. Shute would inform the Ladies and Gentlemen of Plattsburgh (New York) that she has taken a room at John M'Kee's Hotel where she will remain for a short time. All who may employ her may rest assured that a correct likeness of the original will be obtained. Ladies and Gentlemen are requested to call and examine the paintings. Price from $5.00–$10.00. Miniatures from $5.00–$8.00."

The Shutes are thought to have collaborated in their work, one doing the rough sketching and the other the finished painting in oils, watercolors, pencil, and various other media. Their portraits include several paintings featuring fashionably attired ladies wearing their combs and all show the sitter with at least two visible combs of enormous size. They show

a number of hair styles, but the giant sausage-like curls with hair parted in the middle predominate.

The combs, both clear and imitation spotted tortoise arise from the back of the head. One entitled *"Woman With Two Canaries"* has the hair arranged in a plane across the top, giving the woman a curiously flat headed appearance. One of their best known, *"Dolly Hackett,"* dated Nov. 27, 1832, can be viewed at Fruitlands, where it seems admirably suited to its pleasant surroundings. It presents a cheerfully forthright lady wearing combs which are quite unalike, earrings, laces, and a ribbon neck tie. [*See Plate 19.*]

This work is interesting as it presents one of the problems primitive artists struggled with and seldom solved: how to model the human hand so it was not disproportionately large when compared to the rest of the body. They usually had the sitter holding an object to disguise any shortcoming in this respect. The Shutes nearly always followed this practice, but this not too ungainly hand is shown holding a slim book, with the name of the sitter prominently lettered on its cover. A gaily painted Hitchcock chair appears to the right of the sitter's back in Shute works in order to indicate the client is seated and to add perspective. These prosperous ladies show a fondness for necklaces, dangling earbobs, rings worn on the index finger, fine lace collars and cuffs, and other fineries which one does not usually associate with Puritanical New England in all its grim aspects. The facial similarities, rigid poses, almost identical clothing, and the simple pastel watercolored backgrounds make the Shutes' work instantly recognizable. One cannot help liking Dolly Hackett.

THE HISTORY OF the comb making industry in America was concentrated largely in the hands of a few families who for over one hundred and fifty years saw the industry evolve from a limited, spare-time, cottage occupation, through its heyday when comb making was a full time occupation for hundreds of workers, to its current status. At present it occupies a steady but certainly minor place in fashion accessories with a limited number of factories producing both combs and other products suitable to induction molding.

When horn and tortoise were in vogue the fascinating W. K. Potter catalogue dated April, 1879, lists such diverse items as jewelry, belts, cases, chatelaines, cane handles, coats of arms, dice, optical items, fans, whistles, visors, smelling bottles; in fact 78 categories (including rather surprisingly, cigarette cases). By-products were then as now a necessity to success.

Among the prominent comb making families are the Noyes family of West Newbury, Massachusetts, whose members included the first comb maker

PLATE 19. Portrait of Dolly Hackett by Ruth Shute, 1832 (*Fruitlands Museum, Harvard, Massachusetts. Photo by George M. Cushing, Boston*).

Enoch Noyes and his descendants Elfameo, Joseph, Somerby, Francis and William, whom Doyle considers the most remarkable of this talented family saying, ''Indeed he surpassed him (Enoch) for while Enoch made but one article, William Noyes invented many and mastered the most complicated problems of mechanics. His career and accomplishments in the comb industry have never been equalled by any man since his time.'' Their contributions to the industry lay in the field of numerous improvements in machinery and production techniques.

In Leominster the most celebrated family was the Hills family who first established themselves there in 1774 and the last of the great families, Tilton and Cook Co., has closed its doors almost as this book is being written. Although I knew none of these people, there is a sadness about such finality and the passing of an era which can never return. So extensive is the list that only a few names can be mentioned here and it is suggested anyone interested in the origin and development of the comb industry in Leominster consult Doyle's book which offers an outstanding account. Other early comb making families included the following: Morse, Bennett, Cook, Joslin, Howe, Blodgett, Tisdale, Kingman, Patch, Damon, Colburn, Adams, Spill, Smith and Chase. Doyle reveals intimate details of the apprenticeship of numerous young men who were guided by these comb making families and follows their progress as they in turn became employers, though the ''live in'' aspects of the training period vanished when production moved from the home to the factory building. A few of the original structures may still be viewed in the Pleasant Street area of Leominster.

In 1893, Caleb C. Field, M.D. wrote a short paper on the statistics of comb making in Leominster in 1852, in which he states that the manufacture of combs from horns was begun in Leominster about the year 1770 by Obadiah Hills who went to that place from the town of Newbury. ''The business was then pursued on a small scale compared with the present operations. With a cash capital of $100.00, each man employed could make about $500.00 worth of combs in a year. Almost the only combs made then were the old fashioned kind with coarse teeth on one side and fine teeth on the other. No fancy combs were manufactured in Leominster until the commencement of the present century. The tools used by the workmen were few and were worked by hand and not by machines. The wooden wedge press had not been supplanted by the more perfect machine of the present time. In this press the pieces of horn when taken from hot water in which they were softened, were placed between cold iron plates and pressed by driving with force a large wooden wedge. About 30 years ago, in 1822, the iron

PLATE 19-A. Some famous U.S. combmakers, as shown in the book ''Comb Making In America'' by Bernard Doyle *(provided courtesy Louise Doyle)*. *Fig. 1:* Edwin A. Harris, Clinton, Massachusetts. *Fig. 2:* William Noyes, Newburyport, Massachusetts. *Fig. 3:* Capt. Thomas Hills, Leominster, Massachusetts. *Fig. 4:* Bernard Doyle, Leominster. *Fig. 5:* Edward Tilton, Leominster. *Fig. 6:* Aldrich Cook, Leominster.

FIGURE 1   FIGURE 2

FIGURE 3   FIGURE 4

FIGURE 5   FIGURE 6

screw press was introduced from Jabez B. Low. In this press, heat was applied to the iron plates to aid the process of pressing.

"In preparing the horns in their rough state almost the only tool then used was the hatchet, while their division into sections was accomplished in a tedious manner by the hand saw. The horns were clarified by hot water instead of oil as the latter article was too expensive for general use. All the various processes in the manufacture of combs were slow and imperfect, and all the implements used were ill adapted to their purposes, except the grail, which was then and is now, a perfect finishing tool for the comb. It is said that previous to the use of the cold press, the horns were softened by hot water, were stamped upon by the feet on the floor and then placed under a heavy flat stone to be pressed. Then, as the combs were made without machinery, the labor was performed by each comb maker in an apartment of his dwelling house or in a small shop attached to the same; but now the work is done mostly in large factories by the aid of steam or water power. In one factory 50 or 60 persons are employed, and in 5 or 6 others 20 or 30 labor together."

Dr. Field quotes from Whitney's *History of Leominster,* published in 1793, "And beside the manufacturing of combs is here established in 2 or 3 places and the work is carried on to a great perfection and profit. About 20 persons work more or less at this trade. About 10 persons are constantly employed and they manufacture about 6 thousand dozen combs a year. Among them is one Nathaniel Low, who makes ivory combs equally good, perhaps, as any imported from any country."

In 1845 there were 24 shops or factories, 146 persons employed (women were employed in some capacities) value of the combs was set at $77,400 and capital employed was $22,000.

In this connection it is amusing to note that the good doctor surmises that the capital was deliberately understated in order to reduce the assessed valuation owed to the state. The true valuation of combs produced was closer to $100,000 annually, he estimated. This ruse could more easily be accomplished 140 years ago than today!

By 1852 the annual valuation had quadrupled and Leominster was the leading comb manufacturer in Massachusetts, and for that matter, in the United States. Again quoting from Dr. Field: "Fancy combs of all kinds constitute the chief part of the manufacture. They are made from horns, and are called side, tuck, and pocket combs. Raw horn pocket combs are made to some extent, and, within the past year, the manufacture of shell combs has been commenced." This is a valuable statement as it establishes a reliable, actual date for the manufacture of domestic tortoise

shell combs, at least in Leominster.

From Dr. Field we learn that South American horns were preferred early in the manufacture of combs and were purchased chiefly in New York, which was also the leading market place for the finished product, though some were sold in Boston and Philadelphia. Men were paid $1.00 a day for a 10 hour work day but some men worked a 12 or 15 hour day and were paid on a per dozen basis earning nearly $14.00 a week. Women were paid $3.00 a week and out of these wages men boarded for $2.25 a week and women for $1.50 a week respectively.

DR. FIELD'S AIM in this paper (in which he evidences a talent for generalizing, moralizing, and making value judgements which no serious researcher would dare proclaim today), was to show the harmful effects of poor diet, lack of exercise, and tenement housing on the families of comb workers, rather than the workers themselves. He notes the wives and children of these workers had a 50% higher mortality rate and were more susceptible to disease than the rest of the population. His remarks on the comb industry itself are incidental but fortunately establish a source of reference which may be regarded as reliable owing to his stature in the community and his scientific training.

Dr. Field's paper yields a few noteworthy observations which should not be passed over lightly. First: in 1770, combs were still being made with a center division (though they were too crude to have had ornamentation) with fine teeth on one side of the comb and coarse on the other. Second: the Leominster area turned late to the production of tortoise shell combs, if we are to believe Dr. Field, as areas such as Boston, Philadelphia and Providence were all advertising tortoise goods a century previous to the commencement of such production in Leominster in 1851. Third: some raw horn combs were still being manufactured in 1852 which is surprising. Fourth: "fancy combs" constituted the bulk of the production in 1852 but such comb production originated early in the 19th century.

Horn continued to be used as a substitute for expensive tortoise shell until the discovery of celluloid in 1868, (though some countries continue to use horn even to the present day).

Not all species of tortoise could be suitably worked, and most if not all commercial shell, came from the hawksbill turtle found in the Indian and Pacific Oceans. The hawksbill reaches a length of 2-3 feet and weighs 500-600 pounds.

The shell on the back consists of 13 overlapping plates varying in thickness from 1/8-1/4 of an inch according to the age and size of the turtle. These uper plates determine the general conformation and size of the finished comb though it is possible to weld shells

by pressing them between hot iron plates, thus increasing the size or the thickness.

In 1836 it was noted the quantity of useable shell obtained from a single tortoise of average size was about 8 pounds, then worth between sixty and seventy dollars. The shell was so valuable workmen were careful not to waste any; much shell must have been joined which required considerable skill.

The upper plates are a darker color than those on the underside of the body, sometimes called blonde shell. The blonde variety was greatly prized for making Spanish combs in the 17th and 18th centuries. Later combs were made of the darker and mottled plates as the hawksbill became scarcer. These combs were enormous reaching a height of 12–16 inches and a width of two feet.

Tortoise was a highly prized material for a number of reasons. It was plastic, meaning it could be carved, welded, sawn, softened, impressed with metal inlays and twisted into various shapes. Each comb produced was as individual as the tortoise markings, and had a mellow glow achieved by much hand rubbing. Tortoise is highly durable, far more so than horn, which tends to become brittle with age. It was easily worked and required no coloring or streaking as horn often did. The finished product was handsomer than horn or bone and therefore commanded a higher price.

Tortoise shell was processed almost exactly as horn, but considerably greater care was taken not to apply too much heat to the sheets thereby discoloring them.

Warden's *History of the United States* Part II tells us on June 30th, 1816 there were 598,860 horn combs produced in the United States at a value of $80,624. As the horn cost only 1/10 of a cent per comb the selling price of 13¢ per comb was almost entirely for the labor involved. Import records reveal that tin combs and vellum combs were popular then though they are so rare today I cannot recall ever having seen a vellum comb anywhere, and tin combs might be mistaken for badly tarnished plated combs.

ADVERTISEMENTS APPEARING IN Colonial newspapers make fascinating reading for they indicate prices, materials, locations, offerings, and many little known oddities of our forebears, some using the antiquated type setters ''f'' in lieu of ''s''.

The earliest, from the *Pennsylvania Gazette,* * appeared on August 16, 1764: ''Christopher Ainger, comb maker, is lately removed out of Strawberry Alley into Fourth Street, five doors below the Academy, near Market Street, who has all Sorts of Combs, Powder Horns and Punch Ladles, to sell Wholesale

Historical files of Mercer County Museum, Doylestown, Pennsylvania.

and Retail, at reasonable Rates. Whoever has any tortoiseshell to dispose of may have money for it, or if to make up in Combs, done well by said Christopher Ainger.'' Accompanying this ad was a drawing of a comb which drew the reader's attention, as it was the only non-textual item on the page.

Graham's of Charter Street, North-end of Boston, seems to have specialized in ivory combs offering ''to pay the same price in Cash, for IVORY, (from Africa) as in London.'' in his ad which appeared in the *Massachusetts Centinel* on December 23, 1789.

John Federhem Jr.'s ad is most intriguing as it gives an accurate figure for the repair of combs and a willingness to barter. The ad appeared on April 19, 1833, in the Boston *Daily Evening Transcript.* The ''Pearl Ornaments'' he touts may have been mother-of-pearl; the copy does not clearly indicate what the pearl substance was.

''Court Street Comb Store. The subscriber has on hand a good assortment of Combs. Shell and Horn, which will be sold low for cash, or in exchange for Old Shell, Gold or Silver.

''Laides wanting Combs repaired, either carved or plain, at the very reduced price (in plain combs) of ten cents for each inside tooth, are respectively invited to call; and all the Combs repaired at this store are warranted strong and a fine polish for 6 cents, when the comb is repaired.

''Pearl Ornaments, new and splendid patterns, just finished by the subscriber, and are offered wholesale and retail, cheap for cash at 89 Court Street, under the N.E. Museum.''

We are inclined to think some of the claims made for commercial products today are deliberate falsehoods and the promised merits excessive beyond reason, but they are bland indeed when compared to the wild assertations and warnings of the 19th century manufacturers and merchants. Consider the notice of one A. S. Jordan of 191 Washington Street, Boston, whose wholesale and retail establishment offered ''the best preparations for dyeing and restoring the hair.''

''A.S.J. will pay particular attention to the Manufacture of Shell Combs of every description and keep on hand a large assortment of all the latest and most fashionable French and English styles and having received 9 silver medals at exhibitions of different Mechanical Institutions throughout the United States for best Shell Combs, feels warranted in saying that his facilities for manufacturing are superior to any in the country and none but the best workmen are employed.

''In this assortment the most fastidious cannot help being suited either as to style or to price. Combs manufactured to order in any style and neatly repaired however badly broken. He also keeps every variety of Brazilian, Buffalo, Horn, Ivory and Silver Combs. In order that purchasers be not deceived by attempts to sell them the work of other and irresponsible makers using patterns and imitations of mine, I would caution them, that hereafter they will see my name stamped upon every comb made in my factory.''

We can only conjecture as to what was meant by ''Brazilian'', but it probably was a particular grade of horn, as Doyle later tells his readers that some of the finest horn was obtained from South America. It is a point of interest that these comb makers were purchasers of quality materials, and aged tortoise was much in demand. The scarcity of hard money is reflected in the lower price when deals were struck with gold or silver, paper currency being held suspect by the merchants and the public at large.

ISAAC DAVIS ANNOUNCED January 1, 1823, that he had ''received a large shipment of wrought top India Combs, of the newest patterns, singly or in sets, with side combs. Also 50 dozen large plain Tops, of the circular or high patterns, manufactured from the richest colored Shell, expressly for retailing and comprising the handsomest assortment to be found in Boston, and will be sold at the lowest prices wholesale or retail. Also 100 dozen best Imitation (tortoise) combs from 25¢ to $1 each with the common horn combs of every description. Cash paid for Tortoise Shell, Ivory and Horn.'' Even at this early date tortoise combs were costly for Davis cunningly does not state their price, but tries to entice the reader with the lesser quality horn comb.

The most amusing advertisement is credited to John Noyes of Sudbury, whose January 23, 1764 ad solicited, ''Any person that will bring to John Noyes, living in Sudbury, a Quantity of good Ashes, shall have Four shillings or Ten per Bushel.'' It would appear ashes would have been so readily available that there would have been no need to advertise for them! These ''good ashes'' mixed with water were used in hand polishing horn and tortoise shell combs.

In addition to newspapers, journals, histories, governmental reports, treatises, and the like, merchants' account books and catalogs listing available services and tools are an invaluable aid to the researcher and had it not been for such as the F.H. Cook & Company and the William K. Potter, Providence Shell Works pamphlets, much background material would have been forever lost to those of us involved in recording and preserving Americana.

Doyle states that Edward B. Tilton and George H. Cook began to make combs in Leominster, Massachusetts in the spring of 1878, calling their company Tilton and Cook, (which company remained in operation until 1981, with some changes in titles and personnel of course). George was a descendant of the first

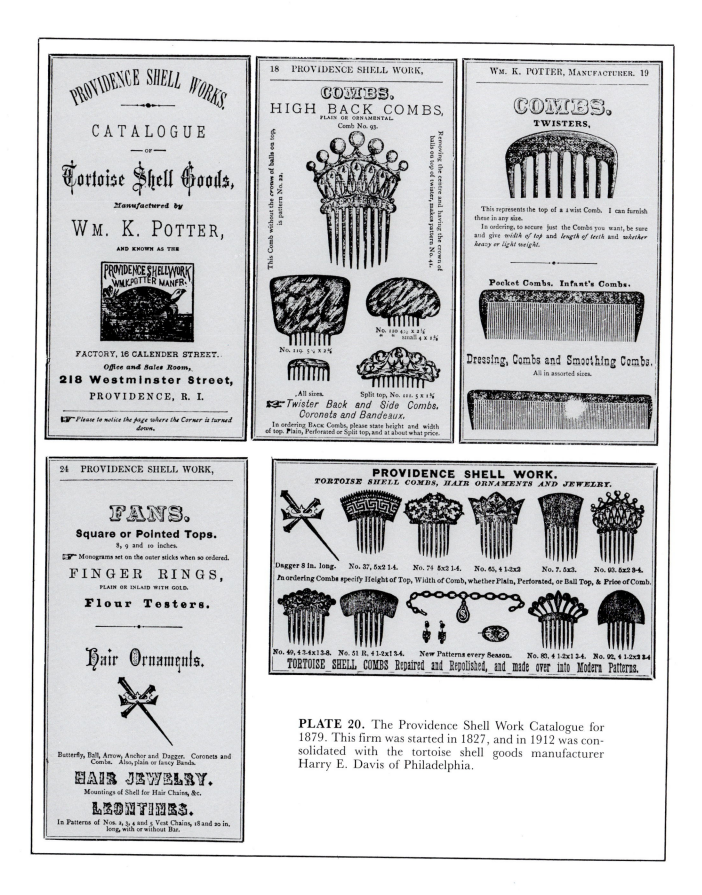

PLATE 20. The Providence Shell Work Catalogue for 1879. This firm was started in 1827, and in 1912 was consolidated with the tortoise shell goods manufacturer Harry E. Davis of Philadelphia.

comb maker in America. Exactly who the F.H. was in the Cook family (Frank H. or Horace F. or Fredrick H.) is unclear, but it is known that they were the first company to use hydraulic pressure for clarifying horn and the machinery which they offered in this booklet, dated 1894, was still used in every comb manufactury in the United States as late as 1926.

Machinery may or may not hold a fascination for each of us, but who can resist the wealth of information provided in the illustrative material and the curious marginal notes, let alone the obvious impor-

PLATE 20-A. A photo of a dagger and crown pin as shown in the Providence Shell works. (*The Metropolitan Museum of Art, gift of Dr. Walter L. Hildburgh*).

PLATE 21. Combmaking tools as shown in the Mercer Museum of the Bucks County Historical Society, Doylestown, Pennsylvania. *Fig. 1:* Cutters, shaves, grail, tongs, poker, horn pieces, and clamps. *Fig. 2:* A comb maker's bench with crude horn combs, horn stock, tools and presses. *Fig. 3:* Hand operated horn splitting machine and twinning machine with fire box. *Fig. 4:* Cauldron, clarified horn combs and work bench.

FIGURE 1

FIGURE 2

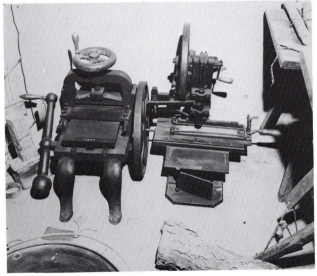

FIGURE 3

FIGURE 4

tance of this little book as the clerks were instructed to, "Keep this Book in drawer in the Safe".

It Is Difficult to use superlatives in connection with combs for there are so many interesting and historic ones, but surely the most fascinating American comb has to be the case comb in the form of an American Indian made of tortoise (at least the teeth are of tortoise); there is a difference of opinion as to the material used in the case section; some claiming it is baleen and some affirming it is blonde tortoise. Whatever the material, its unique shape is undeniable.

Only two examples are known to be in private

hands (one shown here in *Plate 23*) and no museum I am acquainted with has an example. The cost was prohibitive in accord with its rarity and was unobtainable to me. Even though there is a great deal of damage to the teeth, the body is in fine condition considering its great age, as they were made for the French and Indian trade during the 17th and 18th centuries. It is of average dimensions, approximately 4-1/4 inches long and 1-3/4 inches wide with an ornamented bridge. The double sided figure into which the comb folds may be decorated in a fashion identifiable to the purchaser of Indian antiquities rather than being an accurate portrayal of any particular tribe or section

PLATE 22. Some of the comb making machinery offered by the W. H. Cook & Company in 1894.

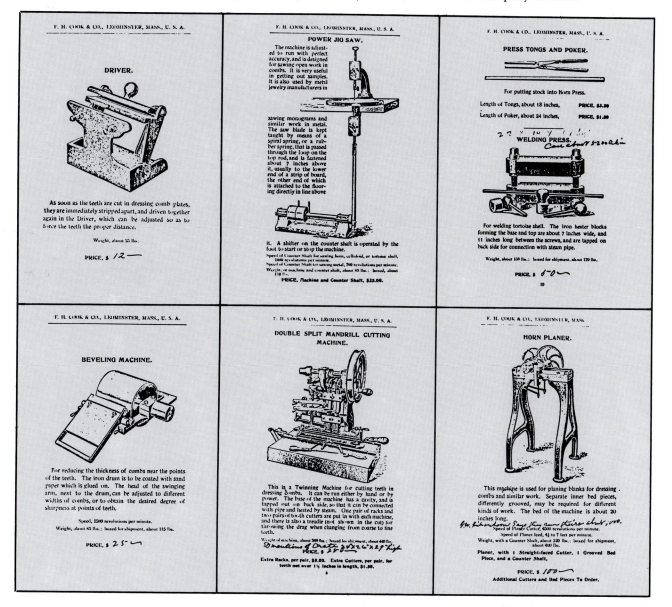

of the country, as the costume seems overly ornate and stylized. The warrior has a bow and arrow in hand and two arrows in the quiver on his shoulder. Similar figures were used in making wooden and/or metal weathervanes. His long hair is bound pony-tail fashion and he appears to be wearing earrings, shell necklaces, bracelets, and an ornament of some kind on the upper thigh. Feathers are shown in his headdress, skirt, and calf adornment. All this ornamentation is nicely incised though the comb appears to be in need of an application of oil.

The difficulty of determining the age of an object which has no patent date or other positive means of identification was recently demonstrated when a startlingly similar comb to the Indian was encountered.

The cased figure was that of a Civil War soldier holding a rifle and ammunition so the comb could not logically have been made prior to 1861. Made of well defined hand carved clarified horn, it was rather clumsily spotted to resemble tortoise. A number of the teeth and some of the embellishment along the outer edge was missing, however, only the design plainly showed the difference of nearly a century between the two combs—the size, casing, and style were all identical. The price quoted was approximately $275.00; a bargain indeed for a comb as rare as this,

PLATE 23. 18th Century tortoise shell folding comb with case in the shape of an Indian figure *(Courtesy Augenstein King).*

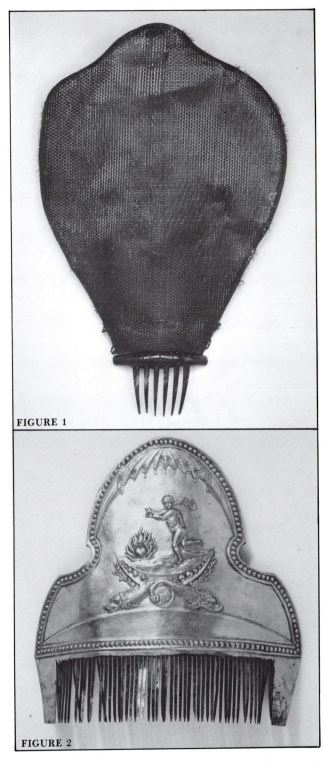

FIGURE 1

FIGURE 2

PLATE 25. *Fig. 1:* A comb made from hair or fiber which is 16½ inches high! C. 1900 *(The Metropolitan Museum of Art, Marcia Sand Fund).* **Fig. 2:** 19th Century European brass comb *(Museum of Fine Arts, Boston, Elizabeth Day McCormick Fund).*

even more so in light of the value assigned to the Indian comb.

THESE COMBS ARE so enormous and outrageous in design, material, construction, and size that it has been suggested they must have been made for theatrical purposes, for even in the 19th century when bizarre headdress was more the rule than the exception, they would have been cumbersome, impractical, and even ugly. They were found in the Metropolitan Museum and Boston Museum of Fine Arts Costume Institutes.

The most puzzling is the six tooth semi pear-shaped comb [*Plate 25, Fig. 1*] made of horse hair or some very coarse, stiff, woven black material which rises 16-1/2 inches above the head, so dwarfing the tortoise teeth that they do not appear sufficiently long nor strong enough to support such immense height. Couple this with the sheer ugliness of the comb and one wonders why anyone would want to wear it. Could it have been decorated in some appropriate manner so its outsize proportions could be visible for some distance from a stage? Was it specially made for an opera, a specific play, a costume ball, or some type of buffoonery? In any event it is one of the most comical combs one will ever encounter; circa believed to be 1900–1925; country of origin, the United States.

The 19th century brass comb [*Plate 25, Fig. 2*] shows the unmistakable European metal teeth, in this case brass and with uncharacteristic square end teeth, though the center teeth are pointed, and very flexible, which accounts for their bent and wavy condition. The shape of this comb, which is more like a tiara than comb, is unique, and the band of raised beading and cupolas are most attractive and pleasing. Cupid or Eros, like his mother Venus on the half shell, a theme extensively used by Renaissance painters, is in the act of rescuing a heart or soul. The symbolism is as obtuse as the dog-headed fish supporting the sea upon which Cupid is walking. Again, such a dramatic comb would seem appropriate to the opera singer, actress, a costume event of some sort, but hardly fitting for afternoon or formal evening wear.

The tortoise comb with floral foliate carving [*Plate 26, Fig. 1*] is from the 19th century and although the country of origin is unassigned, it strongly resembles several combs from the German-Austrian regions which are documented by Gerlach in his *Primitive Jewelry* (1903). It is a large comb measuring 12 inches high and 14 inches wide, the teeth constituting only a fraction of the overall dimensions. The curve of the teeth indicate it is a back comb, nicely executed, but again of towering loftiness. It might be suitable for a mantilla.

The graceful brass comb at *Figure 2*, though credited to Western Europe, 19th century, is made

PLATE 26. *Fig. 1:*High-backed European comb of tortoise shell from the 19th Century *(The Metropolitan Museum of Art, gift of Miss Harriet Leslie Wilcox).* ***Fig. 2:*** 19th Century European metal comb similar to Indo-Arabic styles *(Museum of Fine Arts, Boston, Elizabeth Day McCormick Fund).*

PLATE 24. Portrait of Miss Harriet Leavens, c. 1815, by folk artist Ammi Phillips. The young girl is winsome, but her jewelry seems too sophisticated. The two combs she wears are awkwardly placed, one holding the curls at the back of her head (there is perhaps another out of sight on the side) while a barette holds wispy curls drawn across her forehead. Note the brilliant scarlet reticule she holds. *(Fogg Art Museum, Harvard University, gift of the estate of Harriet Anna Niel).*

44

of white metal in a style which is reminiscent of Indo-Arabic themes. The teeth are long compared to the top, which is arched and rayed much like the head-dress worn by Balinese dancers, but the length of the teeth would preclude its being effectively worn as a tiara.

In determining whether a comb is of man-made or natural materials it is helpful to examine the decorative heading and teeth. A hand carved comb of natural materials such as amber, mother-of-pearl, rubber, ivory, bone, tortoise, or wood usually reveals crude irregular spacing, teeth of varying widths, and the charming imbalanced patterns typical of all hand work of whatever medium. The marks of the carver's tools are often visible in the spaces between the teeth. The ends of the spaces are squarish rather than those rounded or pointed by using the pointer, grail, or the topper. The spacing in celluloid combs will be smooth, sharply pointed between the teeth, and the teeth will have the perfection of a machined object.

DURING THE MID 1800's exquisite sterling silver embossed combs were popular in the United States [*Plate 27*]. Custom made, they were decorated with

FIGURE 2

PLATE 27. *Fig. 1:* Early American sterling silver comb. Head decoration shows classical influence popular in the late 18th Century *(author's collection).* *Fig. 2:* 19th Century metal comb—possibly lead—set with French paste ornament *(The Metropolitan Museum of Art).*

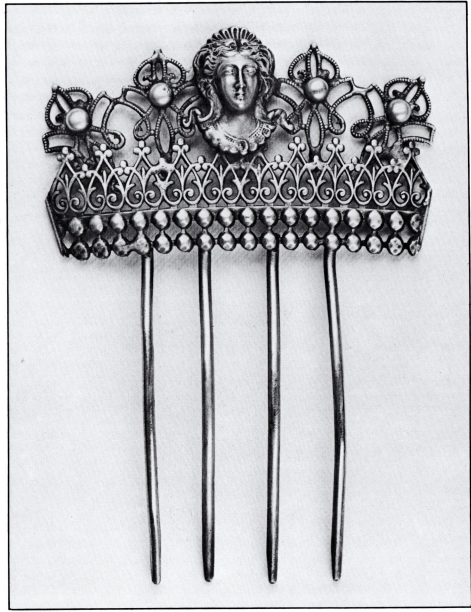

FIGURE 1

45

pin point fine designs which when closely examined reveal slight variations on the opposing sides of a central portion. The teeth are fine, wide set, curved and made separately from the top or bridge; then the two sections were soldered together. There were engravings of leaves, fans, petals, baskets of fruit and sheaves, along with beaded oval escutcheons for the owners' initials. The monograms were separated from and outlined by intricate-scrolled and serrated edges and small round baubles which gave a crown like effect. Some were engraved on both the face and the reverse side, the patterns not necessarily identical. These would have been worn with a hair style which permitted them to stand away from the head so both decorations would be visible.

Very few manufacturers signed their creations, but these custom pieces were a noteable exception, as leading silversmiths of the day made them along with traditional flatware, stemware, serving pieces, and other accessories. The primitive designs show originality and spontaneity, unlike the precise designs used later in die stamped patterns. Occasionally sterling combs were set with a single, large, paste brilliant stone centered amidst the florals or rows of clear rhinestones. An occasional comb is found with a large central motif which will be encircled by clear rhinestones or paste which sets off the motif and adds radiance and elegance. These combs are rather small compared to more spectacular back combs and measure a mere 4 inches long by 5 inches wide in the extreme; but their delicacy, originality, fine craftsmanship and light weight make them a most refined, desirable sort of comb among American combs. I believe them to be original to the American silversmith as they are invariably stamped "sterling", a term not widely used in Europe, as Europeans prefer the use of numbers to indicate silver content.

Steel cut bridges were also attached to horn teeth by a series of three pins. Like many products which imitate a more expensive and superior article, the cut steel comb is easily distinguished from the sterling comb by its heavier weight, dull finish, stamped patterns, and sometimes exposed brass areas where the finish has been removed. They simply lack the finesse of sterling combs.

In contrast to the sterling combs, aluminum combs, pins, and back combs were set in the 1870's with marcasites, rhinestones, semi-precious stones, flat back pieces, filagree work and cut work. The soft grey finish was ideally suited to marcasites in particular which resembled small diamond chips.

HAIRPINS

That which separates the hairpin from the hair ornament appears to be a tooth; one tooth, tine, or prong, is used in Western style ornaments and two

are used in those items referred to as "pins". It is a slight differentiation and many times no distinction whatsoever was made in advertisements, catalogues, and other references. Often the pin was as decorative and ornate as the ornament, but the function was different, as the pin was a utilitarian device for holding the hair—however it was arranged—securely in place, assuring the wearer of a neat appearance. The ornament was primarily intended as a decorative accessory and the wearer did not depend upon it to maintain her coiffure. The Oriental pin is worn in connection with the comb also as a decoration but it is almost inseparable from the comb which itself is purely decorative. Both are considered in another chapter. There is hardly a substance which has not been used in making the hairpin. Records show it was made of bone, ivory, bronze, steel, wood, silver, gold, platinum, glass, aluminum, mother-of-pearl, brass, tortoise, horn, iron, tin, copper; the list seems endless. Gerlach in his fine book, *Primitive and Folk Jewelry*, shows them in an infinite variety of shapes, sizes, and materials; each significant to a culture.

HAIRPINS OF HORN were probably the first American pins. Later we note President George Washington sent to England ordering pins for his family. They were plain, had straight teeth and were quite thick compared to the wire varieties of later years. The upper classes were able to afford delicately thin sterling silver and gold pins, approximately 2-1/2 inches long. Some had crimped tines which it was hoped would grip the hair fast, others were tapered and spread much like a miniature comb and were finished with filagree tops so enormous they dwarfed the tines. The filagree section was attached to the mother-of-pearl, sterling, horn, aluminum, or celluloid teeth with pins or a metal cap. Gilt was widely used in intricate shapes above a single or double shaft of abalone shell. Aluminum pins were set with a simple scattering of rhinestones or marcasites.

There were hairpins intended to be seen and those it was fervently hoped would remain invisible. The latter came in a wide range of shades to blend as closely as possible with individual hair colors. Celluloid, and later molded acetate, was a great boon to manufacturers as the points were gentler to the scalp, pins made of it were more pliable, they could be made at a fraction of the cost of natural materials, and they were feather light.

With the exception of the aluminum barrette set with clear rhinestones, and the paste set celluloid barrette [*Plate 28, Fig. 1*] the hairpins shown span a good 150 years. The first two, bottom left are aluminum, set with colored rhinestones to contrast with the metal. The remaining pins are sterling. The third has a hinged, filagree, fold-over top, marcasite mounts, a

very fragile pin which could not be subjected to the strain of constant use such as the next three whose Spartan decoration is most appealing. Each is a variation of the rope twist and is notably thicker than the gold pins in [*Plate 28, Fig. 2*]. The remaining pin has a cascade of small balls, chain suspended, emerging from bell shaped flowers which sound faintly when swayed. Decorations of this sort were used by virtually every folk culture during the 18th and 19th centuries, though they seem less than typical of European arts.

The tiny gold pins [*Plate 28, Fig. 2*] were treasured in the closing years of the 19th century to such an extent they were drilled at the top and attached to fine chains, which in turn were fitted with pince-

PLATE 28. An assortment of hairpins from the author's collection. *Fig. 1:* Aluminum pins and barettes set with rhinestones. *Fig. 2:* Gold and silver hairpins. *Fig. 3:* Ornaments of mother-of-pearl and French celluloid.

FIGURE 1

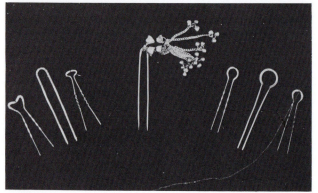

FIGURE 2

FIGURE 3

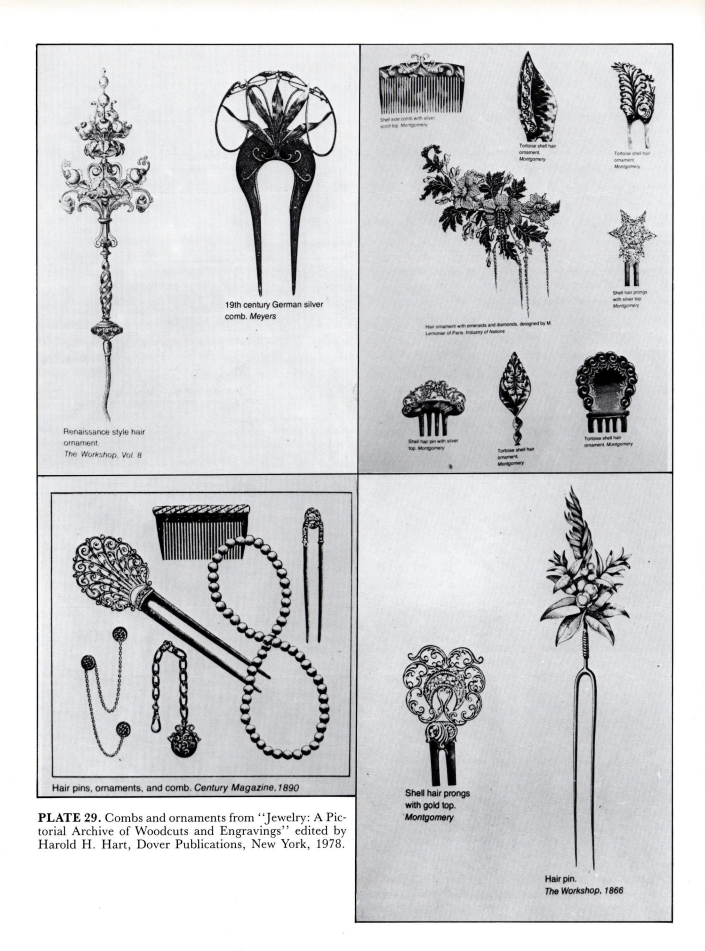

19th century German silver comb. *Meyers*

Renaissance style hair ornament. *The Workshop, Vol. 8*

Shell side comb with silver scroll top. *Montgomery*

Tortoise shell hair ornament. *Montgomery*

Tortoise shell hair ornament. *Montgomery*

Hair ornament with emeralds and diamonds, designed by M. Lemonier of Paris. *Industry of Nations*

Shell hair prongs with silver top. *Montgomery*

Shell hair pin with silver top. *Montgomery*

Tortoise shell hair ornament. *Montgomery*

Tortoise shell hair ornament. *Montgomery*

Hair pins, ornaments, and comb. *Century Magazine, 1890*

Shell hair prongs with gold top. *Montgomery*

Hair pin. *The Workshop, 1866*

PLATE 29. Combs and ornaments from ''Jewelry: A Pictorial Archive of Woodcuts and Engravings'' edited by Harold H. Hart, Dover Publications, New York, 1978.

nez hooks. Whether the hair pin secured the glasses when they were temporarily removed, or the glasses acted as a guard against the loss of the hairpin, is a toss up. Each gold hairpin is approximately 2–3 inches long, has a simple stippled top and gently rippled tines for improved grip, (though the improvement is doubtful).

The gold and sterling topped pins are mother-of-pearl [*Plate 28, Fig. 3*] two of which (single prong) are technically ornaments but could serve as pins depending on hair styles and the thickness of the hair. The center celluloid pin has artificial, wired-on pearl decoration and the remaining two prong celluloid pin is stamped, "Made in France" by the Regina Novelty Company. It resembles a miniature shoe horn and is a most attractive pin; in some respects more appealing than the iridescent genuine shell, though they are easily distinguished from one another if held side by side. Their average length is five inches.

Many single prong metal hairpins from Hungary and Russia were wide, and flat looking, more like wavy letter openers than hair pins. European museums house ancient Roman hairpins resembling fibulas which have a single slender shaft and delicate gold or silver filagree. Some from Switzerland are unusually lacy filagree work as are the larger decorative combs whose attached chains connect terminal points. The use of chains was characteristic of Western European combs in the 18th century.

MONTGOMERY WARD'S CATALOGUE #57, 1895, proudly touted as the "Largest Mail Order Business in the U.S." with "Supplies for Every Trade and Calling on Earth" contained 2 full pages of combs and ornaments which varied from those offered by Marshall Fields in two significant respects: 1. imitation tortoise items cost a mere 10¢–$1.50. Sterling silver raised ornamentation was applied to both combs and ornaments. Brilliant rhinestones or paste sets make their initial appearance in a rolled plate ornament shaped like a sword priced at 48¢. Two pronged combs approximately 3 inches in length were ornamented with solid gold sprays and leaves for $3.75–$4.00 each. All the combs were shown half size and were quite diminutive.

Sears Roebuck catalogue for 1902 fails to show any high back combs or ornaments and the few combs they do feature are of the circlet type or low back combs now set with rhinestones; all are of imitation tortoise. Without sets they ranged from 10¢–22¢ each. Clearly they are insignificant sellers. Both catalogues featured the aluminum dressing and pocket comb which was intaglio engraved. Celluloid combs were now available in pastel shades and sold for mere pennies. Curiously, both raw horn and clarified horn continued to be sold, but genuine tortoise shell had by

now become a thing of the past. Horn was beginning to be outdistanced by hard rubber, which Montgomery Ward refers to as "Goodyear" and Sears coins "Ebonite." A rose by any other name....

The 1896, Marshall Fields Jewelry and Fashion catalogue offered merchandise of a higher caliber to the well-to-do Chicagoan and other fortunate midwesterners. Wholesale merchants of Marshall Fields solicited their patrons through fine woodcut illustrations, many full sized. Among the items found were genuine tortoise shell combs and hair ornaments with filagreed tops ranging from $2.00–$13.00 and sterling silver mounted hair ornaments in intricately delicate traceries resembling the Mexican silver jewelry of the 1940's. There were small battle axes, roses in full bloom, olive wreaths on fine wire scroll fields and the ubiquitous several tiered mock ostrich feathered designs. Prices ranged from $2.50–$6.00. Combs of genuine tortoise, variously termed bang combs and side combs with sterling silver trimmings were sold in pairs. They appeared with curved teeth and curiously graduated teeth, shorter at either end and longer in the center, and sold for as little as $1.00–$4.00.

Dressing sets comprised of as many as 77 pieces were sold by Unger Brothers, manufacturers of elaborate Art Nouveau sterling silverwares. Their 1900 catalogue contained tortoise combs with sterling silver tops gorgeously embossed which sold for surprisingly high prices; $9.00–$11.50, a princely sum when one remembers the depression of 1893 was barely ended and unemployment was high. The white collar worker was lucky to earn much in excess of $20.00 a month. This is further indication of the importance and quality of this toilet article and why so many are still obtainable to the collector nearly a century later. On today's antique market an Art Nouveau dressing set containing a mere 13 pieces in mint condition and of matched pattern might sell for $2,000, depending, of course, on the sterling weight and the market value of silver at any given time.

Their 1904 catalogue listed, incredibly, 111 different types and styles of combs, 1 hair curler, 40 clothes brushes, 14 hair brushes, 25 bonnet brushes, 3 chatelaine sterling bags, 23 button hooks, 23 mirrors, 14 toothbrushes, 40 bonbon and chatelaine boxes, 46 scissors, and 32 pages of jewelry in addition to numerous other items.

Unger Brothers assigned names to their various designs which were as romantic and sensuous as the items themselves such as: "Stolen Kiss", "Wild Rose", "Man in the Moon", "He Loves Me", "Love's Voyage", "Love's Dream", "Dawn", "Bride of the Wave", "Peep O' Day", "Le Secret des Fleurs", "Lily", "Evangeline", "Reine des Fleurs", among them. Many of these patterns

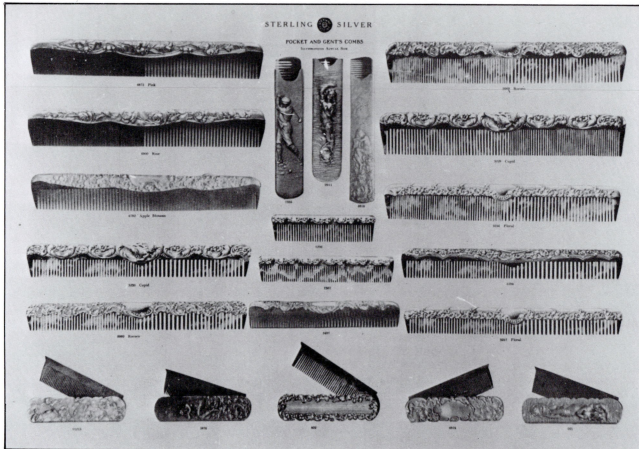

FIGURE 1

PLATE 30. *Fig. 1:* A sampling of sterling silver combs and cases. ***Fig. 2:*** This handsome 5-inch sterling silver comb (celluloid teeth) with matching case was made about 1925 for Tiffany & Co. It was obtained at auction in mint condition, still inside its original anti-tarnish protective sleeve. Louis Comfort Tiffany (1848–1933) son of the wealthy New York jeweler, was one of the few American artists involved in the Art Nouveau movement, and is of course famous for the Tiffany Art Glass Co. and its spectacular products.

depicted beautiful women with long wind swept tresses, cupids and cherubs tenderly kissing a woman or other cherub, flowers and buds with long curving stems, delicately posed full female nude figures, an occasional Indian chief in full headress, and a few designs which combined humor with the aesthetic. All were repousse work and rather fragile as they tend to flatten with use or abuse and are difficult, if not impossible, to repair.

OCCASIONALLY AMONG THE odds and ends found in attics and basements will be a small notebook in which random thoughts, notes, accounts, and purchases were kept from year-to-year by those fortunate enough to read and write. The spelling is often outrageous and the materials so incohesive it is difficult to determine

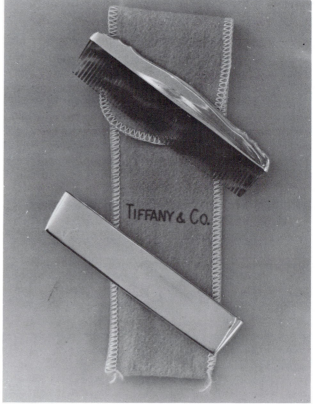

FIGURE 2

50

the purpose of the intriguing, diary-like, penciled entries. Recently just such a tiny book dated 1852 was found. Written in a wavering hand by an unknown lady from New Harmony, Indiana, it tells of the highlights of an otherwise unexciting life, train trips, overnight visits to friends and relatives, sketchy accounts which she jotted down from time-to-time. Among the calicos, buttons, soap recipes, shoe repairs and lofty quotations from lectures she attended, was an entry for a comb. Its size, composition and kind can merely be speculated upon, but the price was clearly marked: five cents. It probably was a horn comb as tortoise would have cost several dollars, even then.

Benjamin Franklin facetiously objected to the choice of the bald eagle as the national symbol, commenting that the eagle is "a bird of bad moral character. The turkey is a bird of courage and would not hesitate to attack a grenadier of the British Guards." The "turkey" today has a quite different,

less attractive connotation!

Immediately after its adoption in 1782, the bald eagle appeared as a motif on such diverse decorative art objects as candle table inlays, Amelung glass, oil paintings, watch charms, fraternal symbols, gilt girandoles, vase handles, mirrored plateaus, clock finials, and an endless variety of objects, among them, all types of horn, tortoise combs, and later, celluloid back combs. One early tortoise comb (1810–1840) displayed an eagle with outstretched wings; a shield bearing the thirteen stars and stripes across its chest. It is a regal, if unfeminine decoration, amidst the oak and acanthus leaves. Though the comb maker is unknown, it is contemporary in time and feeling with an equally fine yet considerably larger comb attributed to Alfred Willard, of Boston. This comb is owned by Winterthur Museum, Winterthur, Delaware [*Plate 33*].

Possibly the most fabulous comb of this type, is the one carved by Harris and Sons in Clinton, Massachusetts, for the Centennial of 1876 (see frontispiece).

PLATE 31. Beautifully executed in tortoise shell, this commemorative comb is by the Harris Co. of Clinton, Massachusetts. The pony express and train symbolize a century of progress, 1776–1876. *(Clinton Historical Society, Clinton, Massachusetts).*

PLATE 33. Tortoise shell comb and comb box, c. 1810–40, United States *(Henry Francis du Pont Winterthur Museum).*

FIGURE 1

FIGURE 2

FIGURE 3

PLATE 32. Three eagle motif back combs of celluloid. The elaborate decoration indicates their use was for evening affairs *(author's collection)*.

The carving of the name, the town, the dates 1776–1876 in intricate scroll work, along with an enormous eagle and shield having the symbolic eight stars (also shown on a small horn comb owned by Mercer Museum) and stripes, is unequaled among existing American combs. It is presently owned by the Clinton Historical Society where it may be viewed by appointment. Few combs can be directly attributed to a given carver but it is entirely possible that this comb could have been done by Joel Sawtell, for Doyle tells us, "Joel Sawtell was born in Doylston, Massachusetts in 1809. As a young man he worked for Nathaniel Lowe and in all probability learned the trade from him. Later he worked for Emory Harris for several years. From 1829–1837 he was in business for himself, and it is supposed that at one time he entered into a partnership with Sidney Harris. During the last years of his life until his death in 1887, he was employed at the Harris Comb Shops."

THE COMB BOX housing the Winterthur comb resembles an antique hat box. This one made by Joseph Freeman protected the delicate teeth and carved bridge when its owner travelled by coach. It appears ideally suited to this purpose. Other comb boxes resembling envelope purses were made of wool, heavily embroidered. They held double sided combs already cased such as those tortoise Jamaican examples dated 1673 and 1683. Both are incised with coconut trees, leaves and florals, the comb partitions of which are remarkably similar. Perhaps the same craftsman made both combs, the overall dimensions of which are approximately 7 inches by 5 inches [*Plate 17*].

A less common case of lightly tooled sections which slip over one another, has velvet covered strips embroidered with silver thread across wheat sheaves and small golden beads. The German phrase reads, "In Remembrance" or "Memory of" and is frequently found on beaded funeral bags made between 1800–1830. The case which has deep grooves top and bottom, can accommodate only a slightly curved comb measuring 3-1/2 × 5 inches and could have been carried in a reticule if the need arose [*Plate 34*].

Literally hundreds of comb manufacturers are listed in one source or another, but only Smith and Moore in East Ware, New Hampshire and Freeman of New Bedford, are known to be manufacturers of comb cases. Possibly, like reticules and other types of purses, they were home made to fit particularly beloved combs.

Celluloid back combs continued to use a modified form of the eagle motif, though its historical significance was little noted. The eagle becomes any bird outlined in fine, large, rhinestones set in brass mounts [*Plate 32, Fig. 1*] attached to the bridge of the comb, traditionally with 3 small pins. Some were works of

FIGURE 3

FIGURE 1

FIGURE 2

PLATE 34. *Fig. 1:* Comb case with motto "In memory of..." Thought to be Pennsylvania Dutch *(author's collection).* *Figs. 2 and 3:* Elegantly carved horn combs from the Mercer Museum. 1776 date may mean a commemorative comb. *(Leominster Historical Society, Leominster, Massachusetts, former collection of Mrs. Alice Sawyer).*

FIGURE 1

FIGURE 2

PLATE 36. *Fig. 1:* Early 19th Century American clarified horn comb with irregular teeth *(author's collection).* *Fig. 2:* Early 19th Century American hinged brass comb with hooks for veiling or netting. Teeth are of horn. This rare example was sometimes called a "bride's comb" *(ibid Fig. 1).*

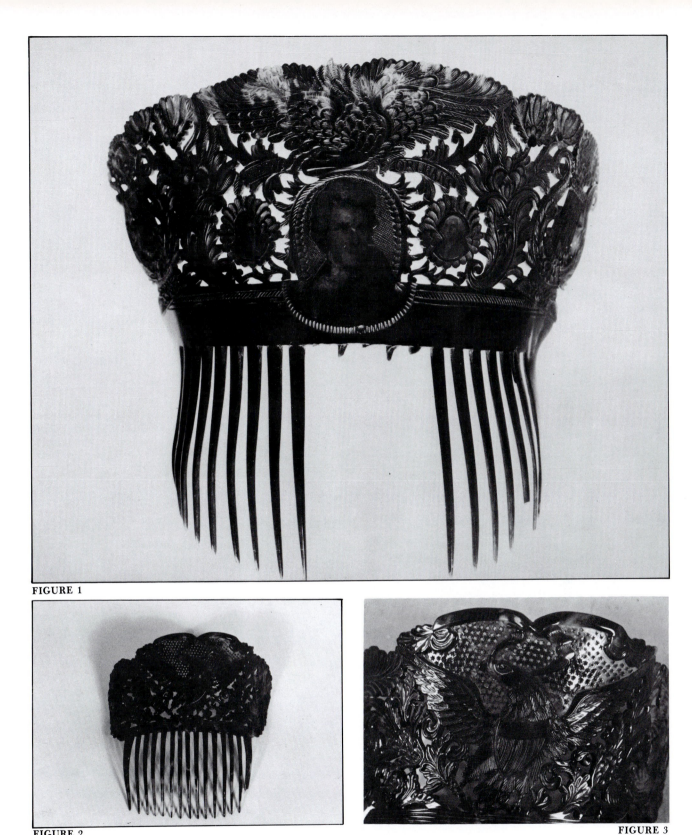

FIGURE 1

FIGURE 2

FIGURE 3

PLATE 35. *Fig. 1:* Tortoise comb for President Andrew Jackson made by John Evans Jones *(Smithsonian Institute photo).* ***Figs. 2 and 3:*** Eagle motif comb for Dolly Madison by John Evans Jones *(Daughters of the American Revolution Museum, gift of Mrs. Charlotte Shanklin and Miss Harriette E. Niese).*

54

art such as the stylized pair gracing the honey colored comb in [*Plate 32, Fig. 2*].

When Andrew Jackson was elected 7th president of the United States in 1829, he received toward the end of his first term of office, a magnificent high back tortoise shell comb as a presentation piece. Presentation pieces are a tangible recognition of the state of an artisan's ability and are not necessarily intended for use. This fact escaped a group of irate citizens who protested to the press that it was "inappropriate for a bachelor to have such a gift," (Jackson's wife Rachel had died two weeks previous to his taking office and he did not remarry.) Jackson escaped further criticism by presenting the handsome comb to his niece Emily Tennessee Donelson, who acted as his First Lady until poor health forced her to withdraw. The comb can be seen at the Smithsonian Institute in Washington, D.C.

The central figure in the group is a likeness of Jackson, flanked on the right by George Washington and on the left by the Marquis de Lafayette. Over all is the ubiquitous bald eagle carrying the banner "New Orleans" in its beak [*Plate 35*].

Mr. John Evans of Roxbury, Massachusetts, also presented to the fashionable Dolly Madison a comb along the same basic lines now in the possession of the Daughters of the American Revolution, also based in Washington, D.C. [*Plate 35, Figs. 1 & 2*]

SOME STRANGE DRESSING combs were made from time-to-time such as the novelty of a certain Mr. Griffith whose patent in 1852 called for, "Galvanic combs of which the teeth are alternately of copper and zinc while the handle is hollowed into a chamber for containing a roll of flannel moistened in acid solution. The inventor expects a beneficial galvanic action by combing the hair with this apparatus."

Other oddities included a comb with an oil dispenser which was to lubricate the scalp when combing the hair. Little wonder that this invention failed to catch on as the inventor had hoped.

A hinged ivory comb folded neatly into 3 sections for storage and extended rigidly into a straight comb with fine, medium and coarse teeth, much like a folding rule.

One interesting comb was fitted with a metallic mechanism which somehow cut and combed the hair in one operation, as the feather cut did in the 1940's. Monogrammed sterling cased combs with ivory teeth were worn on ribbons or cords about the neck like a pendant or lavalier for a quick repair job if the need arose.

No dresser set was complete without the oversized comb of celluloid or tortoise, some with sterling mounts in embossed patterns to match the countless pieces which were so popular in the last quarter of the 19th and early 20th centuries. Some sets included as many as 52 pieces, several pieces of which seemed little more than exact duplicates of others.

Comb, mirror, and nail files in little leather cases were standard equipment for every female in the days just preceding the general use of cosmetics.

For years merchants had used the calendar for spreading good will among their clientele but one enterprising company wished their customers a Merry Christmas in 1903 with a 4-3/4 × 3/4 inch aluminum dressing comb bearing the date and greeting on one side and the firm's name, Rfhker and Kiers, on the other. It is not known what their line was, but the idea was unique. [*Plate 40, Fig. 4*]

The etui, which contains a silk winder, needle, awl, and hook made of ivory, most importantly contains a comb so small that at first glance it would seem to belong to a doll's set. It is, in fact, a silk comb used to comb the silk from the silk cocoon and is a mere 1-3/4 inches long and 5/16ths of an inch wide. The gold thread-covered case was made in England in the early 19th century and was a treasured gift from a friend of mine. There was an attempt to produce silk domestically nearly a century ago and Doyle tells of a certain Rufus Kendall, "who was perhaps the largest manufacturer (of combs) of his day, but retired to experiment upon raising silkworms. His mulberry orchard stood on Central Street opposite Litchfield Street, where a garage has recently been built. One of the original mulberry trees remains today (1925) and blooms every year."

The white metal case comb [*Plate 38, Fig. 4*] has mock tortoise teeth and a high relief scene which

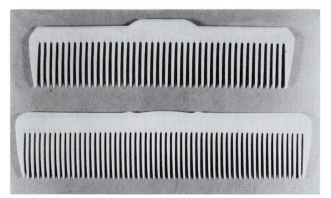

PLATE 37-A. These utility combs were manufactured by the millions at the turn of the century and can still be found for a few dollars. They were intended, however, for grooming the massive tresses of those times, and are not really suitable for today's hair styles. (*Author's collection.*)

FIGURE 2

PLATE 40. *Fig. 1:* Folding ivory comb *(Collection of Kathe Kilot). Fig. 2:* Miniature etui. Gold thread with silk comb *(author's collection). Fig. 3:* Liberty of London side comb *(courtesy Pierre Olivier Co., Tiburon, California). Fig. 4:* 1903 advertising comb *(Collection of Evelyn Wittsell). Fig. 5:* African and Oriental wood

FIGURE 7   FIGURE 1

FIGURE 3   FIGURE 5

1860
First Rubber Combs made
in West Newburyport, Mass.
William Noyes invented the
first machine that would
cut teeth in rubber in 1860.

FIGURE 4

combs *(ibid Fig. 1). Fig. 6:* Early rubber combs *(Leominster Historical Society, Leominster, Massachusetts). Fig. 7:* Enameled comb *(ibid Fig. 1). Fig. 8:* Mustache comb with sterling silver rim *(ibid Fig. 2).*

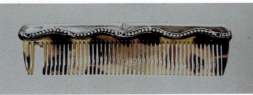

FIGURE 6   FIGURE 8

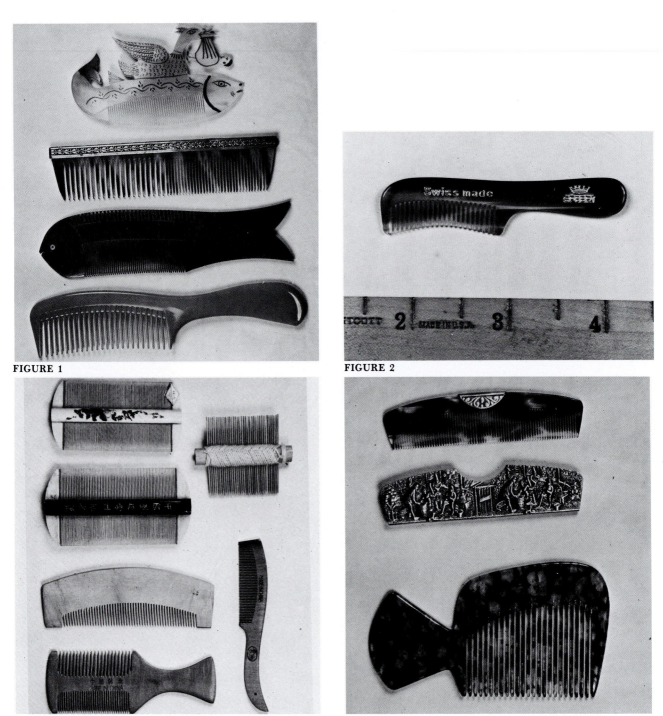

FIGURE 1

FIGURE 2

FIGURE 3

FIGURE 4

PLATE 38. Modern combs from around the world. *Fig. 1:* Top comb is of raw horn from Mexico, hand decorated with folk pattern. Third from the top is a dyed horn comb from Bangladesh with an inlaid ivory eye. *Fig. 2:* A modern mustache comb made from acetate. *Fig. 3:* Composition and bamboo tooth combs from China, decorated with symbols, plus a bamboo and cotton "toothpick-type" from Ceylon. *Fig. 4:* Three more modern combs. The one at the bottom is the Liberty of London comb *(courtesy Pierre Olivier Co., Tiburon, California).*

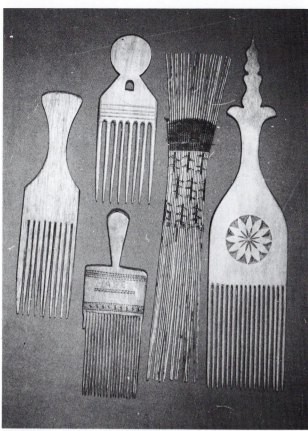

FIGURE 1

FIGURE 2

PLATE 39. *Fig. 1:* African wooden combs *(Collection of Kathe Kilot). Figs. 2 & 3:* Oriental wooden combs *(author's collection). Fig. 4:* Sterling silver cased comb and barber's comb *(ibid Fig. 1).*

FIGURE 3

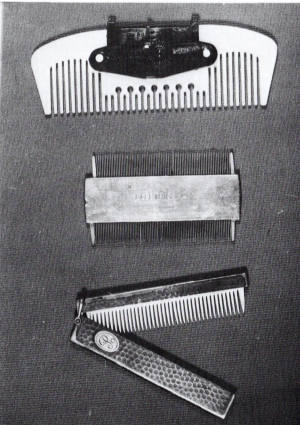

FIGURE 4

reminds one of a centuries old Breughel village group. It was recently offered for sale by a prestigious Western women's apparel shop for about $10.00, and was imported from Holland. It is not attached as the sterling comb [Plate 39, Fig. 4] nor intended to be worn about the neck, but the style is quite similar and revives in popularity from time-to-time.

California based Pierre Olivier Company is currently producing an unusual line of combs both decorative and utilitarian using a special patented process allowing printed cotton fabric by Liberty of London to be laminated between layers of acetate to produce a unique yet modestly priced comb such as shown in [Plate 40, Fig. 3]. Their exceptionally high quality line includes numerous sizes, shapes, and designs which are still hand made and hand polished in France. Hand polishing insures the hair is not split, the comb is more durable, and it is quite handsome. Some of the shapes are ultra modern and the overall patterns are subdued pastels. Each is script signed "Pierre Olivier" and could not easily be confused with antique combs.

THE PRESENT DAY rage for mustaches has resulted in the recent manufacture of the old time mustache comb. This diminutive comb measures 1-1/2 inches in the tooth section and is 3-1/16th inches overall. The Swiss model shown was expensive for such a novelty ($5.00) as antique sterling topped versions can run upwards of $30.00 + . The older ones are devoid of handles and may or may not have teeth which are arched in the center. The wooden curved handled comb, [Plate 38, Fig. 2] has about the same dimensions but it may be intended for use by a small child rather than a bearded adult male. The three wooden combs at the bottom of [Plate 38, Fig. 2] made of wood polished as smooth as glass, are made in China.

With some notable exceptions, wooden combs will have been made outside the United States, some cultures favoring them above all other materials. They will be found in boxwood, sandalwood, ebony, bamboo, and other easily carved woods. Combs from the African continent and the South Sea Islands are nearly always of wood and tend to be repetitive in design and material, so only a few are shown [Plate 39, Fig. 1]. Like the combs from Near and Far Eastern countries they tend to be traditional, and ancient designs and forms remain as popular today as they were centuries ago. As a case in point several combs were recently purchased at the United Nations in New York City which are representative of the arts and crafts exported from member nations. It is significant that these combs are hardly distinguishable from genuine antique combs. Their extremely modest prices for hand made goods do not reflect the additional taxes and duties which would add substantially to their cost had they

not been duty free. Such nations as Colombia, Bangladesh, and Mexico still work horn combs for export, as their technological progress allows for hand labor not feasible in the more advanced nations. I was recently approached to examine some of these combs by an inexperienced dealer who was shocked when presented with the selection shown here, as identical combs were mistakenly thought to be antique. Always look for signs of wear!

THE MANUFACTURE OF ivory combs requires greater skill, judgment, and painstaking attention to detail, far in excess of the expertise required for making either horn or tortoise combs.

All the raw materials had to be imported, the tusks warped and fractured easily and the grain was often uneven. Every step in the early manufacture of ivory combs was done by hand; saws and other machinery were used from 1849 till the turn of the century. Today no ivory combs are manufactured in the United States, nor in any other country, in all probability, as sadly the elephant itself is in danger of becoming an extinct species. Chemicals have been developed which are suitable; but by no means are they as durable, beautiful, nor aesthetically pleasing as the genuine dressing or decorative ivory comb.

Doyle tells us, "To make an ivory comb, a tusk was sawed by hand into blocks of varying lengths which were again sawed into rectangular bars about half an inch in thickness. The bars were then rounded and on a narrow, flat surface left on one side, a row of tiny sockets was carefully drilled. The teeth, which had been sawed separately, were shaped and pointed by means of delicate tools similar to those used in the making of horn combs. They were then driven with a small hammer into the sockets which they had been shaped to fit. Into the holes drilled through the back of the comb, brass pieces were inserted. Last of all came smoothing and polishing. The result was a very beautiful dressing-comb that would last a lifetime."

Just as a few towns in Massachusetts became the centers of tortoise and horn comb production, so Saybrook, Litchfield, Middletown, Deep River, Mansfield, and Meriden, Connecticut gradually became the centers for ivory comb manufacture. Meriden made 2/3 of all the domestic ivory combs in 1849, and in 1845 an astounding 4,800,000 ivory dressing-combs were produced in the United States. No mention is made of decorative combs, but it is safe to assume they were imported from China, as this was the same era in which great quantities of these exquisitely carved combs were brought by clipper ships from the Far East. It is doubtful that many American craftsmen were capable of executing such involved designs nor could they compete with the cheap Oriental labor of that period.

PLATE 37. *Figs. 1 & 2:* A selection of tortoise shell, elephant ivory, vegetable ivory and horn combs from the collection of the Leominster Historical Society, Leominster, Massachusetts.

FIGURE 1

FIGURE 2

FIGURE 1

FIGURE 2

FIGURE 4

PLATE 41. *Fig. 1:* Carved ivory comb *(courtesy Elizabeth Anne Buzzell).* *Fig. 2:* Carved Chinese comb *(Collection of Kathe Kilot).* *Fig. 3:* American ivory comb *(Costume Institute of The Metropolitan Museum of Art, gift of Mrs. Grace Rainey Rogers).* *Fig. 4:* Carved ivory Chinese comb, damaged *(author's collection).*

AMONG THE NOTABLE producers of ivory combs the following Connecticut based companies were synonymous with high standards of quality: Pratt, Williams, Reed, Rogers, Merriman, Murdoch, Bush, Webb, and Batsford. Of the millions of ivory dressing combs which were made in Connecticut one would be hard pressed to find a single example today so we can appreciate the small ivory one from the Leominster Historical Society's collection all the more, [*Plate 37, Fig. 1*] even though it is unimpressive by itself.

Each of the ivory combs on *Plate 41* is representative of the handsome decorative type which the adroit Chinese exported to the Western world in great numbers in the early 19th century. The decorative aspects were rather rigidly prescribed. *Figure 1.* is said to have been made in France and except for the stunning rose and leaf decoration which is certainly atypical of Chinese motifs, note the similarities in *Figures 1, 2, and 4.* Each has ultra long sharply pointed teeth, the spacing between the teeth has been topped or pointed by hand, each has a framework surrounding a lattice worked design, each has the bridgework decoration done well above the lengthy teeth, each

FIGURE 3

FIGURE 1

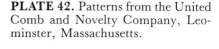

PLATE 42. Patterns from the United Comb and Novelty Company, Leominster, Massachusetts.

has an uneven number of teeth, and each is approximately the same size. *Figure 3.* is American and differs in every respect from the others. The forest scenes, shorter teeth—centered to allow the bridge to extend beyond them—the freer form, square unfinished spacing of the thick teeth—all distinguish this fine Occidental comb from the equally fine Oriental examples.

The forerunner of the most frequently used comb substance, celluloid, was the natural resin, rubber. Until 1839, when Charles Goodyear added sulphur to masticated, heated rubber masses and discovered it would retain its shape when molded, rubber had been little more than an interesting but useless curiousity. So called ''hard rubber'' combs were jet black in color and can be distinguished from celluloid only with great difficulty. Hard rubber tends to be somewhat lighter weight and in decorative combs and hair pins has a matte finish. It is also softer to the touch and is much scarcer than celluloid; those examples I am acquainted with have been imported chiefly from England or France, both of which countries had extensive and high grade comb manufacturies.

Although John Wesley Hyatt patented ''celluloid'' in 1868 in the United States, an Englishman, Alexander Parkes, had pioneered with a similar substance which he called ''Parkesine''. Parkes was a metallurgist and is credited with developing a technique for electro-plating strange things such as spider webs and fresh cut roses, novelties he presented to Queen Victoria and Prince Albert, presumably for their amusement. Incidentally, those roses and other flowers were captured in hatpin heads which are real collector's gems today.

Celluloid, as it is commonly known today, was made in England by treating wood flour, nitric and sulphuric acids which made a tough cellulose. Parkes discovered the addition of molten camphor would dissolve the solution which when cooled would harden to form. Reheated it could be drilled, sawed, planed, molded, and shaped. Among the first objects made from cellulose were dressing and fancy combs. By a process of trial and error, Parkes had hit upon celluloid just as Goodyear had made rubber a useful, almost indispensable material, and both were extensively hailed as superior to tortoise, horn, and ivory, by several virtues.

Celluloid could be made in an endless variety of shapes, it required no particular skills such as all previous materials had, it could be mass produced in huge quantities, required less hand labor, it could be

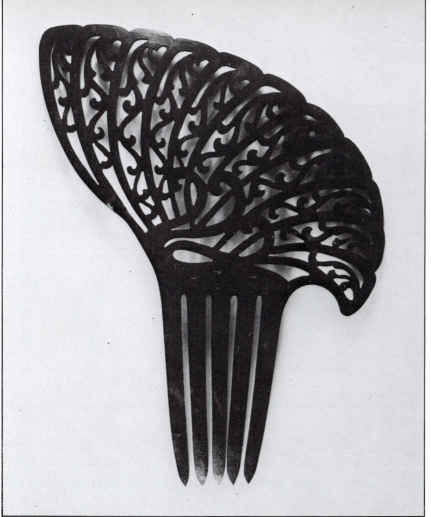

FIGURE 2

made in any desired colors or combinations of colors, it could easily be decorated with gems, metallics or inlays, it took a high polish, it was lightweight, and best of all, it could be made cheaply.

AT FIRST CONSIDERED a great boon to the comb and other industries which rapidly were completely mechanized, it had one serious flaw which ultimately led to its demise and eventually removed it from the market by federal law; it was dangerously flammable. In 1934, it was supplanted by the advent of the induction mold method using sophisticated cellulose acetate. Very simply stated, in injection molding, the plastic is heated to a fluid and molten state. It is then injected through a nozzle into a cold mold just long enough to take the shape of the mold before cooling and setting solid. Once set, the comb is ejected from the mold immediately and the mold may be used for the next batch, the whole process taking only a few minutes. The cheap, flimsy product is well adapted to a modern age where novelty takes precedence over quality to please a fickle, frenetic society. Luckily we are concerned with a gentler age when quality and beauty counted for something.

Each comb manufacturer of any size employed a pattern maker who designed the comb, drawing it by hand on an oiled paper made especially for this purpose. This pattern was carefully cut out and glued to the back of a master pattern made of heavy scrap material, then jig sawed with great precision so a perfect metal die could be made from it. These dies were expensive and the original patterns were retained for future use if the die was damaged or wore out. These original patterns were stamped with the pattern number on the face for easy identification; one factory alone had over 1,400 patterns when it ceased operations. *Figures 1 and 2, Plate 42,* are probably much older than those which show both the pattern and the finished combs. *Figure 2 of Plate 42A* shows a two section comb which was welded together by heat and pressure rather than the traditional pin and hinge arrangement.

On August 24, 1923, when a certain William H. Durant delivered an address to the Leominster Historical Society, he could not have foreseen how soon the comb industry would end, nor could he know how invaluable his seemingly trivial remarks would be to researchers in this field nearly sixty years hence, particularly in reference to the celluloid comb. ''Celluloid is made by taking tissue paper of the finest

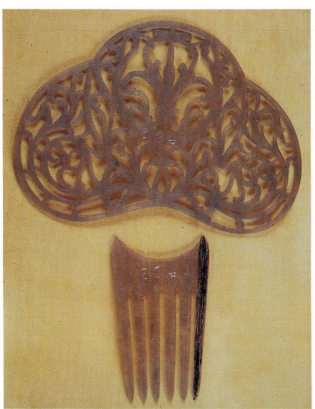

FIGURE 1

FIGURE 2

FIGURE 3

PLATE 42-A. Patterns and combs from the United Comb and Novelty Co. Note the 2-part comb in particular.

quality and immersing it in sulphuric and nitric acids, which convert it into nitro-cellulose. This is washed and bleached and passed thorough a roller-mill with the addition of a certain amount of camphor or its substitutes. It is colored and pressed into cakes 50 × 21 inches, then cut into sheets of any required thickness and hung up to dry, after which it is polished by pressure between highly polished nickeled plates until it is as smooth as a sheet of glass. Celluloid softens at 178°F when it can be molded, turned or bent into almost any shape. It is very inflammable and great care is used in working it.

"In making a comb, a sheet of stock 50 × 21 inches, from a minimum thickness of .005 inches to any desired thickness, is cut with a 40 or 50 inch knife into 4 × 5 inch plates. These plates are then taken to the quiller, who puts a V shaped groove just above where the teeth will come, then the plate goes to the teeth-cutting machine, where two combs are made of the 4 × 5 inch plate.

"If the comb is very fancy, it may go to the jig-saw where the design is jig-sawed out and then hand engraved. The comb may go to the swedge-room where a very fine or elaborate design may be pressed in the stock by steel dies, and then pierced out with punches, making a fine looking design at very little cost. The comb may be plain and then it is trimmed up to shape by cutters on a foot-power polking machine. The teeth are then circled, that is, the four or five end teeth are trimmed off a little, giving a graceful appearance to the comb. The comb is pointed on machine burrs which draw the teeth lengthwise over revolving burrs, with teeth on their circumference. This rounds over the front of the teeth. Now the comb is bent on wooden blocks as previously. The comb is then sent to the rubbing room, where it is rubbed by passing over buffs made of woolen carpet, and run in "mud" made of finely sifted coal ashes and water. This rubbing is rather a dirty job, but it wears down the rough edges and the comb comes out completely smooth. It is then washed in warm water and dried in a revolving dryer. The comb was polished on cotton buffs or dipped in glacial acetic acid to add a fine gloss.

The comb is now finished and goes to the packing room, where it is inspected and wrapped in tissue paper, placed in boxes, labeled, and packed in cartons ready to be shipped to all points of the globe."

ASIDE FROM THE preparation of the stock, it is obvious that the celluloid decorative comb required almost as much hand labor as had the tortoise, horn, and ivory which had preceded it. It is amazing it could have been sold for so modest a price, considering its elegant patterns, wide range of lovely colors, overlaid colors, and sheer beauty.

In his book *Manual for the Manufacture of Celluloid Combs and Buttons* (Paris, 1923) a French chemical engineer with the unlikely name of F. Schmitt relates the advantages of making combs of celluloid viewed from the production standpoint. Translated from the French (with some difficulty) he made the following points:
1. As the raw material could be accurately controlled, the quality as well as the quantity of combs could be standardized.
2. Any other material could be imitated with ease.
3. Both cost and selling price could be predetermined as nothing was governed by chance as when using natural materials.
4. Waste of materials was almost non existent.
5. Since uniformity of the combs could be guaranteed each and every time, packing boxes, and other shipping materials could be standardized.
6. The storage of raw materials was minimized.

Many of the other points such as color, rigidity yet pliability, resistance to the elements, low production cost, wide selection of patterns, the ease with which intricate shapes and sizes could be produced (compared to natural substances), etc., have all been dealt with elsewhere in the book.

The French had recognized the one great drawback to celluloid-inflammability—and had like other nations experimented with numerous other chemical compositions and natural substances and found each wanting. Until the discovery and practical application of acetates the problem was not to be overcome.

England, France and other European countries produced combs with less ornate patterns than Americans, their styles were more conventional, and they had a decided preference for barrettes. Some very elegant combs decorated with piqué work, gold inlays, and pearl and gold decorations were made which have a distinctly European flavor.

Chapter III contains a selection of celluloid low back combs and high back combs with imaginative stone set and unset patterns from the collection of Evelyn Wittsell which can be viewed by appointment. (See listing in the back of the book). An attempt has been made to show a wide range of shapes and patterns; the high decorative combs with a few exceptions are approximately the same dimensions, 4-5 inches wide by 7-8 inches high. The tremendous cost of color photography prevented the use of countless others which were equally fine. Some general observations concerning them should be noted. This is a fairly representative selection of celluloid combs which might be found in a collection though others might be more or less ornate, or differ in some small details.

CHAPTER 3
TYPES AND STYLES OF POPULAR COMBS

There is a tendency to refer to all large combs from 60–200 years old or older as mantilla combs. This is a fallacy, as few, if any of the combs made in the United States at least, were intended for the purpose of supporting the mantilla, (a lacy head covering such as is worn by Lillian Russell in [*Plate 80, Fig. 1*] which was habitual to the Spanish culture. An inheritance from the Moorish Islamic traditions, the Spanish custom of wearing lavishly embroidered silk shawls and fine white or black lace mantillas as head coverings when ladies ventured from the confines of their homes and most especially to church services, was not generally practiced in other parts of the continent, nor in North America.

This is not to say that these romantic trappings were taboo, but rather that they were foreign to the English and Northern European peoples who populated the Eastern part of the United States where the first settlements were established and where the comb industry initiated. Mantillas were also very costly and only the rich could afford to indulge themselves with these hand made laces.

Since the mantilla comb is the most impressive of all combs it should be considered at the outset.

FIGURE 1

FIGURE 2

Doyle tells us in his *Comb Making in America,* "A century ago, (1826) Spanish women would pay as much as $14.00 for a comb of plain tortoise shell, as the plain was considered superior to the mottled which, when made into a comb, brought only about $6.00. Today plain tortoise shell combs are rarely seen, and combs of mottled shell often sell for several hundred dollars."

In 1981, the mantilla tortoise shell comb [*Plate 43, Fig. 2*] with some mottling and a great deal of intricate carving brought at auction about 1/3 of its actual value at $250.00 and was a real bargain. An immense comb by any standards, it has a slick polish; the blotches are easily seen; the tortoise is only 1/16 of an inch thick, so it is very delicate despite its size. It resembles European combs made in the 18th and 19th centuries, and since its former owner was an entertainer it is possible it was either a gift or was purchased there. Divided into four sections, the center square is uncarved and the remaining squares are composed of leaves and florals framing the widest section showing a cross-hatched flower pot with classic entwined floral motif, masterfully executed and scored for emphasis.

The fourth and final section is a stylized border. All the carving has been done by hand, as the irregularities of pattern show and some knife lines which missed their mark are evident. Most indicative of hand work is the square spacing between the 5 long teeth.

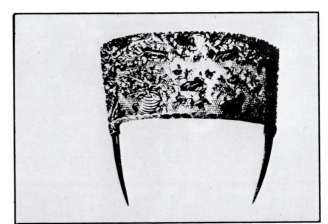

FIGURE 5

PLATE 43. *Fig. 1:* Imitation tortoise mantilla comb, 19th Century *(author's collection).* *Fig. 2:* European tortoise high back comb with intricate carving, 19th Century *(ibid Fig. 1).* *Fig. 3:* 19th Century tortoise shell, probably Chinese *(Leominster Historical Society).* *Fig. 4:* Modern acetate comb with rhinestones *(ibid Fig. 1).* *Fig. 5:* This strange comb with end teeth only has carvings seemingly identical to the comb shown in Fig. 3. It is Chinese also *(ibid Fig. 3).*

FIGURE 3

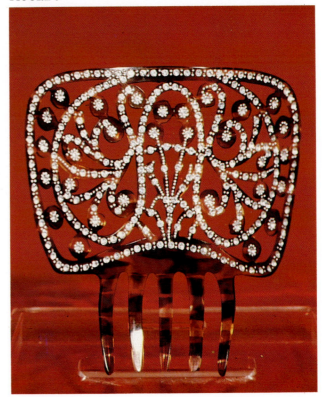

FIGURE 4

67

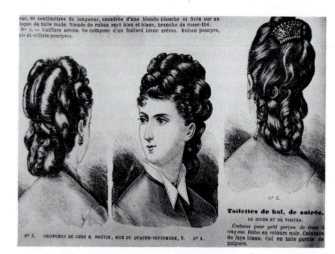

COIFFURE N° 3.

PLATE 44. International hair styles as shown in "La Mode Illustré" from 1875.

It is uneven and so are the teeth, but this in no way diminishes the value of the comb, in fact it enhances it, for hand work need not apologize for itself in minor imperfections; rather marvel at the skill required to execute it for it is a work of art as fine as any oil painting or superbly mounted gem. It would have held the mantilla high off the head and allowed the lace to fall gracefully about the face and shoulders. The curve of the comb follows the shape of the back of the wearer's head so the inside or reverse side of the comb is seen by those facing the wearer. In this case the pattern is clearly visible and is as interesting as the outer or "right" side.

Merely to contrast with this fine antique comb of genuine tortoise shell, the imitation modern comb is shown not entirely for contrast of materials and workmanship, but to present an attempt to show the inner side of a comb to full advantage [Plate 43, Fig. 4]. As this is an acetate molded comb; (note the short stubby teeth) it needed something novel which it has in the striking rhinestone pattern of circles and swirls. The overall dimensions are 5 × 5 inches, the teeth being 1-3/4 inches long. The cost a few years ago was $60.00.

LOOKING AT THE ladies magazines from a century ago one cannot help but be astonished at the profusion of things which were used to ornament the hair under the guise of fashion. Fashion was dictated by that far away and magical city, Paris, and no suggestion was too absurd to prevent its immediate adoption by those not fortunate enough to live there. It must be remembered that the leisure classes were obsessed by clothing and hair fashions and by the time the latest thing had trickled down to the masses the styles had changed again. It was inevitable that each spring last year's clothing was passé and some new craze or outrage would be the "rage." It was a strange passion this love affair between Paris and the rest of the

PLATE 45. Hair styles and accessories, 1858–1875 (from ''La Mode Illustré'').

PLATE 46. Hair styles and accessories, 1858–1875 (from ''La Mode Illustré'').

civilized world which is difficult for those emancipated from its grip to comprehend. Woe be to her who did not conform!

Consider the hair styles as a case in point. Lest anyone think for a moment this madness was confined to the weaker sex alone, it was the male animal who in the 18th century went to such lengths that they could scarcely think of anything other than personal adornment and the time and money that was squandered in their pursuit of vanity was unmatched by even the most profligate woman, then or now. Men maintained their own personal hairdressers who, if the cartoon is to be believed were in almost constant attendance. Note the combs in the hairdresser's wig and the scissors in his pocket [*Plate 47, Fig. 1*].

When Louis XIV lost much of his natural hair he turned to wearing wigs which were made of human hair, then of wool and horsehair when human hair became scarce. Called a *peruke* it rose above the brow, was parted and arranged in two peaks flowing in long curls nearly to the waist. Under Louis XVI the tight round curls of the periwig hung over the shoulder, down the back and surrounded the face. There were literally hundreds of wig styles and no 18th century gentleman appeared in public without his perfumed, powdered, shaped, styled, ribboned, jeweled, and dyed wig. In Hogarth's *The Five Orders of Perriwigs* (1761), four of the orders are wigs for men and the

gigantic curled, banged, rolled affairs cause those made for women to pale into insignificance by comparison. Such wigs are used in English (judicial) courts even to the present day.

Ribbons called ''falbalas'' were used by men to tie the hair in the back and it was considered the height of good manners to comb the wig in public using elegant combs in the process, making sure to attract as much attention as possible.

Every profession had its style of wig and wig snatching was equivalent to purse snatching today.

FIGURE 1

FIGURE 2

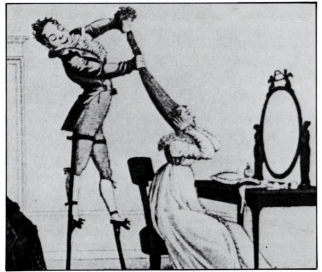

FIGURE 3

PLATE 47. Caricatures ridiculing 18th Century French fashions. *Fig. 1:* A fashionable gentleman is followed by his hairdresser, who is protecting the elaborate wig from possible damage or disarray. Note the combs in the hairdresser's wig and scissors protruding from his pocket. Hairdressers were not considered part of the service class and were highly paid, pampered, privy to their employers' most intimate secrets and much sought after. *Fig. 2:* These outrageously complicated coiffeurs from the French court are symptomatic of the excesses which would lead to the French Revolution. Once arranged these ridiculous creations were left undisturbed for weeks at a time, as they were time consuming and costly to prepare and only the wealthiest could afford them. They must have been hot, uncomfortable, lice-ridden and sure to prevent the noble, albeit sophisticated, lady from enjoying a decent night's sleep. *Fig. 3:* Though both sexes were enamored of their hair styles, women were more frequently the butt of the contemporary caricaturists.

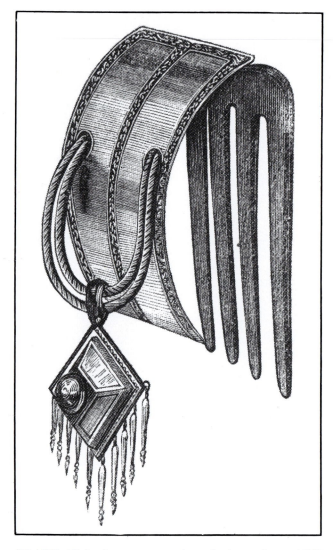

PLATE 47-A. A very unusual comb shown in an 1857 "Lady Godey" magazine. The curved buckle with its ornament attached by metallic cord fell over the knot or chignon in the hair. Teeth of the comb are horn.

Gay wrote a ditty on the perils of wig snatching:
"Nor is thy wig with safety worn;
High on the shoulder, in a basket born,
Lurkes the small boy, whose hand to rapine bred,
Plucks off the curling honors of thy head."

Styles for both men and women became so involved that the advantages of the wig were realized early, for by the mid 17th century wig making was a most profitable business. For those who could afford to have their hair dressed it is believed in 1769 there were 1,200 hair dressers in Paris alone.

During the Renaissance barber shops served as social centers for intellectuals, medical and surgical assistance was given by barbers (who became the doctors of the future) and barber shops were the gathering places for masculine sport in general. Today this vestige of masculine domination has crumbled, indeed women patrons must bridle the tongue in beauty shops as the occupant of the adjacent booth is as likely to be a man as a woman. A form of liberation in reverse, as it were. . . . Hairdressing schools were established and hair dressers and wig makers became an essential professional group from the 17th century onward, many famous hairdressing personalities evolving. Peter Gilchrist, in 1760, published *A Treatise on Hair or Every Lady her own Hair-Dresser,* in which he advises ladies on current styles, preparations and techniques for arranging the hair. An incredible 3,744 hair styles were contained and illustrated in several volumes entitled *L'Elonge de coiffeurs adresse au dames* (1772). Coiffeur dolls were exhibited to popularize a hair style, much like the exquisite dressmaker's dolls which were exported from France to acquaint foreigners with the latest in clothing styles.

LATE IN THE 17th century and throughout the 18th century until the French Revolution, the headdress of stylish women reached a height of two or three feet, decorated with ribbons, feathers, jewels, swags, artificial flowers, miniature golden bird's nests, ships, carriages, in short anything which would cause an overnight sensation at court functions and balls. This must have been no easy feat in such a sophisticated and jaded society. Hairdressers actually mounted ladders to arrange the hair; that they wore stilts as well is quite plausible. The favored color for both men and women was blonde or snow white, possibly because few people had such natural hair color.

Mid 18th and 19th century publications for women devoted space to the hair styles currently in vogue, ornaments, hats and other headgear. Even a glance at the styles shown on the preceding pages proves the absolute necessity for pins, combs, barrettes and all manner of devices to keep these masses of natural and/or additional tresses in a manageable state. Researching the various tools used to support,

curl, frizz, roll, wave, puff, thicken, and separate the hair would constitute a lengthy book in itself.

This exerpt from *Mr. Godey's Ladies* discusses the *waterfall*, ''The dressing of the hair is of course a subject of importance now that the back hair is no longer covered. The waterfall is the usual style and as some persons may be at a loss to arrange it, we will give

PLATE 48. Hair fashions c. 1870.

them a hint on the subject. Tie the back hair rather low on the neck. If a braid is required, tie it under the natural hair, letting it rest on the neck. Then roll the front hair and fasten the ends at the back. Comb the front locks, which are fastened at the back with the back hair. Pin on a frizette and turn the hair up over the comb, which must be entirely concealed. Then put on a net and tie a ribbon around the waterfall.'' Sounds simple, doesn't it?

Despite the fact that virtually all women wore combs before 1921, it is difficult to find suitable photographs of them worn in the hair, as they were usually placed at the back of the head and by the 1870's they had shrunk to the smaller versions then popular. Having one's photograph taken was a fearful business in the days of flashes, black hoods over huge box cameras, artificial backdrops and props of plush Victorian parlors and a general unfamiliarity with the whole puzzling process.

This accounts at least in part, for the wide eyed stare and rigid stance shown by most subjects brave enough to undergo the ordeal. These portraits were taken by the time photography was reasonably well established and neither a frightening nor novel experience, though judging from the expressions, still a grim one.

Literally thousands of wedding and family portraits from old heirloom albums were examined in order to locate even these few, as vintage pictures are often damaged, of extremely poor quality, faded, uninteresting, or they just lack combs!

The combs shown are rather nondescript but are representative of those being worn by the middle class between 1870-1890. The varied hair styles show how mightily these ladies struggled for individuality and generally achieved it, though few were fortunate

PLATE 49. The misses Amity Angell, Belle Cooper and Ethel Seavey, graduates of Southbridge High School, Southbridge, Massachusetts, Class of 1898.

PLATE 51. Representative hair styles from the close of the 19th Century.

FIGURE 4

FIGURE 5

FIGURE 6

playing instruments and the larger central figure is dancing. Each wears loose trousers and jacket.

Fig. 3: Is a beautifully cast pair of winged griffins set with topaz colored stones and carefully attached with almost miniscule brass pins to the amber colored celluloid. This comb commands a value of about $150.

Fig. 4: An imposing comb with a large, deep topaz faceted oval in the center of brass fretwork set with clear rhinestones. Like the preceding combs, it is a distinctive style as the the applied decoration is formed to match the outlines of the comb exactly and the decoration is hand applied, which would have put these combs into a price range far in excess of the average molded comb.

Fig. 5: Has a delicate feeling compared to the massive combs which have preceded it and is indeed much lighter weight. Each of the floral swirls contains a small Persian turquoise set and the brass designs are mounted on a celluloid petal shaped extension of the bridge.

Fig. 6: Has a deep bridge with heart shaped brass leaves which intertwine to make a strip which is attached to the celluloid by small pins. The flowers or berries are of pink glass, pitted for visual effect.

Fig. 7: Is a delicate Art Noveau comb showing brass daisies in full bloom. It is smaller than the other examples but equally fine.

Fig. 8: Among the beloved decorations for these combs was the grape pattern, and at least one is found in

77

nearly every collection. Green jade or green glass beads, arranged so as to simulate a bunch of grapes were used, along with pearls or moonstones to make an impressive comb.

Fig. 9 & 10: These are of European origin, usually stamped "Made in England" or "Made in France" on the back of the comb, and are good examples of gold deposit work. The cabochon oval insets of #9 are cleverly made of glass to resemble black opals. Those in #10 are curiously "painted on" over a substance which may be blue dyed horn to look like turquoise. Gold and silver deposit combs are rarely found in mint condition as almost all will show some degree of wear.

Fig. 11: To prevent the inevitable damage, an Ameri-

PLATE 53. Ornamented low back combs from the author's collection.

FIGURE 7

FIGURE 8

FIGURE 9

can firm patented a plastic overlay similar to verathane which was found on comb #11; whether the process was widely accepted is doubtful.

Fig. 12: Sterling silver set with aquamarine colored faceted stones and a shaped bridge make this an attractive comb. The teeth are longer on this comb than the others.

THE CELLULOID BACK comb was particularly effective when decorated and as it was a pliable, cheap substance which unlike tortoise did not have to be imported, availed a wide array of styles and colors to the middle class woman.

Some low back combs were set directly with colored glass particles, precious and semi-precious

FIGURE 10

FIGURE 11

FIGURE 12

stones, French paste, and other bits of decorative materials. Mr. John Sheehan, for many years an employee of DuPont Manufacturing Company in Leominster, Massachusetts, relates, "The stones were for the most part made of glass with faceted tops and conical shaped bottoms and sometimes straight round bottoms (flat back). These stones were set into pre-drilled holes in the comb using a solvent that momentarily softened the plastic in the drilled hole and acted like a glue to hold the stone in place. The drilling and setting could be combined in one operation, but was usually separated for convenience and/or efficiency as much stone setting was accomplished on the kitchen table in homes where all the grownups and older children would participate. This was called 'homework', but such practices were declared to be illegal in the 1930's and this kind of moonlighting was eliminated along with most stone setting and similar decorative effects on combs which were slow to accomplish and therefore expensive. The stone setting was accomplished with a pair of tweezers to pick up the stone, dip the bottom of the stone in solvent, and set the stone in the drilled hole of the comb which was held in a simple fixture. A skilled operator could set a dozen or so stones a minute. The drilling was accomplished by a drill press arrangement actuated by a foot treadle, the comb being set in a fixture and the operator would move the fixture with both hands to the desired location beneath the drill. Sometimes precious and semi-precious stones were used for decorative purposes and these were heated and impressed into the plastic which would cool after the impresison and hold the stone in place. The heat method could also be used with glass stones."

If the hole expanded too much, a larger size stone could be used to fill the depression, but frequently a comb will appear to have been damaged, when this may have been the initial cause for the irregularity of holes.

The designs used were relatively simple such as a few stones to imitate stars, tiny flowers, rows of alternating colored stones, stones set in impressed patterns, diamond shapes, bands of stones divided by smaller sets, and the like. Many combs were plain in an attempt to imitate tortoise more closely and for those prim ladies who would not tolerate any decoration because of religious or other principles. These unadorned combs lack appeal for most collectors as the decorative motifs tend to differentiate the combs from one another. The most elaborate combs were undoubtedly the high back sorts which most people associate with distant relatives in the latter half of the 1800's and early 1900's.

There is something so supremely feminine and elegant about the high back comb there is little wonder they appeal to the collector over all other types of combs. High back combs, not to be confused with mantilla combs, reached a height of 12 inches, (some theatrical combs were 16 inches or more but were not intended for wear outside the theatre). No high back comb reached the mammoth widths of the ugly clarified horn combs of the late 18th and early 19th centuries, for the teeth were 3-1/2 inches long and the comb extended for 9 inches along the head! As was noted in Chapter II, as huge as these combs were, they were worn in pairs or greater numbers, as side and back combs, in support of the heavy heads of hair that were then in vogue. These combs, incidentally, weigh virtually nothing.

Aside from the fine carved tortoise shell versions of the high back comb, celluloid combs were far and away the most gracefully proportioned, fanciful, colorful and charming. They do not compare with those magnificent custom creations of such master craftsmen as René Lalique, Henri Vever, Orazzi, Veazey, Elsa Unger, Harald Slott-Moller, Lucien Gaillard, Paul Lienard, and others, but combs of this sort discussed in Chapter VI, are in a class removed and are found only in museum collections, for sale by exclusive dealers to the fabulously wealthy, or are already in the private collections of the very rich.

Mr. John Sheehan [*Plate 54*] is shown with a display of DuPont and Viscaloid combs which were popular in the last quarter of the 19th century up to that fateful day in 1921 when Irene Castle, an internationally famous ballroom dancer, decided to "bob" her hair. Almost overnight, the manufacture of combs such as the one held by Mr. Sheehan ceased, and while those such as are shown below it continued to be produced, the days of the "fancy comb" were numbered.

Manufacturers placed increased emphasis on the utility comb. Dressing combs with rat tails, combinations of combs and brushes, handled combs, purse-sized combs, combs cased in mock tortoise, sterling, and other substances to be worn as jewelry about the neck on chains, handled combs with giant teeth, and combs so inexpensive they were almost "throw away price" appeared.

Exotic and beautiful high back combs were doomed but many manufacturers continued to make celluloid and acetate hair pins and barettes; some simply ceased operations altogether. Improvements in hair pins, which were still required by those die hard ladies who refused to wear the marcelled bob and frizzy permanents, water wavers which promised to wave the hair while the wearer slept, and a myriad of hair curlers and similar devices were produced by comb manufacturers faced with near ruin. Eventually such companies as The Diadem of Leominster and others, made puff combs which have enjoyed a modest comeback in recent years. The smart shops are sell-

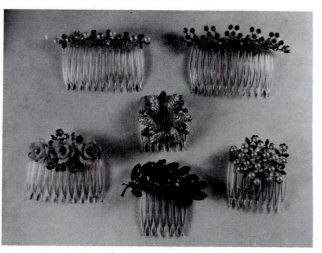

PLATE 54-A. When the marcel wave ruled the land every woman owned a set of water wavers.

PLATE 55. Modern split tooth decorative combs *(Courtesy Mrs. Alice Sawyer, Leominster, Massachusetts)*.

ing them for stiff prices, and department stores, boutiques, and bargain stores alike sell them for evening wear. They will invariably have split teeth, that is to say, the teeth are rounded and separated so there is an oval space between the teeth which is supposed to hold the hair more firmly and prevent loss and slipping. This invention was variously termed Grip-Tuth, and Magik Grip by Diadem, whose acetate combs had a metal rolled and stamped hinged decorative top containing good quality glass stones and rhinestones in a wide range of colors. "These stones were still hand

set," asserted Mrs. Alice Sawyer who along with her husband and father-in-law operated the firm for many years. "Today they are strips of stones glued to the comb."

A current manufacturer of combs in the Leominster area who inherited a long established factory found in his basement a quantity of celluloid combs and the patterns from which they had been created. None of these combs had been set with stones as they surely would have been had the process just described by Mr. Sheehan been followed. They were

PLATE 54. Mr. John Sheehan presents a variety of DuPont and Viscaloid combs in the early 1930's.

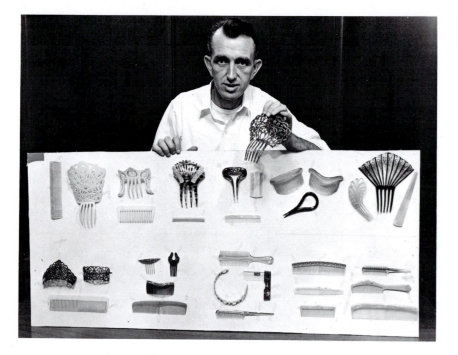

of random sizes but those which I purchased were the large high back variety which would have been striking had they been set with the appropriate stones. Some were found with the original salesman's sample cloth attached and the wholesale prices indicated they would have cost the merchant an average of a dollar each. Fortunately the sample was dated 11/23 and the model numbers and other pertinent data were also included. Though they are nearly 60 years old, they have the appearance of having just come off the assembly line, for indeed in one sense they have, for they have never been used and provide an excellent opportunity for study.

The purpose of the high back comb was primarily for visual effect and toward that end they are found in various treatments as well as shapes and embellishments. One of the most effective methods was to treat only the front side which was to be decorated, with an acid which gave a "frosted" appearance and

greatly enhanced the detail of flowers, butterflies, abstract designs and lacy patterns on which such motifs as the fleur-de-lis shown on *Plate 57* were formed.

The practice of overlaying the clear celluloid with black, imitation tortoise, pastel colors with a watered appearance, and filling certain areas with shiny fragments which simulated flecks of gold or silver was popular. Impressing naturalistic forms such as parrots with jeweled eyes and outlined or solidly encrusted butterflies, stressing certain areas with white lines and dots of enameling added depth and price in the process, as this also was hand applied. Hand coloring areas such as petals or stamens was occasionally done, and enameling in bright colors an entire fretted top which was then set in matching brilliants, as in bow knots, were effective decorative additions.

Figures 1 and 3 on *Plate 61* are very different examples of celluloid treated to resemble tortoise. Each is very attractive but careful observations of genuine

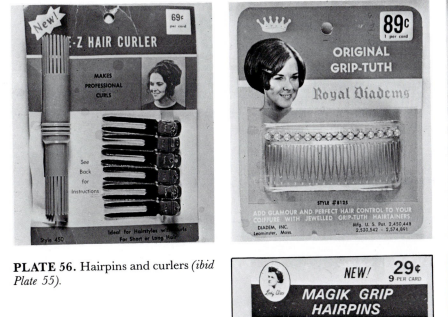

PLATE 56. Hairpins and curlers *(ibid Plate 55).*

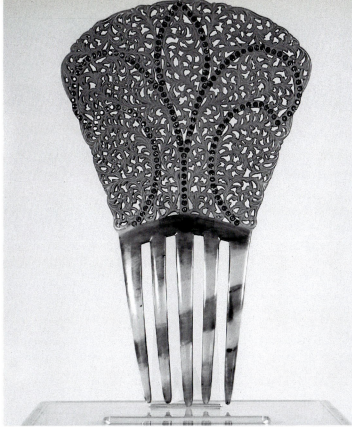

FIGURE 2

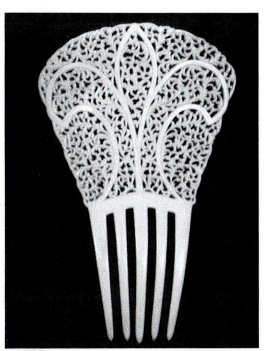

FIGURE 1

PLATE 57. Fleur-de-lis celluloid combs. *Fig. 1:* Ivory *(Leominster Historical Society). Fig. 2: (Collection of Evelyn Wittsell). Fig. 3: (author's collection).*

FIGURE 3

tortoise throughout the book will show the vast difference between the two substances. Since this is the question most frequently asked, the point is stressed to familiarize the reader with examples to aid in identification.

A GOOD EXAMPLE of the variations which were achieved using a single motif, the fleur-de-lis, are noteworthy. *Figure 1 of Plate 57* is an ivory comb and has the fleur-de-lis solidly outlined against a background for sharp contrast, and is characteristically unset, as previously noted, ivory was considered elegant enough in its own right and was left plain save for the carving.

The celluloid examples *(Figures 2 and 3)* show the fleur-de-lis outlined in green or blue rhinestones against an acid treated or "frosted" ground, with plain

FIGURE 1

FIGURE 2

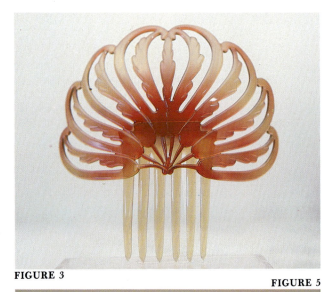

FIGURE 3

FIGURE 4

FIGURE 5

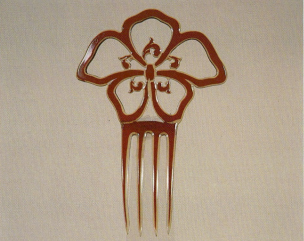

FIGURE 6

PLATE 58. Unset celluloid combs from the United Comb and Novelty Co., Leominster, Massachusetts.

84

FIGURE 7

FIGURE 8

FIGURE 9

teeth on one and imitation tortoise teeth on the other. Bright colored stones were pavé set in this motif on an uncarved ground to produce a brilliant effect for wear at ultra social events such as the opera. The lacy ground could be treated, light or dark colored, untreated, set with rhinestones, plain or any number of color combinations, but the size (5-1/2W × 8H) and the number of teeth remained relatively constant.

Though the pattern was identical, the use of gold colored flecks, various colored sets and/or combinations thereof, overlaying colors, background enameling, outlining, acid etching, and the basic celluloid tint, so individualized a comb that it could hardly be recognized as the same initial pattern. A manufacturer could thus produce an infinite range of combinations from a limited supply of patterns once the die was formed. The retail price was dependent upon the amount of embellishment requiring hand labor; however, an elaborate and outstanding comb must have commanded the top dollar.

Pattern makers were hard pressed to create original designs for pins and combs, so the variations are slight indeed. Original combs were designed for those willing to pay the price, but for the collector to find a genuinely unique example even among the hundreds of thousands of them, is most unlikely. A purely arbitrary list of 20 shapes which were mass produced would have to include the following, though the list is by no means totally inclusive, nor could it be, given the countless patterns available at one time. The near prohibitive cost of color plates does not permit as wide an inclusion of exceptional examples as desired, but a representative sampling is shown.

1. Abstracts	11. Flowers
2. Ball tops	12. Geometrics
3. Birds	13. Hearts
4. Bows and knots	14. Insects
5. Celestial motifs	15. Modified horseshoe
6. Circles	16. Nautical motifs
7. Enamels	17. Scrolls
8. Fans	18. Stylized leaves
9. Feathers	19. Symbols
10. Filagrees	20. Wings

THE COMB IN the middle of *Plate 58,* is intriguing for it is actually a simple tiara and when worn fits neatly across the crown of the head between the ears, and if the hair is arranged surrounding the tips it is surprisingly becoming. *Figure 3* on *Plate 60* is an example of the effective use of brilliants against a lacy background. Often over-ornamentation produces a gaudy comb not suitable for day wear but quite effective for an evening event. These sets were used in celluloid combs rather than other substances (there may be exceptions but this is as near a truism as one can get) and the pattern created by the stones was of

paramount importance. Stone set combs are a great deal of fun to collect and as their purpose was to create an illusion for the average person who could not afford diamonds and precious gems set in their hair ornaments, they did an admirable job.

Novelty combs such as the crescent on [*Plate 59, Fig. 3*], the bow on the same page, the peacock feathers on [*Plate 61, Fig. 6*], the pair of parrots on [*Plate 62, Fig. 5*], and the stylized insect on the same page are combs which were worn in the top knot in the 1890's. Of course they could have been and were worn anywhere the wearer chose.

Red combs are most distinctive, *Figures 4 and 9* on *Plate 61* are unset but their charm lies in the simplicity of the design. Both are outsized combs, as is the rather Art Deco comb of *Plate 60*, with its alternating plain and unset spokes. Several of these combs show

FIGURE 1　　　　　**FIGURE 2**

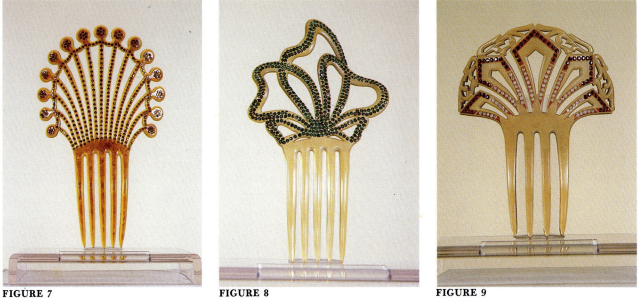

FIGURE 7　　　　**FIGURE 8**　　　　**FIGURE 9**

PLATE 59. Novel designs in rhinestone set combs (*Collection of Evelyn Wittsell*).

the overlay of color upon a clear base. *Plate 62, Fig. 8* has gold flecks, which were used rather sparingly, as they tended toward ostentatious display.

No one can deny the attractiveness of the celluloid comb, nor its usefulness and place as an accessory of dress.

A word about hinged combs is in order, whether of celluloid or natural materials. Those shown on *Plate 68D* are the type which formed tiaras or bands which were worn across the crown of the head as indicated by the curve of the ornamentation. Those which were straight and much narrower in width were intended to be worn with the teeth inserted into the

chignon. Whether worn at the front of the head or the back depended on how the comb was hinged, how the hair was arranged, personal likes and dislikes, the formality of the occasion, as well as the prevailing fashion. Coiffures were created for the comb, or perhaps it was the other way around. Celluloid tiaras such as the one worn by the girl shown *in Figure 1, Plate 51* are usually plain, and if set, the design is simple. Very popular was the single row of pearls, coral, or gold balls attached to teeth of tortoise, metals, celluloid, or horn. Though celluloid became the most often employed for everyday use and for those who could not afford other substances, it did not cause the

FIGURE 3

FIGURE 4

FIGURE 5

FIGURE 6

FIGURE 10

FIGURE 1

FIGURE 2

FIGURE 3

FIGURE 5

overnight disappearance of other substances; there is a decided overlapping of materials, designs, styles, and kinds of combs as with any other facet of life in which change occurs.

It cannot be stressed too frequently that these celluloid combs are substantial in nature and there was much hand labor involved in their creation as opposed to the cheap, flimsy, obviously stamped combs with stubby, broad teeth which are currently found in import stores. The high back celluloid comb contained from 2–6 teeth which were straight, curved, or wavy, but they were almost without exception made

PLATE 60. Leaf and fan designs from the collection of Evelyn Wittsell *(except Fig. 1)*.

FIGURE 6

FIGURE 7

FIGURE 8

FIGURE 4

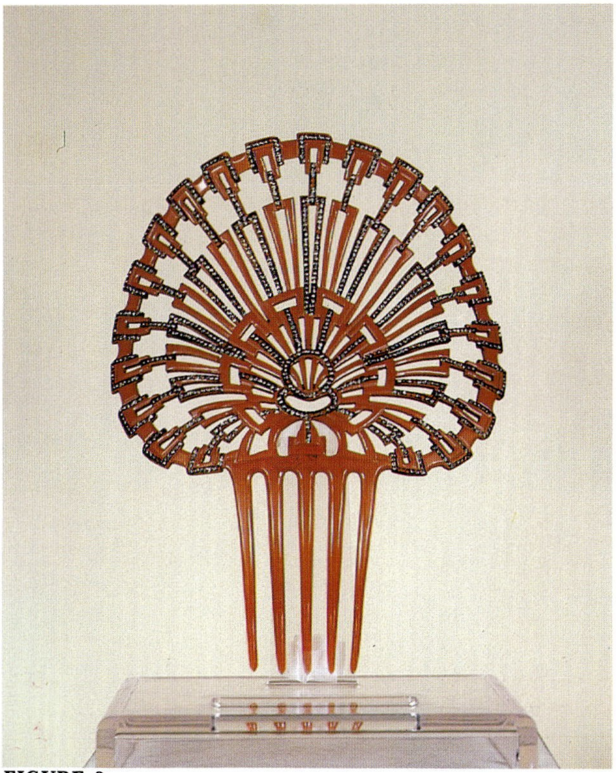

FIGURE 9

89

FIGURE 1

FIGURE 2

FIGURE 3

FIGURE 4

FIGURE 5

FIGURE 6

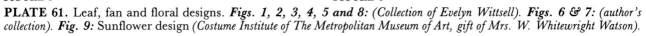

PLATE 61. Leaf, fan and floral designs. *Figs. 1, 2, 3, 4, 5 and 8: (Collection of Evelyn Wittsell). Figs. 6 & 7: (author's collection). Fig. 9: Sunflower design (Costume Institute of The Metropolitan Museum of Art, gift of Mrs. W. Whitewright Watson).*

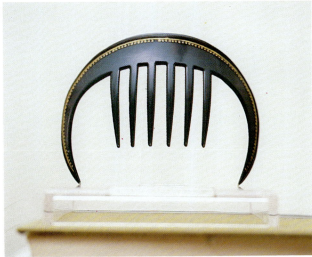

FIGURE 7

FIGURE 8

FIGURE 9

with solid teeth, that is not split as they are today.

Teeth often exceeded 4 inches in length, in the carved and pierced ivory beauties from China, and were at least 2-1/4 inches long. They tapered from nearly 1/2 inch at the widest end tooth to about 1/4 inch at the base of the slenderest tooth. Those combs which have only 1 tooth are not considered combs but hair ornaments, and they are in a class by themselves.

There are as many curves in the high back comb as there are combs, but the most graceful stand away from the natural shape of the head to enable the design and the ornamentation to be fully appreciated. The teeth were inserted into the puffs, curls, bun, rolls, or other hair arrangements so only that part of the comb above the teeth was visible. It is evident that those with scant tresses were forced to resort to switches, rats, and other forms of additional locks to pad their natural hair if they were to display their combs to full advantage. The open fan shape was the most adopted but the semi circle, oval, pyramid, spread wings, leaf shapes, cones, horseshoes, scallops, full circles, feathers, crowns, triangles, side swirls, and a myriad of other shapes were used. They were not always worn completely perpendicular to the back of the head but were slanted to the side, reversed so the curve ran counter to the shape of the head and the front of the comb was fully visible from the front face. There appears to have been no absolute requirement as to how combs should be worn and some ladies exhibited much individuality in wearing their combs.

FROM PAT HATHAWAY'S historic photograph collection comes this extraordinary picture of an anonymous lady from the 1870's wearing a low back comb as a coronet [*Plate 63*]. Its almost exact duplicate can be seen in [*Plate 88, Fig. 1*] in black bakelite, Goodyear,

FIGURE 1

FIGURE 2

FIGURE 3

FIGURE 5

FIGURE 6

ebonite, or a wide range of other trade names for this hard rubber substance invented in 1863. Each prong is surmounted by a large pearlized sphere which contrasts sharply with the jet black teeth and bridge. The unusual hair style has probably been arranged specifically to show the comb to best advantage, and as portrait pictures presented the subject in their finest attire, it is safe to assume the comb was, among her other jewelry, considered rather choice.

In connection with ebonite combs it is curious that many of the backcombs have much longer teeth than those made in any other substance and are both stunning and versatile. They appear to have been

worn as other than low back combs as the nice selection found on *Plate 88* will illustrate.

No BOOK ON combs can overlook one of the most exquisite forms of combs. Found on the heads of clay images unearthed from Japanese tombs thought to be at least 1,000 years old, were the representative coiffure and ornamentation which until recently was worn by all Oriental ladies.

Unlike the Occidental combs which can be worn in any manner on a wide variety of hair styles which change with dizzying rapidity, Japanese ladies wore their hair in particular traditional styles (originally

FIGURE 4

FIGURE 7

FIGURE 8

FIGURE 9

PLATE 62. Floral, insect and bird designs. *Figs. 1, 2, 3 & 7: (Collection of Evelyn Wittsell). Figs. 4, 5, 6, 8 & 9: (author's collection).*

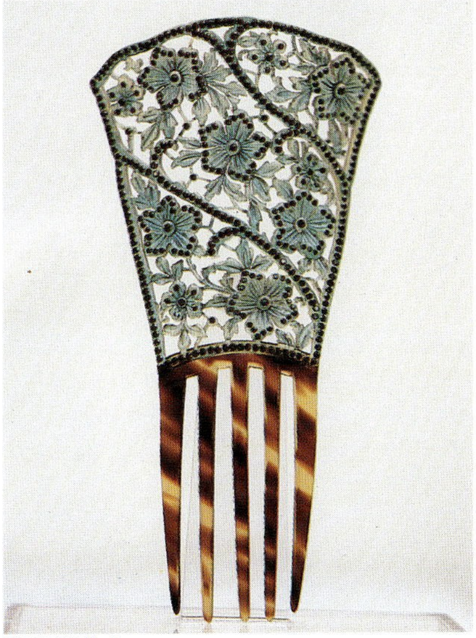

93

PLATE 63. This woman is wearing a button or ball comb, popular in the U.S. in the 1870's *(Historical Photograph Collection of Pat Hathaway, Pacific Grove, California)*.

PLATE 63-A. Contemporary Japanese bride wearing traditional Japanese wedding headdress.

there were scores of them) that at a glance revealed the age and/or marital status of the wearer. Some styles were considered appropriate only for unmarried girls and others were reserved for older women or particular classes of women. So complicated were these hair styles that only experts were able to arrange them and the process was a lengthy one. Accomplished by the use of hard fat cosmetic paste, thick dark blue paper was pasted to the underside of the chignon and puffed sidelocks, which gave the wearer height as well as fullness and stability. Depending on the formality of the occasion, white, silver, or gold strings were used to secure the chignon.

Mr. R. Saito of the Japanese Board of Tourist Industry, writing in 1939 provides us with an accurate description of Japanese coiffure. "For hair ornaments, combs, and hairpins are required, the hairpins (kanzasi) being of two kinds: those stuck in from the front and those inserted in the back. The combs are usually of raised lacquer work, while the ornamental front hairpins are generally fanciful representations of flowers and the back hairpins, of beaten silver. As a rule no bar or kogai is used in this style; but for a bride in full wedding costume a tortoise shell bar of considerable size is inserted at the bottom of the knot. At both ends of this bar are engraved pine, bamboo, and plum, cranes and turtles, and other objects popularly regarded as auspicious signs or omens. Combs and hairpins must also be all of spotless tortoise shell of a pale yellow hue, since all other materials such as metal are considered absolutely inappropriate." A style favored by the geisha, but avoided

94

FIGURE 2

FIGURE 3

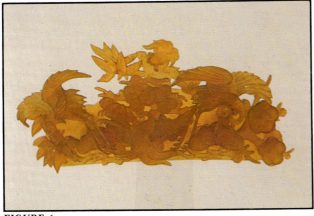

FIGURE 1

PLATE 64. *Fig. 1:* Blonde tortoise shell decorative combs and Japanese bridal headdress *(author's collection).* ***Fig. 2:*** Japanese bridal hair ornaments, probably Meji period *(Collection of Miss Chiyo Okazaki).* ***Fig. 3:*** Enameled and mother-of-pearl inlay comb of amber *(author's collection).*

in households with austere and refined taste, since it is even more informal or less ceremonial than the ordinary style called ''simada'', was the ''tubusi-simada.'' One who has her hair done in ''tubusi-simada'' enjoys great freedom in the choice of combs and hairpins so that she can depend on her own individual taste and discretion as her chief guide.

FIFTY YEARS AGO the most representative of all native Japanese styles of hairdressing was the ''maru-mage.'' All married women wore this style and waitresses, whether married or not, though some slight modifications were permitted the serving groups. At this point in time Japan was a very traditionally oriented nation and the social class structure was rigidly followed. Unless an Occidental were apprised of the significance of the minor differences in headdress they would go unnoticed, though every Japanese person would instantly recognize their importance to the wearer. ''As in the simada, combs, bars and hairpins used in the ''maru-mage'' should be of spotless tortoise shell for ceremonial occasions, but for most other occasions one may use spotted tortoise shell, raised lacquer ware, gold or silver, precious stones, or any other substance

in fact, that suits one's taste or inclination. Here, then, one enjoys freedom of choice among a wide variety of materials.''

The style appropriate for young girls from 13–18 years of age was called the ''momo-ware'', meaning ''a peach cut in two'', and of all the styles it is the prettiest. The hair was drawn up in a continuous roll around the head and a full rounded chignon was worn atop the head. It was, ''adorned with a comb having an artificial flower on the upper edge or with a hair-pin also decorated with an artificial flower or flowers.''

The elegant comb [*Plate 64, Fig. 3*] shown actual size (3-1/2 × 2-1/4) is hand carved of amber decorated on the face with many petaled flowers, leaves, and stems traced in gold. The symbolic dragonflies have iridescent wings and bulging eyes. The reverse side shows the same pair of insects with solid gold and white enameled wings. The workmanship is delicate beyond belief and the motif is clearly that which influenced the French artists in the late 1880's. The accompanying pin has matching florals and typical of the attention to detail exemplified by Japanese workmen, even the vertical ends hold gold inlaid flowers.

Prints made between 1700–1900 would verify the common practice among upper class ladies to compete with one another to see who could wear the most combs. A 19th century European visitor to Japan

PLATE 64-A. Examples of the Japanese use of combs (*from ''Japanese Prints'' by James A. Michener*).

noted in, "Japanese Art Lacquers" Kushi Kogai, "The ladies stuck elaborate small combs into the forepart of their piled up coiffure with sundry fanciful pins behind. Such ornaments were their pride and joy and often cost the husband the income of several months. Jewelry of our kind was not worn."

During these centuries noted artists drew sketches for decorating these combs and pins which ranged from golden maps of the Japanese isles, kite flying, sailing ships at anchor in the bay, garden scenes, views of Mt. Fuji, and seasonal motifs to an occasional bit of comical subject matter. As an island people, there is much use of water, birds, marshes and pampas grass, blossoms and bamboo against the moon, each significant to the culture.

A very brief glimpse of Japanese history will show, as the European above noted, the robes of both upper class Japanese and Chinese women were lavishly embroidered in brilliantly colored silks and satins, so the use of jewelry was confined almost exclusively to hair ornaments and combs. In the prehistoric Jomon period bent and lacquered bamboo combs and carved bone hairpins were used. During the Nara period the Japanese were influenced by the Chinese who were wearing boxwood and ivory combs as well as forked hairpins. As they developed a culture of their own during the Heian period, the hair was worn long, flowing over the shoulders and completely unadorned. The elaborate hairdos fashionable during the Edo period necessitated the use of restrained but elegant combs made of boxwood, ivory, tortoise, horn, glass and lacquered work. Featured were inlays of mother-of-pearl, openwork, and continuous designs sprinkled with gold and silver powder.

Dates For Japanese Periods	
Yamato	300–592 A.D.
Asuka	592–710 A.D.
Nara	740–794 A.D.
Heian	794–1192 A.D.
Kamakura	1192–1333 A.D.
Namboku	1334–1392 A.D.
Muromachi	1392–1573 A.D.
Momoyama	1578–1603 A.D.
Edo	1603–1867 A.D.
Meji	1868–1912 A.D.
Taisho	1912–1926 A.D.
Showa	1926–Present

THE WEDDING HEADDRESS shown in [Plate 64, Fig. 1] was originally thought to be baleen but careful comparison with a similar comb from the vast collection of Miss Chiyo Okazaki (Kushi Kanzashi Ten, Kyoto, Japan, 1978, Pg. 246) would definitely establish it as blonde tortoise from the Meji (1868–1912) or Taisho (1912–1926) periods. It conforms to the requirement that the head ornaments used in the Japanese wedding ceremony be of spotless materials and depict symbols of longevity and happiness. The graceful long legged cranes stand on a single pedestal 3/4 of an inch above the lower bamboo, plum blossoms and branches. The entire 5-1/2 inch wide ornament rises from the head on four teeth or prongs measuring about one inch high; how it is secured to the head is unclear. Compared to the colorfully inlaid combs worn on other occasions it is rather monotonous as to nuances, but the delicacy of the carving is exquisite. Though elaborate and large, it is very lightweight and would not prove cumbersome to the wearer.

Miss Okazaki's bridal hair ornaments are forked pins rather than the tiara type but the cranes, plum blossoms and branches are almost identical.

Blonde tortoise strongly resembles honey amber when photographed so a determination of material or circa on this basis alone is not foolproof. More convincing is the Japanese tradition of using only plain rather than mottled tortoise in wedding headdress and the nearly identical motifs.

Observations concerning Japanese combs are as follows:

1. Shape is nearly always the same, arched or square with wide square tipped end teeth with very fine teeth, some no longer that 1/2 an inch long.

2. Did fine inlay work in mother-of-pearl, coral, jade, enamels and lacquers.

3. Unlike other cultures enameled some combs made of ivory and tortoise.

4. Often ran the pattern in miniature over the teeth as well as the shallow bridge with nice effect.

5. Size of comb and number of teeth fairly standard to conform to hair styles.

6. Pin accompanying comb is identically decorated.

7. Used designs which are recognized part of the artistic culture.

8. Never used shapes popular in Western World such as high or low back comb.

9. Hanging decorations were common from Edo period on.

10. Teeth serve no useful purpose as they do not enter hair as in Western combs.

11. Often decorated in ivory, carving away the portions surrounding the decoration and coloring area. Used jade and coral affixed to the ivory itself. Not done elsewhere.

12. Pins inserted horizontally so the decorative portion extends from the side of the head and dangles.

13. Hairpins forked into two tines very close

together; at times both ends were decorated.

14. Exhibited fondness for coral, abalone, colored beads, jade, but used pearls sparingly. Did not use diamonds, emeralds, sapphires, etc. as other cultures did.

15. Auspicious symbols used such as crane, tortoise, moon, fortune ship, etc.

16. Motifs seldom, if ever, geometrical, but drawn from nature; abstract; or fanciful.

17. Large proportion have an earpick terminal on one end resembling a tiny mustard spoon which was traditional. Once used to scratch the scalp, as the costly headdress once set, was to last for some time.

18. Older combs tend to be less colorful but more intricate.

19. Use of wood is prevalent, not so with Western world.

20. Combs were purely decorative.

21. Some combs and pins are absolutely plain.

22. Narrow bridges made for delicate designs.

FIGURE 2

FIGURE 4

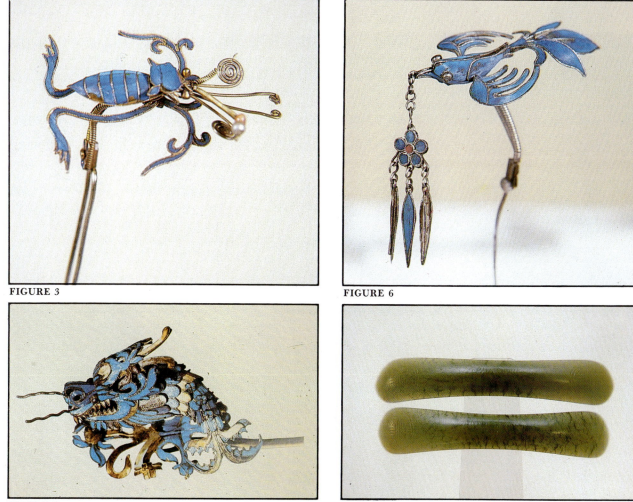

FIGURE 3

FIGURE 6

FIGURE 5

FIGURE 1

PLATE 65. *Fig. 1:* Toothless Chinese hair pins of jade, worn at the base of the head through a heavy chignon *(author's collection). Figs. 2, 3, 5 & 6:* Kingfisher feathered ornaments mounted on metal springs, 19th Century Chinese *(author's collection). Fig. 4:* Jeweled kingfisher feathered hair ornaments, c. 18th–19th Century, Chinese *(Courtesy Augenstein King, Manor House Antiques).*

CHINESE JEWELRY WAS dominated from the earliest times to the 19th century by tiaras and hairpins, the designs of which were not dictated by the hair styles to the extent that Japanese ornaments were. The value of the materials used was of minor importance as bamboo, wood, ivory and the feathers of the tiny kingfisher bird were greatly favored. Jewelry tended to be traditional in the extreme in this highly structured society. Though they are quite inexpensive, the fanciful bird and fish shaped ornaments shown here are none the less, genuine, and show the brilliance of the turquoise blue feathers which are characteristic of Chinese jewelry. They are not difficult to find in China today,

but those made of gold, and/or silver and ornamented with jade, moonstones, pearls, rose quartz, and rubies are rare and exceedingly costly. Originally they were worn by the Mandarins and ruling class. They were mounted on springs which caused the tiny metallic pieces cascading from the sides to sway at the slightest movement of the head. In many respects they are reminiscent of the hatpins called "nodders" which were worn by Western women and today command a premium price among hat pin collectors.

Among the Oriental combs and ornaments are a most unusual pair of jade sticks or ornaments which are Chinese in origin, although their exact age is still

in doubt. The symbols of good fortune and longevity carved at each end are crudely executed and the jade is not the finest; however, assurance that they are old has been given by authorities in Chinese artifacts. One is slightly longer than the other which may indicate they were intended to be worn in pairs, one above the other, or through the thickest part of the chignon or side locks. It is also interesting that they are curved to fit the back of the head to perfection, they were apparently intended to extend beyond the chignon at each end. They are lighter in weight than they appear and for a woman with heavy hair would not be unduly uncomfortable. Should they fall from the head they would shatter or chip as jade is a hard mineral but will crack if damaged in a certain fashion.

THE FOLLOWING GENERAL observations apply to Chinese jewelry of all sorts:

1. Because of the elaborateness of Chinese garments, little jewelry was worn aside from hair ornaments, pins, and combs.

2. Early gold work was influenced by the Persian and Indian cultures because the Chinese valued bronze over gold until the 7th century.

3. Much punch work, filagree, pierced work was done both on gold, ivory, tortoise, silver and other metals which shows the strong influence of the Near Eastern lands.

4. The favorite jewels or gem stones of the Chinese and the Japanese (who adopted the methods and skills of the Chinese artisans though not all of their

Nº 1. ÉCRAN. (BRODERIE EN APPLICATION DE DIVERSES ÉTOFFES.)

designs), were coral, pearls, jade, and turquoise. Very few other stones were used.

5. Decorative themes involved animals, dragons, birds, good luck symbols, clouds, flowers, branches, leaves and abstract decorative shapes.

6. Tiaras, diadems, and decorated combs indicated the social rank and standing of the wearer. The more powerful the family, the more richly decorated the headdress.

7. Headdresses were long, terminating in four points form which hung strings of pearls, coral, and colored beads on either side of the face. These massive head ornaments were worn atop the head rather than in the back and were not really intended to contain the hair but to add a regal touch and stature. Gold

phoenix birds with pearls in the feathers were used at court during the Sung dynasty, 960–1279.

8. The Chinese alone used the brilliant blue feathers of a bird (Fei Ts'ui) which they mounted in gold or silver and used extensively for hairpins. So iridescent are these feathers that they appear to be enameled work and are distinguished from enamel by the missing tiny flakes exposing the metal beneath. There is usually some damage to the feathers as they are quite fragile and the combs are from the 18th and 19th centuries. The more valuable versions were made in gold and contained jade, pearls, and coral stones. It is interesting to note they are still available in China and are astonishingly inexpensive; those below were obtained only last year by an acquaintance traveling

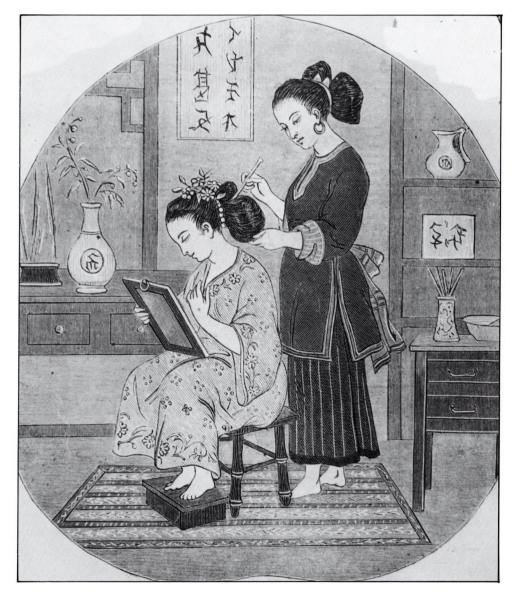

PLATE 65-A. These amusing engravings purportedly showing Japanese society appeared in "La Mode Illustré 1875," and show how cultures viewed one another in the days when rapid communication prevented accurate dissemination of information and ideas. The women are barefoot, the costumes a strange Euro-Japanese mix, and neither facial features or hair arrangement are characteristic of the Japanese.

101

FIGURE 1

PLATE 66. Jeweled combs and hair ornaments from the Orient. *Fig. 1:* The faint outline of the Phoenix bird can be detected on the outer ornaments *(Courtesy Augenstein King, Manor House Antiques).* *Fig. 2: (ibid Fig. 1).* *Fig. 3:* Jade and enamel Chinese pin. Ruby-eyed bats are a symbol of good fortune *(author's collection).*

in China. They are made in the shape of a tiny bird set on a pair of springs which cause the dangling bits of metal to swing back and forth and the birds to move slightly when jarred. The frog has small bits of coral and pearls attached to the antennae.

Not all pins and combs bear the traditional Chinese decoration. The beautiful and elegant ivory comb shown in *Plate 41, Fig. 1* was mistakenly described as of French origin as it is unlike other Chinese combs, but if the teeth and the band above the teeth are observed there is little doubt of its age or origination. It could well have been especially commissioned by a sea captain's wife or other relative as it is a rare design and beautifully executed.

This fine jade pi (circular shape with a hole in the middle like a doughnut) barrette was found among an assortment of inexpensive costume jewelry. It is noteworthy for the azure blue enameled bats, a symbol of good luck. It is 4½ inches long by 2 inches wide

with a gold bar catch. The eyes are small but good quality rubies; the center is the favorable omen of longevity [*Plate 66, Fig. 3*].

The pins above [*Plate 66*] are set in the legendary phoenix shape and feature pearls, jade, lapiz lazuli, moon stone, rose quartz, and an unidentified reddish-pink stone. Only if one looks with care and uses his imagination can the wings, head, and tail of the bird be perceived. Note also the use of the kingfisher feathers, a treasured art form of the Orient in lieu of enameling or inlaying of stone or other background material. Each of the combs and pins is slightly different though at first glance they appear identical. The filagree to which they are attached by pins and wire is gold and the teeth are probably tortoise, though they resemble celluloid. It is easy to be fooled concerning shell used in the Orient, as it was often selected and treated differently than that used for imported combs and uncarved shells imported for domestic use.

Each of the items is valued at several hundred dollars.

FIGURE 2

FIGURE 3

CHAPTER 4
HAIR ORNAMENTS OF ALL KINDS

Webster's Unabridged Dictionary, Second Edition, 1934, refers to the comb as, "An instrument consisting of a thin strip, as of metal, bone, wood, etc., with a row of teeth on one or both sides or edges, used for adjusting, cleaning, or confining the hair or for adornment." The essential part of this definition is the words, *'row of teeth'*, which effectively divides the comb from other hair ornaments such as pins or decorative arrangements including the aigrette, plumes, jewels, circlets i.e. (crowns, diadems, frontlets, ferronnieres, tiaras, fillets,) and the like. The pin may arbitrarily be thought of as any one or two pronged device primarily intended for containing the hair; some hair pins are hardly decorative by any interpretation of the word, whereas others which are large, have ornamented bridges (the section of the comb which rises above the teeth and is intended to be seen, as opposed to the teeth which are inserted into the hair) and having teeth as long as those found in many decorative combs. As stated numerous times, combs are subdivided into straight or utility combs and decorative combs, which may or may not be essential to the maintenance of the hair style.

As the terms pin, comb, and ornament are often used incorrectly by compilers of commercial catalogues, authors, dealers, and collectors alike, it seemed advisable to make these distinctions, for this chapter will deal exclusively with headdress other than combs.

Considering pins in the foregoing context, their recognition presents no problem; the distinction between the types of circlets which are commonly regarded collectively as crowns, is not so easily made, nor does the picture become any less confused by resorting to glossaries and dictionaries. The average person will probably never have to struggle with their identification, but these elaborate symbols of wealth and social station are steeped in history and remarkable for their symbolism, incalculable value, antiquity,

superb jewels, and workmanship which is the state of the jeweler's art.

If combs were seldom set with precious jewels the reverse is true of crowns and other circlets. The original headband was a wreath of flowers or leaves which the Greeks awarded to the winners of athletic contests. Both natural and imitation leaves were used by the Classical Greeks who favored ivy, palmette, laurel, and oak clusters made of beaten gold when the actual leaves were not used. Following Caesar Augustus, the Romans used the same motifs in gold and silver, the execution of which was somewhat heavier, with a suggestion of regal overtones.

From the tomb of Queen Shubad of Ur (Mesopotamia 3,000 B.C.) came three long gold hair pins with lapiz lazuli heads and a headdress consisting of a wide gold band topped by three gold diadems each one of a smaller diameter, on top of one another. The first (worn low on the forehead) of gold circles and blue faience beads, the second band ws made of three embossed golden willow leaves, also divided by blue beads; the final grouping was of beech leaves, veined and realistic in thin sheet gold. There was also a five tooth comb decorated with golden flowers which secured the wig which it is thought Queen Shubad wore. Frescos indicate both men and women wore wigs and shaved their heads, as did their Egyptian contemporaries.

In the early days of the Roman Empire, the suggestion of a monarchy or title of king was studiously avoided as abhorrent to the Romans who had had unhappy experiences with kings; but ancient Roman coins, statuary, and writings concerning the emperors leave little doubt that they considered themselves regal, were absolute dictators and lived on a scale so lavish it would stagger the imagination. The only difference was the power to rule was not obtained through the right of accession or direct lineage as would be the case in an established monarchy. The imperial crown as we know it today would be traced to the Iron Crown

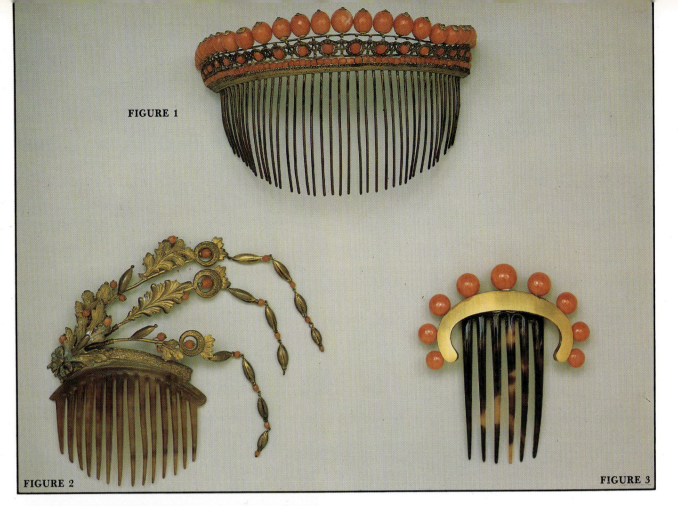

FIGURE 1

FIGURE 2

FIGURE 3

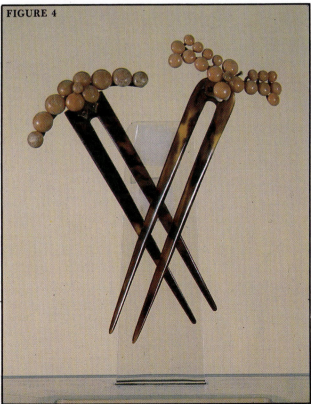

FIGURE 4

PLATE 67. Coral set ornamental combs and pins. *Fig. 1:* Pierced brass set with beads, late 18th Century, France. Shows the wire teeth characteristic of 18th Century European combs. Faceted button, ball and oval shapes were widely used, gold plated in medium priced articles such as these. *(The Metropolitan Museum of Art, gift of Mrs. William Floyd Nichols and Mrs. Langdon Tyler). Fig. 2:* American coral trembler of gilt metal *(Costume Institute of The Metropolitan Museum of Art, gift of Miss Caroline Ferriday.) Fig. 3:* Brass with circular cut coral beads, 19th Century, United States *(Costume Institute of The Metropolitan Museum of Art, gift of Dr. Walter L. Hildburgh). Fig. 4:* Mediterranean coral pins of a relatively common style *(author's collection).*

of Lombardy dating from the 9th century. It is composed of six curved plates each set with a central large cabochon surrounded with rosettes and set off by deep green enameling. It is not too impressive when compared to modern crowns. The Holy Roman emperor's crown more accurately fits the definition of a diadem which is a circlet, one of the jewel studded arches which rises from the rim of a crown and unites over the center front.

FIGURE 1

FIGURE 2

PLATE 68-A. *Fig. 1:* European and Asian combs were often decorated with swag chains which crossed the teeth and contained the hair. Chain ends were hung with shorter chains and suspended ornaments such as jewels, coins, etc. *(Cooper Hewitt Museum of Smithsonian Institution's National Museum of Design). Fig. 2:* Carved 19th Century tortoise shell comb, European. Note the sharp pointed teeth, square spacing and motif, all of which differ greatly from Chinese tortoise shell combs.

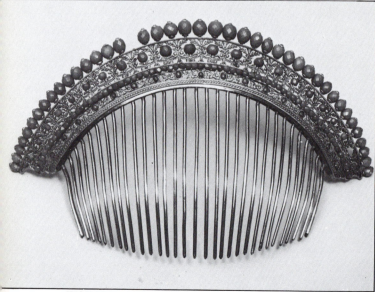

FIGURE 1

FIGURE 2

PLATE 68-B. *Fig. 1:* An 18th Century coral comb with metal teeth *(Bremen Gallery, Bremen, Germany). Fig. 2:* A horn comb with enameled, pierced silver overlays, 19th Century *(ibid Fig. 1).*

THE TIARA IS a bee-hive shaped triple crowned head decoration such as is worn by the Pope at ceremonial functions. It symbolizes the Pope's authority over heaven, earth and hell. The three sections are easily recognized in the tiaras worn by the British monarch and the Pope and they do adhere to the formal definition of a tiara. However, a host of diamond, pearl, sapphire, ruby and emerald creations worn at all European court functions, especially from the 18th century through the period immediately preceding World War I, do not.

It seems easier to think of the crown as being worn by monarchs only, diadems and tiaras as being worn by nobility, high ranking members of the clergy and persons of great wealth—at social functions—as late as the first quarter of the 20th century. There is no pattern of development which can be traced, but starting with the Egyptians a simple gold band was worn tied at the back of the head. Later empires wore more lavish inlaid varieties. The Greeks awarded them to athletes in the form of olive wreaths. The Romans used the tiara chiefly to honor their heroes, awarding them the laurel wreath of natural leaves during the republic and under the empire, gold leaves. Late in Roman history awards were given as a symbol of favor from the supreme ruler and no deeds of valor needed to be achieved to receive one. This may be the root of the expression, "To rest on one's laurels."

During the Dark and Middle Ages women wore the hair covered with jeweled silk cauls, cloth nets, caps, lace nets, hoods, wimples, hennins, veils, hats, headbands, wigs, scarves, snoods, gauzes, tressons, dorelets, crespines; the list is endless, but for five centuries for all intents and purposes the hair itself was largely hidden from view. By the mid-18th century women had begun to expose more of their tresses and the hair was worn in the countless styles which long hair permitted.

Imperial crowns are thought to have originated in England over a thousand years ago with the coronation of Alfred The Great, in 886 A.D. at Winchester. Once unified many European nations adopted the custom. These crowns were usually centered with a cross or a ball and cross, though often a fleur-de-lis replaced the cross. This is understandable considering the close connections between France which used the fleur-de-lis and England's much older symbol. The cross was incorporated into the crowns of Christian nations from the time of Charlemagne.

Many crowns were made in sections which could easily be separated to accommodate the various monarchs who used them on state occasions. This made for ease of storage and transport as well.

ENGLAND'S QUEEN VICTORIA was crowned on June 28, 1838 and reigned until her death in 1901, the period loosely termed the "Victorian Era." She complained that the five pound crown she wore "hurt her a great deal." Like other crowns it had been made originally for George IV and was remounted as Victoria's Imperial State Crown. Victoria preferred much simpler crowns such as the two tiered one surmounted by round balls similar to those coral ones shown here [*Plate 68C*], though the balls were gem stones or pearls rather than coral which were very fashionable materials from 1840–1870. Revivals of styles, materials, and gems are constantly initiated, so it is not surprising that coral decorations in the form of single, double, and even triple rows of uniformly sized beads had been used in the 17th and 18th centuries, separated by fine, ornate filagree work. The unfaceted ball decoration is much larger, the balls fewer in number, and it should be noted that the numerous metal teeth in [*Plate 67, Fig. 1*] indicate it is unmistakably of European origin. A tiara of branch coral, somewhat resembling a crown of thorns, was made in 1850 which is of interest because it was a complete circlet and rested upon the head like a crown; the various sections being attached to a gold band terminating in interlocking rings.

The Empress Josephine is credited with favoring a beautiful comb named after her [*Plate 68, Fig. 2*] called the "Peigne Josephine" which also featured coral in many instances. It consisted of approximately 7 teeth of material other than metal, topped by a medium wide metal filagree bridge decorated with two or more rows of coral beads. Rings were attached at intervals to the filagree and strands of coral beads were suspended from them terminating in a larger sized bead or one of a contrasting shape. These were interlocked in a web-like pattern and hung over the chignon when the teeth were inserted into the hair. They must have been very attractive. Few of the chains have survived for when hair styles changed they were remodeled and used for other purposes or melted down. Coral was also used in the small pins such as those from the author's collection, [*Plate 67, Fig. 4*] which were hinged and mounted with button-like bits of Mediterranean coral.

Less common are decorations of the type shown as berries or flower centers to the sprays of leaves and beads spring set in *Figure 2, Plate 67.* Note the comb is hinged forward.

The wearing of jewelry has several purposes. It is made to embellish and beautify, to impress others with the wearer's financial and social success, to signify engagement and/or marriage status to the general public, to detract from some physical deformity or shortcoming, to make an artistic and/or aesthetic statement, to indicate the wearer is cognizant of current styles and trends, to conform to socially acceptable patterns of behavior, to insure ones valuables are safe

FIGURE 1

PLATE 68. *Fig. 1:* Superbly carved tortoise shell hairpins are from a single piece of shell, without separately attached teeth *(author's collection)*. *Fig. 2:* A ''Peigne Josephine.'' Named for Napoleon's wife, the Empress Josephine, it is made of tortoise shell with the large ball ornaments popular in 1860–70 *(Leominster Historical Society)*.

FIGURE 2

when worn on the person, (how safe they are today is a moot point) and in some primitive countries where banking practices are suspect, women wear the wealth of the family in the form of jewelry and precious gems.

Victorian society was one of the most rigidly proscribed of all times. Correct dress was determined by court procedures for those prominent persons invited to attend these events, and for the average man there was always an Emily Post, or her equivalent, whose rules of etiquette were studied for each and every occasion. These rules tended to fluctuate where jewelry was concerned; what was ''proper'' one season was ''out'' the next. generally the tiara of coral, ivory, or

Comb ornament; lotus flowers filled with blue and red stones, designed by O. Weber of Hanau. *The Workshop, Vol. 7*

The crown of Charlemagne. *Terms in Art*

Various crowns. *French Ad Art*

Diadem in silver and silver gilt with pearls and emeralds. *The Workshop, Vol. 8*

PLATE 68-C. Crowns, diadem and comb from *Jewelry: A Pictorial Archive of Woodcuts and Engravings,* edited by Harold H. Hart, Dover Publications, NY, 1978.

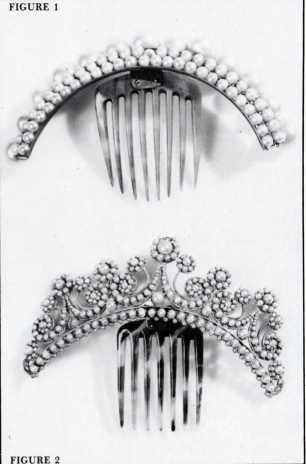

FIGURE 1

FIGURE 2

PLATE 68-D. *Figs. 1 & 2:* Two different designs of 19th Century hinged combs which could also be used as tiaras. They are of tortoise shell with imitation pearls. *(Museum of Fine Arts, Boston, Elizabeth Day McCormick Collection).*

semi-precious stones was considered correct for day wear, and diamonds were a matter of course for evening wear.

From 1845–1865 coral was used in great quantities and it continued to be favored throughout the 19th century. Most nationalities preferred the polished, carved, faceted, type in either the deep reddish or the pale pinkish shades. Maragret Flower shows a charming diadem in her *Victorian Jewelry (Plate II)* in which the coral beads are scored to resemble gold tipped berries resting on a row of smaller balls, also scored. Almost all books concerning antique jewelry will show numerous examples of coral combs and tiaras, and they are invariably attractive.

The tiara does not fall into the category of jewelry which we know as costume or novelty as it was ordinarily of fine workmanship, was costly, and was

intended to endure for many years, if not generations. Of all the kinds of jewelry, the tiara is least likely to be presently worn yet it may contain some of the finest gems and should be left unaltered if at all possible. Old saws about the diamond tiara are commonplace, but the diamond tiara was considered essential for evening costume in Europe where there were many royal functions and a class system was well defined. The discovery of the Kimberly Diamond Mines in 1867 made the diamond so plentiful that women literally dripped diamonds from their aigrettes, diadems, tiaras and other ornaments. It is said the diamond became popular after the introduction of the electric light which reflected their faceted brilliance and made the wearer sparkle.

Electricity fostered the bizarre, for in 1867, the Paris Exhibition featured electric hair ornaments

109

which glowed or moved, powered by a battery worn inside the back of the dress. Imagine a skull of diamonds which winked or scowled and animals which played instruments hidden in the hair. These were status symbols beyond compare!

A DIAMOND TIARA created in the late 19th century had the distinct advantage of a relatively cheap diamond market, new diamond finds allowed for the use of huge and choice diamonds which would a few years hence be prohibitively expensive. A recent new find in South America has already had a depressing effect on the diamond market so a flawless 2 carat diamond which just a few years ago brought as much as $40,000 may sell for a fraction of that amount today. In the 20th century diamonds were a girl's best friend, in the 19th century they were relegated to married women only and as such were a symbol of marital solidity. (See *Plate 90A* for a traditional diamond tiara).

Late in the 19th century diamond tiaras with showers of diamonds falling over the ears, speared on spikes of platinum and silver, made into artificial flower arrangements, in wreaths, bands which ran straight across the forehead, diamond leaves, diamonds set on wires so fine as to be almost invisible swayed and sparked on heads powdered with gold and

FIGURE 2

FIGURE 1

PLATE 69. *Fig. 1:* Hardstone cameo parure consisting of earrings, tiara and comb *(courtesy Sotheby Parke Bernet, New York).* *Fig. 2:* The Empress Josephine with diadem, necklace and earrings *(Musee de l'Armee, Paris).* *Fig. 3:* A stunning classical cameo oval tiara with gold acorns and leaves *(The Metropolitan Museum of Art, gift of Mrs. Ethel Weil Worgelt).*

FIGURE 3

110

silver dust. Diamonds appeared in the shape of berries, grapes, stars, balls, flowers, bees, butterflies, beetles, swords, doves, circles, knots, owls, musical instruments, dragonflies, it would appear the stranger the representation the better. Imagine a wedding at which the bride wore a diadem trimmed with trembling flowers dotted with diamond dew drops.

Not all tiaras and diadems were as splendidly ornate and costly as the diamond tiara, which was often combined with pearls, sapphires, emeralds, and rubies; as witness the exquisitely simple moonstone, pearl, and garnet diadem made by May Morris of the Pre-Raphaelite group, (circa 1908). The tiara made for Fanny Cerrito in 1843 by Serretti, which is very similar to that designed by Castellani for the Countess of Crawford, of gold leaves in a wreath interspersed with pearls, is also a classic.

DURING THE MIDDLE AGES women wore a head covering, and a diadem was often worn by the upper classes at least, as an anchor, much like the headdress used by the men in the Arab world today.

One of the strangest ways of wearing hair ornaments was introduced in 1865—lasting a mere five years—in which wreaths of flowers or chains hung from the headdress or tiara and passed under the chin to the chest, or the hair itself was braided and took the place of the chains. Some very humorous situations must have arisen from this fad as the braids could easily have become entangled with all manner of objects ranging from food on serving dishes, to hooks and closures which happened to be on the same plane, however momentarily.

The closing years of the 18th and throughout the 19th century saw so many revolutions political, social, and industrial it is nigh well impossible to know whether a style was flourishing or declining. The most important single revolution occurred in France in 1793, ending the monarchy and leading to the eventual rise of Napoleon and his court. Up to this time jewels had been manufactured for nobility and now they were worn by the wealthy bourgeois and for a brief period were out of favor completely. They were reestablished with a vengeance when Emperor Napoleon repossessed the crown jewels, and the court, led by Empress Josephine, became as lavish as under the Louis.

A series of revivals began on the Continent and in England which ran through nearly every known antiquity including the Egyptian, Roman, Greek, Etruscan, Gothic, Rococo, and Near Eastern. Diadems of laurel wreaths, Greek key and garland motifs, all of the classical style, combined pearls, diamonds, and other precious stones along with the cameo much beloved by Josephine. A traveler to France noted in 1810, ''Spanish combs were popular with prongs of tortoise shell or metal, the heads of gold scrollwork set with three stones, often cameos. At the end of the Empire period a gallery of gold filagree was finished with a row of gold or amber knobs or most often coral beads engraved with criss-cross hatching. A parure of jewelry was not complete without a comb!'' Actually it was not complete without a tiara or diadem for the most part, as in this stunning hardstone cameo parure [Plate 69, Fig. 1] composed of three tiered earrings, comb and diadem. An unusual combination, as parures consisted usually of brooches, rings, bracelets, etc., but seldom included both comb and diadem.

The diadem and tiara really became chic during the reign of Empress Josephine and Napoleon in France from 1804–1815, for Josephine adored jewels especially cameos, crowns and tiaras of diamonds, pearls, rubies, and other precious gems. In the 1850's the antique styles she initiated were revived and by the 1890's with the discovery of the diamond mines in South Africa, diamond tiaras had become fashionable for the very wealthy as well as court circles. Not only Europeans wore these elegant headdresses but American socialites as well.

THE EGYPTIAN CAMPAIGNS of Napoleon resulted in the revival of antique styles furthered by archeological excavations and research. Realistic and accurate classically inspired cameos begun by the Greeks in the 4th century B.C., spurred on by the excavations at Pompeii and Roman ruins, became the vogue.

Cameos were so important that the Journal des Dames, 1805, stated, ''A fashionable lady wears cameos in her girdle, cameos in her necklace, cameos on each of her bracelets, a cameo on her tiara. Antique stones were more fashionable than ever, but in default of them, one may employ engraved shells.''

Presently the popularity of cameos is depressed, but like all jewelry styles, it takes only a fashion leader such as Josephine to resurrect their appeal.

One of the handsomest tiaras imaginable is the Italian, 'Toilet of Nausicca' (circa 1850) of carved sardonyx. The design was cut into the lighter colors of the stone, (the layers occur naturally, sometimes white and black, at other times white, black and brown, allowing the darker colors to act as a background) so the female figures stand out in sharp relief. Realistic gold acorns and oak leaves support the wide oval bezel [Plate 69, Fig. 3].

The most popular designer in England was Italian born Fortunato Pio Castellani, who revived the lost art of gold granulation, a most difficult Etruscan technique which he is said to have mastered with the aid of some village craftsmen who had retained the ancient skills. Inspired, he created a new style, but during the 19th century fakes and poor

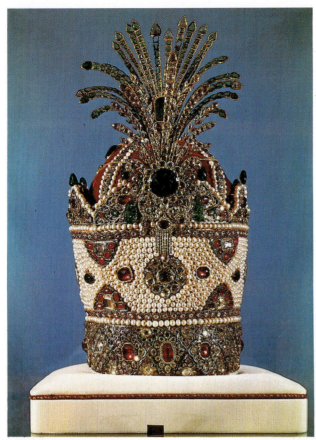

FIGURE 1

FIGURE 2

FIGURE 3

FIGURE 4

PLATE 70. The Persian Crown jewels from *The Crown Jewels of Iran,* University of Toronto. *Fig. 1:* Kiani Crown. *Fig. 2:* Nadir Shah Jiqa. *Fig. 3:* Fath Ali Jiqa. *Fig. 4:* Empress Faraha's Crown.

FIGURE 3

FIGURE 4

FIGURE 5

For The Past three centuries, particularly in Europe, fashionable ladies have worn the aigrette which stood high above the head and was most often made of feathers; the plume egret being the favorite. Stunning jewels and feathery filagrees studded with small diamonds and colored stones fitted with a trembler (a coil spring attached to the ornament and the teeth which shook with the slightest movement of the head) caused the light to reflect the gems much like the prisms on a chandelier. Aigrettes were worn for evening formals, presentation at court, state ceremonies, the opera, ballet, theatre, receptions, balls, and the like, as they were too ornate for any other functions. Colonial American women had their portraits painted wearing feathers which look like turkey feathers they are so large and unattractive. Rufus Hathaway's "Lady with Pets", done in 1790, is an excellent example.

A trembler similar to the one made for Queen Maria Pia of Portugal by Estevas de Sousa in Lisbon in 1878, made of gold and diamonds consisted of a series of various sized diamond stars mounted on gold coils. The one shown here [*Plate 73*] from the Metropolitan Museum, is of cut steel pieces covering the face of each star coil-mounted atop a double row of cut steel bands. The teeth are of celluloid.

In 1913, just prior to the First World War, the wearing of aigrettes made of egret feathers and plumes was very popular in England; coronets were equally fashionable as the English have traditionally "dressed for dinner" and enjoyed formal wear more than we informal Americans.

Possibly The Most famous gem in history is the flawless 45 + carat blue diamond known as the Hope Diamond, named after one of its illustrious owners. Its exact origin is not known but it surfaced in Europe

PLATE 71. Tiaras and combs courtesy of Elizabeth Anne Buzzell. *Fig. 1:* A silver tiara of cabochoned stabilized Persian turquoise with silver accents. The seven crimped teeth are hinged to extend backward rather than down, but it can also be worn as a comb to frame a chignon or cluster of curls. *Fig. 2:* A lacy gold washed silver filagree diadem with faceted citrines. This would add drama to any evening attire. *Fig. 3:* A grape leaf design similar to low backed combs, with squared-off tooth ends and wide end teeth. Material is rolled gold over sterling with seed pearls. *Fig. 4:* An Art Deco design in 14K gold with seed pearls. A stunning contrast against the dark tortoise shell teeth. Three inches high and four inches wide. *Fig. 5:* A tiara of Mother-of-pearl carved Scotch thistle, mounted on a tortoise comb.

FIGURE 1

FIGURE 2

PLATE 73. *Fig. 1:* A 19th Century cut steel trembler tiara *(The Metropolitan Museum of Art).* ***Fig. 2:*** Two black egret feathers.

PLATE 74. A rare diadem comb, c. 1870. The long straight hair is unusual for a married woman of this era *(Historical photo collection of Pat Hathaway, Pacific Grove, California).*

118

FIGURE 2

FIGURE 1

FIGURE 3

FIGURE 4

PLATE 75. Tiaras and hair ornaments from the collection of Evelyn Wittsell. *Fig. 2* has both social and religious significance in Mexico. When a girl reaches 15, the "quinceanera" ceremony is held, signifying that she is ready—and allowed—to be courted. In the strictly observed ceremony, 14 young girls and the celebrant wear white, hoop-skirted gowns, and a tiara (or flower decorated comb) similar to the one shown.

PLATE 77. Evalyn Walsh McLean wearing the Hope Diamond as a hair ornament *(Library of Congress)*.

in the late 1700's. Here it graces the beautiful head of Evalyn Walsh McLean, the adored daughter of Thomas Walsh whose gold mine the "Camp Bird" made the family millions many times over. At age 22, Evalyn married Edward McLean, scion of a newspaper family and as a wedding present her father gave her the $120,000 Star of the East diamond she is shown wearing [Plate 78] attached to a diamond circlet topped with swirling egret feathers.

The Hope, which she was forever enamoured of, [Plate 77] mounted so as to be worn pendant style or as the central part of a diamond tiara, was purchased on January 28, 1912. A description of the infamous gem is found in Cartier's sales sheet dated August 1, 1918, as follows: "1-head ornament composed of oval shaped links all in brilliants, containing in center, the "Hope Diamond" weighing 44¢50 Price agreed following terms of contract signed February 1, 1912.
1917　Interest for April, May and June $625.06
　　　Interest for July, August, and September, $662.56
　　　Interest for October, November, and December $700.03
　　　Total cost $181,987.67

Even millionaires in a tax free era could not pay cash for this gem as the records show the McLeans paid $20,000 down and "traded in" some of Evalyn's jewelry on the Hope. In 1918 the records show they still owed a whopping $58,500.25, and had paid $183,500.25 to that date.

Evalyn was alternately charmed and repelled by the Hope which had brought so much tragedy to its previous owners, and whenever bad luck struck her she blamed it on the diamond. Given to wearing all her famous diamonds at once she visited hospitals so those less fortunate could see it, and as part of her outrageous behavior adorned the neck of her favorite dog Mike with the stone, so as she said, "If I had a dog I wanted him to be a dog people turned to stare at; it was the same with any of my possessions, and with many of my acts."*

The Hope Continued to bring grief to the McLeans as one-by-one of Evalyn's children died prematurely of heartrending causes, her husband lost his sanity, and when Evalyn died in 1947, her estate had so many claims against it her famous collection of jewels had to be sold to Harry Winston, the New York jeweler, rather than being delivered to her grandchildren as her will dictated. The Hope can be seen at the Smithsonian Institute today as it was donated by Mr. Winston to the national museum in 1958.

FROM HER DEBUT in "Pinafore" (1881) until she died in 1922, the most popular actress on the American

*Father Struck It Rich, by Evalyn Walsh McLean, Pg. 143

PLATE 76. Evalyn Walsh McLean, a tiny woman, yet with a remarkable flair for clothes. This hand-crochet ensemble is simply grand, not to mention the feathered hat! (Library of Congress).

PLATE 78. Evalyn Walsh McLean is shown here with a diamond aigrette, and this time the Hope Diamond in a necklace (Library of Congress).

musical stage was the demurely beautiful Lillian Russell. Though a capable singer and actress, her greatest appeal to American women was her fabulous wardrobe and her careful attention to personal beauty maintenance. For American men she was a dream incarnate.

Her special friend and admirer for over 30 years was the free-spending multi-millionaire James Buchanan Brady, familiarly known as Diamond Jim, owing to his penchant for the display of enormous diamonds which he considered proof positive of his success as a salesman of railroad equipment in the heydey of the train. Brady lavished diamonds and other gems on the four-times-wed Lillian, expecting no more in return for his bounty than the public pleasure of her company as escort.

The Library of Congress collection of historic photographs contains many poses of the much

PLATE 79. Lillian Russell is shown here wearing a small crown of pearls dressed for her appearance in ''The Brigands'' *(Library of Congress)*.

photographed Miss Russell in both stage and personal attire, leaving little doubt as to her love of jewelry and finery.

In "The Brigands" she is shown wearing a crown of what appears to be pearls, likely attached to a net of gold. Her numerous admirers showered her with gems, so the crown and other jewels are undoubtedly genuine. [*Plate 79*]

The outrageously elaborate headdress worn in "The Tzigane" [*Plate 80, Fig. 3*] indicates a diamond studded crown, (note the prominent center Maltese cross) with extended side sections which support three dangling pearls at each end. Matching pearls adorn the gown, from the upper arm pearl ropes fall, and no fewer than 6 fingers hold magnificent rings!

Though much of her stage wardrobe was for dramatic effect, she was a fashion pace setter and did much to encourage chic clothing in America.

PLATE 80. Lillian Russell is shown here in a variety of costumes c. 1888 wearing different headdresses (*Library of Congress*).

123

Shades of Theda Bara surround this strangely fascinating headband [*Plate 81, Fig. 1*] and for some absurd reason every lady who sees it has visions of how she would look wearing it. Theda Bara, whose real name was Theodosia Goodman, starred in silent films from 1914–1930, many of which demanded as outrageous a headdress as the one shown. It is a well-made piece of 3 hammered brass bands, secured to a swiveling circle of lotus blossoms, with a suspended

PLATE 81. The following examples are all from the author's collection. *Fig. 1:* A hammered brass circlet, c. 1920. *Fig. 2:* A print taken from the cover of a German music box, showing a revival of classical clothing and a diadem. *Fig. 3:* Brass oak leaf circlet, c. 1860. *Fig. 4:* A fine example of a round or pompadour comb, 19th Century. *Figs. 5 & 6:* A Czechoslovakian glass bridal wreath, c. 1900.

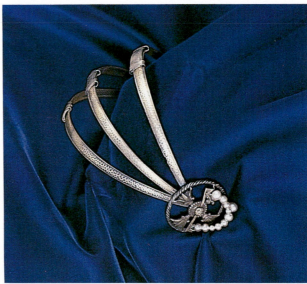

FIGURE 1

FIGURE 3

FIGURE 4

FIGURE 5

pearl decoration covering the wearer's ears. The bands are fitted with a sliding device to increase or decrease the head size. It is the sort of thing one can be grateful was not discarded along with most Art Deco jewelry in a more conservative era!

The Classical revival extended pictorially even to the hand colored plates gracing the inner lid of this German music box [*Figure 2, Plate 81*]. The hair styles shown were worn intermittently for a century, although the clothing is strictly symbolic and sentimental. The diadem being admired by the girls was worn in Europe especially throughout the 19th century, [*Fig. 2*] as was the brass circlet of oak leaves with a central rosette and pierced tab ends for the insertion of cords which tie at the back of the head. It is a soft, easily damaged version of the wreaths which were awarded to Greek athletes and later to victorious Roman warriors. [*Fig. 3*] The round comb at *Fig. 4* shows how effectively 54 teeth would be in contain-

ing the hair, however it was worn.

Although the pearlized orange blossom wedding headdress is not marked in any way it is probably of Czechoslovakian origin. The flowers are sewn to a wooden frame, actually two silk covered bent pieces which slip over one another. The blossoms are made of a wax-like material covered with fish scale centered by beige paper. Less elaborate bridal headdress of orange blossoms and leaves were popular throughout the years, especially during the latter part of the 19th and early part of the 20th centuries.

The 1927 edition of the Sears Roebuck Catalogue shows a display of bridal and confirmation wreaths made of silver cloth over a wire foundation with white wax and muslin flowers and green leaves. One was a triple band offered for $2.25 and others were $3.75. There is no mention of where these wreaths originated but in all probability it was Czechoslovakia which country supplied much of the costume and semi-precious jewelry to the United States, and for that matter, still does.

La Mode Illustré for 1875 featured a pearl ornamented comb in at least one cut on every page indicating its popularity with Parisian women that year. It was particularly suited to the pompadour hair arrangement for it "filled in" the part line created when the hair was divided across the head and was essential to maintaining the upsweep. A few years later there was not one shown—hair and dress styles had radically changed—as they were prone to do annually.

By 1902 THE round comb was the only non-dressing comb shown in Sears Roebuck's Catalogue that year. Decorative combs and pins were momentarily out of fashion. Their sales inducement for the round comb ran as follows: "Ladies' Jeweled Pompadour Comb, imitation tortoise shell, handsomely mounted with 28 turquoise in gilt setting. The latest, most stylish and aristocratically designed comb on the market. Price each 29¢. If by mail, postage extra each 5¢. . . . highly polished, ornamented with 7 baroque pearls, set in gold rim mountings, which are extremely stylish. The comb is a regular 50¢ value. . . . heavier comb, imitation tortoiseshell and very closely set with 42 fine quality brilliant rhinestones, 38¢"

The round comb was used to produce a puffy, blown-out effect and was inserted with the teeth to the front or back of the massed up hair. Its teeth were closely spaced, rounded and numerous, 52 on the average (see *Figure 4, Plate 81*).

Since women acted as their own beauticians for the most part, their success in arranging their hair depended on such factors as the quality and quantity of hair and its manageability, their own native skill, the availability of props such as combs, pins, false hair, barrettes, hair ornaments and the like, as well as an

FIGURE 6

FIGURE 2

FIGURE 1

FIGURE 2

FIGURE 3

PLATE 82. As shown, simple combs, pearl circlets and headbands were popular in the period from 1880 to 1925.

awareness of those styles which were best suited to them. The ideal American girl had been created in 1901 by Charles Dana Gibson, but few women had the perfect facial structure to qualify. So many photographs indicate a styling ineptness coupled with downright plainness which no combs or ornaments could remedy.

At the close of the 19th century neo-classic styles incorporated the Greek fillet, generally a three banded headdress worn in tandem with a metal gilt comb. The comb was attached to the fillet directly above the ears, the band encircled the head and the comb portion was worn across the back; the teeth inserted into the chignon or curls. Presumably this fillet comb combination was more popular in Europe than in the United States where it was referred to as a bandeau. It differed from other forms in that it encircled the head and was worn straight across the forehead or crown of the head.

In the 1920's we see the single gold band being worn by a sad-eyed young woman as part of a simple hair style. [*Plate 82, Fig. 4*]; while a circle of pearls is worn by a beautiful girl around a coil of hair worn high on the back of her head much as the ancient Greeks would have worn a similar circlet centuries ago [*Plate 82, Fig. 2*].

The small standing comb in *Plate 82, Fig. 3* is purely decorative but a careful examination will reveal a round comb contains her upswept back hair. The forelocks are rolled straight across the forehead in a severe fashion which fails to lessen her youthful charm.

The side comb worn by the handsome, albeit plumpish young woman in *Fig. 1.*, complements the

FIGURE 4

short marcel hairdo and shows that not all combs were worn at the back of the head.

Early in the 19th century a revival of a simple headband known as the "ferronniere" after Leonardo DaVinci's "La Belle Ferronniere", enjoyed brief popularity. It consisted of a gold band with a single jewel, cameo, jet or pearl worn directly in the center of the forehead, as it had been in the 15th century, particularly in Italy [*Plate 83, Fig. 2*].

FIGURE 1   FIGURE 2   FIGURE 3

PLATE 83. *Fig. 1:* A French model c. 1900 wearing an ornate diamond headdress and pearl dog collar *(Library of Congress).* *Fig. 2:* A woman with a ''ferronniere'' from a 19th Century style book. A modified form of a ferronniere was popular during the 1960's, when youths wore the device to restrain their long hair. *Fig. 3:* A cut from a French magazine c. 1875 showing the use of the pearl comb or diadem to fill the center part *(''La Mode Illustré'' 1875).*

FIGURE 2

FIGURE 1

FIGURE 3   FIGURE 4

PLATE 84. These American stage beauties at the turn of the century were arbiters of fashion, and publicity photos appeared in the Sunday rotogravure sections of the newspapers as well as in women's magazines. Anna Held *(Fig. 1),* Blanche Bates *(Fig. 2),* Fritzi Scheff *(Fig. 3)* and Frances Starr *(Fig. 4)* were exceptions in 1909 when the pompadour was the rage, often worn in combination with other hair styles such as the top knot, upsweep, ringlets and poufs. Miss Starr is wearing a top knot into which single prong ornaments have been inserted.

DESIGNER'S EXTREMES KNEW no bounds as the ostentatious jewelry worn in 1900 by this French model demonstrates. [*Plate 83, Fig. 1*] Had her jewels been limited to the simple gold fillet set with a central forehead diamond, 14 strand pearl dog collar, then much in vogue, heavy Art Nouveau pendant (probably pilqué-a-jour enameled), diminutive pearl earrings, and gown crisscrossed with passementerie, she would have exceeded the bounds of good taste by present day standards. The addition of what appears to be a pair of huge golden diamond studded horns make the ensemble ludicrous. Actually these curvilinear attachments are modified feather motifs, but as they are constructed of rigid metal pairs on opposite sides of the head, they have a top-heavy and ungraceful look intended to impress the viewer with the opulence of the gems rather than enhancing the beauty of the model. It is hoped this was a one-of-a-kind creation!

PLATE 86. Matching comb and barette sets were mass marketed in the 1890's but are uncommon today, especially magenta colored ones such as this celluloid pair. Found in mint condition they are worth having (*author's collection*). *Fig. 2:* This regal high back comb of imitation turquoise is set with fine French paste jewels. With wide curving teeth and an exquisite design outlined in white enamel, it is one of the author's favorites, though by no means expensive or rare (*ibid Fig. 1*).

FIGURE 1

FIGURE 2

128

FIGURE 2

PLATE 85. *Fig. 1:* Mother-of-pearl hair pins and comb from the Philippine Islands, c. 1919 *(Collection of Kathe Kilot).* ***Fig. 2:*** Carved Mother-of-pearl top, set by three pins to casein teeth, c. 1850 *(author's collection).*

FIGURE 1

PLATE 87. *Figs. 1 & 2:* Aigrettes featuring natural feathers, laces, ribbons and flowers predated the jeweled type shown in Figs. 3 & 4 by about twenty years *(Lady Godey 1859).* **Figs. 3 & 4:** These aigrettes feature diamonds set in gold and platinum and were popular around 1890–1910. *("Jewelry: A Pictorial Archive of Woodcuts and Engravings" edited by Harold H. Hart, Dover Press, New York, 1978).*

FIGURE 1 **FIGURE 2** **FIGURE 3** **FIGURE 4**

129

CHAPTER 5
COLOR, DECORATION AND ARTISTIC GENIUS

The comb collector may be struck by the over-abundance of combs which are decorated with blue or amethyst colored stones. The explanation is relatively simple. Victorian women were a virtuous lot and those who might not have been, like Lady Macbeth, went to great lengths to convince others they were. Blue has traditionally been the color of purity, virginity and morality. Blue also signifies upper class status; consider the bluestocking class, the blue book of the 400 elite, blue blooded, the Blue Laws of New England, made by the puritanical politicians to keep the majority in line, and similar phrases. As a result it is safe to say the majority of combs colored by enamels or sets were blue. Some striking examples were blue enamel over natural colored celluloid set with very nearly the same shade of blue rhinestones or paste stones which enhances the comb.

Combs set with amethyst stones ran a close second in color preference. Long associated with royalty and nobility, this semi-precious stone and color were used by the ancients and royal robes to this day are of deep purple velvet with ermine trimmings. This was the most popular color for hat pins by far, and among the fine paste examples one often finds a genuine stone set in sterling.

Various shades of topaz, yellow, amber, hyacinth, and jonquil are frequently seen today. When set in celluloid of a similar color they were sufficiently neutral to be quite acceptable for evening wear immediately following World War I and into the Flapper Age. When these shades were used it is interesting to note that they were seldom ever used in combination with other colors.

The least popular color worn was red or crimson and one seldom finds a comb, hat pin, purse, or other accessory of dress in this color. This may result from the use of the word in association with women of ill repute as in ''red light district'' or ''scarlet woman'', terms so shocking they were not used in polite society, at least not by the ladies!

MATERIALS

Ivory is obtained from the African and Indian elephant principally, but is also obtained from the hippopotamus, walrus, narwhal, sperm whale, hornbill,

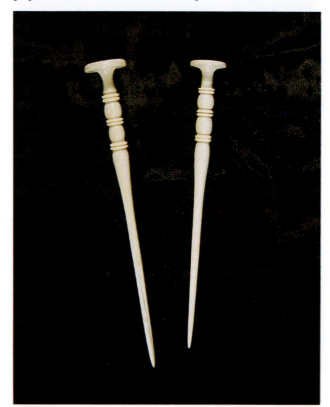

FIGURE 1

PLATE 87-A. Three ivory combs and pins from the 19th Century. The combs are Chinese while the pins are from India. *(Figs. 1 & 2 from the author's collection, Fig. 3 from the collection of Kathe Kilot).*

FIGURE 2

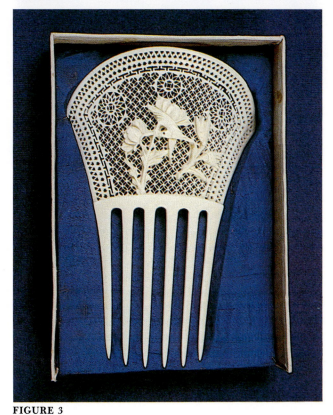

FIGURE 3

and the extinct wooly mammoth (called odontolite). A species of nut called tagua, dom, or jarina nuts are suitable for buttons and small objects only, though they were used for decorations on comb bridges. They are even in texture, take a high polish and are as hard as animal ivory. Large intricately carved combs such as those shown here are from elephant tusks; however, as the elephant is on the endangered species list its ivory is not permitted to be sold except when a proven antique.

Some of the characteristics of ivory are applicable to all the sources; each is white or creamy white in color; each takes a high polish which increases with age, and each is hard enough to be durable yet not so hard as to prevent its being carved effectively.

True or elephant tusk ivory is distinguished by lacking a hard enamel outside cover such as is found in other tooth sources and by the lines or striae running in the arc of a circle making tiny oblong markings. These lines will not run evenly spaced or parallel to one another such as the lines found in celluloid or other imitations.

Over the years such unlikely substances as plaster-of-Paris, celluloid, plastic, and bone, have masqueraded as ivory and to those unacquainted with true ivory have presented a quandary. Bone is most like ivory, but it is dead white in appearance, does not take the polish ivory takes, has small pin hole depressions which are numerous and has not the curved lines found in ivory. Because of the size of ornamental combs it is fairly safe to conclude bone would not have been employed in their manufacture, particularly if they are carved to any degree, the more likely substance being celluloid.

Ivory was used for comb making by the Chinese, ancient Etruscans, and Egyptians, and was the favored substance of comb makers in Europe in the middle ages.

Ivory Combs Carved in China for export have a background of lace-like punch carvings on which are superimposed florals, dragons, garden scenes with strolling figures and abstract designs, often separated by solid borders. They were nicely boxed for shipping often with a glass insert in the top of the box. I recently purchased, to my delight, the huge tortoise comb in its original box [*Plate 15, Fig. 2*], which is somewhat sturdier than the boxes housing the ivory combs but not nearly as attractive. True ivory combs were not set with gems of any sort, depending entirely on the ornate carvings and the purity of the ivory for appeal. If there is a doubt as to the substance and there are gem decorations, it is most unlikely that the comb is genuine ivory. Even those combs made of plastic materials carefully made to imitate ivory, only rarely employed rhinestones and other forms of decoration.

FIGURE 1

stars, attached to spring-mounted hair pins or rather narrow tiaras of relatively simple design. Velvet ribbon trimmed with jet and finished with jet fringes called the "Dubarry coiffure" was worn twined in the hair or encircling it.

The garnets used in Victorian jewelry primarily were obtained from Czechoslovakia (Bohemia was the name then commonly used) and they are superior to those found in other localities, namely: India, Africa, The United States, and Ceylon. They were deep red and less intense in feeling than some other gems and were much admired in the somber society which adhered rigidly to "acceptable behavior" standards. Many combs featured garnets even though they were more costly than imitation stones and the collector who owns a garnet set comb is fortunate indeed. Very few are seen today.

Low back celluloid combs were often decorated with gold and silver applied to shallow depressions and fired. They are still obtainable though more costly than other combs. Unhappily the gold and silver wore off unevenly leaving a patchy appearance. As a rule they will be stamped "18K gold inlay" or a higher karat, and the country of origin, usually France or England. When such wear has occurred they are virtually impossible to repair and the cost would be so excessive it would not warrant the expenditure as these combs can be purchased for less than $100.00 as a general rule, depending of course, on the amount and kind of decoration.

An extraordinary number of the world's most gorgeous combs were produced during the Art Nouveau Period (1895–1910), chiefly in Paris, though not necessarily by French artists. Today the most renowned among these European innovators is the jewelry and glass designer, René Lalique (1860–1945) who at the age of 25 operated his own workshop in Paris where he became a master designer in enamel, gold, and silver creations.

Writing in, *Modern Design in Jewellery and Fans*, Gabriel Mourey and Aymer Vallance remind us of the importance of the comb when they say of Lalique, "His new combs, with pansy and sycamore leaf motifs, in horn and silex, black enamel, and obsidian, with golden insects here and there, show him still anxious to extend the field of his experiments, never tired of seeking fresh subjects and testing new materials. . He is the renovator, or, preferably, the creator, of the art as we know it nowadays, one can easily understand the enthusiasm and the admiration aroused by his work."

All the adjectives one could muster; imaginative, fanciful, original, romantic, infinitely creative, would still not allow us to see the beauty of a Lalique comb. Through the courtesy of Walters Art Gallery, Baltimore, Maryland, we can see one of these priceless

FIGURE 1

FIGURE 2

PLATE 90-A. *Fig. 1:* A trio of puff and back combs of tortoise shell with applied gold decoration (*Sotheby Parke Bernet Inc., New York*). *Fig. 2:* This period photo c. 1920 shows a Mrs. Joseph Ferrara of Chicago wearing a diamond tiara (*Library of Congress*).

masterpieces. [*Plate 90, Fig. 1*] Purchased by Henry Walters at the Saint Louis World's Fair in 1904 for $1,000, the comb is 5½ inches high, 7 inches long, and is signed Lalique along the edge of one of the pliqué-a-jour leaves. The catalya orchid is carved from a single slab of ivory, the pistil delicately tinted, the three ''see through leaves'' are veined with gold and set with graduated diamonds. The three teeth are of lowly horn. The stem is attached by a single gold hinge. Sadly it is not possible to show original photographs of the major combs produced during this period, but in lieu of the originals, which have long since vanished from public view into private collections and museums, some idea of their grandeur may be gotten from these plates from *The Art Nouveau Style*

and Art Nouveau Jewellery and Fans, both Dover Publications. (See Bibliography for specifics).

Lalique, Veazey, Slott-Moller, Vever, Gaillard, Follot, de Monvel, Orazzi, McNair, Unger, and others all embellished their combs with precious stones, and among the jewels one can distinguish realistic pliqué-a-jour, solid gold and silver leaves, wheat sheaves, pansies, and insects of all kinds, especially the dragonfly. Oh how these designers loved the dragonfly whose gossamer wings allowed for rich and varied enamels and even richer jewels!

Proof of Lalique's innovative genius is clearly seen in the diversity of his designs so it is hard to say one is not characteristic of his style. They range from

FIGURE 2

PLATE 90. *Fig. 1:* Ivory orchid with diamond set, pliqué-a-jour leaves on horn teeth. By René Lalique, c. 1900 *(Walters Art Gallery, Baltimore, Maryland).* **Fig. 2:** Another signed René Lalique comb, this with a carved tortoise shell bridge of lions set with rose-cut diamonds *(courtesy Augenstein King, Manor House Antiques).*

FIGURE 1

PLATE 91. All courtesy Sotheby Parke Bernet Inc., New York. *Fig. 1:* Patterned seed pearls on gold mesh are attached to silver gilt teeth, c. 1760. *Fig. 2:* This is possibly a comb by René Lalique, and employs delicate diamond bows and sprays applied to gold mesh. The split teeth are puzzling. *Figs. 3 & 4:* A late 19th Century comb/tiara/brooch combination with diamond and pearl decorations and hinged tortoise shell teeth.

FIGURE 2

FIGURE 4

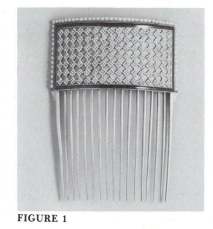

FIGURE 1

FIGURE 3

an ivory face peeking from windblown hair, to the massive golden rooster whose beak holds a Siberian amethyst, to the sycamore leaf comb, impressive in its simplicity. Few of Lalique's combs were actually suitable for wear as they were too ornate, too fragile, and too precious for all but the most elegant occasions. Enamoured of glass, especially the pliqué-a-jour technique, Lalique was less interested in the value of the materials used than in the harmonious combining of such materials as ivory, horn, amber, opals, moonstones and enamels; sometimes in grotesque and strange forms.

It is indicative of the importance of the decorative comb and hair ornament that every major designer and craftsman of the Art Nouveau movement created both in abundance.

When diamonds came into their own at the turn of the century they were set in prong and pavé mountings of ear of wheat, flowers, feather sprays, and ultimately geometric motifs. Silver, palladium and platinum (later white gold) were thought to reflect or set off the diamond more effectively than other metals, so the diamond tiara of wealthy Chicago socialite Mrs. Joseph Ferrara, is the same wheat pattern which

PLATE 92. The six 19th Century tiaras shown here are all copies of far more costly ones, but are nicely executed in gilt brass, imitation pearls, rubies, emeralds and amethysts, plus enameled flower petals. The faceted coral beads are genuine. The amethyst and clear paste examples have removable teeth, while the others have fixed teeth *(Museum of Fine Arts, Boston, Elizabeth Day McCormick Collection).*

was popular a century earlier, and it in turn was renowned at least eighteen centuries before that [*Plate 90A, Fig. 2*].

The Madison Avenue branch of Sotheby, Parke, Bernet, Incorporated, has graciously provided for inclusion and comment four of the most intriguing and lovely combs and tiaras recently sold at their auction house [*Plate 91*].

The most remarkable is the diamond and pearl comb/brooch and tiara combination described in their ''Antique and Period Jewelry'' catalog (February, 1982) as follows: ''Late 19th century. The scroll motif set with three pearls measuring approximately 6.5 to 7mm and 12 smaller pearls measuring approximately 2.9 to 3.7 mm, embellished with numerous old mine, old European cut and rose cut diamonds, with a gold tiara and brooch attachment with a fitted velvet box stamped *Kirkpatrick,* with comb measuring approximately 3¾ inches (90 cm) wide by 4½ inches (110 cm) long, photo reduced slightly.'' As the cover, featuring a photograph of this comb was in color, a magnifying glass was needed to reveal that the diamonds were set in platinum, the pearls set with a pin (which provides maximum insurance against their

139

FIGURE 1

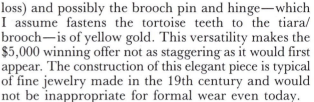

loss) and possibly the brooch pin and hinge—which I assume fastens the tortoise teeth to the tiara/brooch—is of yellow gold. This versatility makes the $5,000 winning offer not as staggering as it would first appear. The construction of this elegant piece is typical of fine jewelry made in the 19th century and would not be inappropriate for formal wear even today.

The silver, gold, and diamond lacework comb with split teeth, has for some time been an enigma to me on several counts. It's the teeth. They are split, and never have I seen an antique comb with split teeth. This does not mean they were not made, but it is strange none have come to my attention among the countless combs observed over the years. The hinged bridge is of gold mesh and the stylized blossoms and sprays of diamonds have the traditional delicacy of French work, but it does not have the freedom of style which characterizes the later work of René Lalique to whom it is tentatively ascribed. It may have been a commissioned piece done by Lalique in his youth, for he had been a goldsmith and designer of jewelry long before his innovative mastery of glass brought him world acclaim.

PLATE 93. These marvelous Art Nouveau combs are reproduced from ''The Art Nouveau Style'' edited by Roberta Waddell, Dover Publications, New York, 1977. *Fig. 1:* René Lalique set an ivory face in natural materials (either horn or tortoise) for this design. *Fig. 2:* Nearly a century old, a sterling silver brush, comb and mirror set created by Mary Galway Houston has figures of great appeal and sensitivity. *Figs. 3 & 4:* Pliqué-a-jour enameled combs from Maison Vever. *Fig. 5:* An enameled swallow pin from George Fouquet.

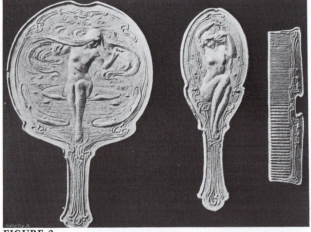

FIGURE 2

FIGURE 3

FIGURE 4

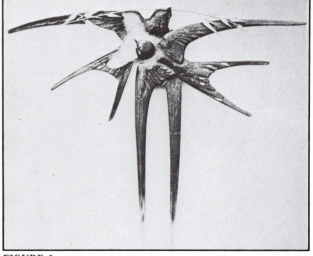

FIGURE 5

140

THE DELICATELY REFINED 18th century comb [*Plate 91, Fig. 1*] is a classic example of European work; the seed pearls are arranged in an interlaced diamond pattern on a gold mesh background bordered by an enameled rectangle, edged on three sides by larger pearls. The teeth are silver gilt. The overall dimensions are approximately 3¼ inches wide by 4½ inches long.

The set of puff and back combs, stamped G.B. on the 18k gold embossed bird-on-bough design artfully applied to tortoise shell, is from the late 19th century. British hallmarks are clearly visible directly to the right above the bird. One tooth is missing from the lower right comb. They are not shown full size for obvious reasons.

PLATE 94. Combs from ''Art Nouveau Jewelry and Fans'' by Gabriel Mourey, Aymer Vallance et al, Dover Publications, New York, 1973. *Figs. 1, 2, 3 & 4:* These are all attributed to René Lalique. *Figure 1* is of horn and silver, signed above the teeth. *Figure 3* is enameled, and the dragonfly bodies are set with diamonds. *Fig. 5:* This novel comb with its pincer-like end teeth is by Orazzi from the Maison Moderne. *Fig. 6:* This horn, gold and turquoise comb uses prominent pins to join the head to the teeth, and is by Boutel De Mouvel.

FIGURE 1 FIGURE 2 FIGURE 3

FIGURE 4 FIGURE 5 FIGURE 6

CHAPTER 6
CARE AND REPAIR OF COMBS

In an effort to aid the reader in the identification of true tortoise, horn, celluloid, and other materials, several combs have been included in full color and it is suggested both the color and the distribution of the light and dark mottling be closely observed as well as the wide variety of shapes, sizes and designs employed in making these combs and ornaments.

In tortoise the larger expanses of brown will be seen to be darker than is generally believed though not so brown as to be considered black and the lighter portions will range from a honey color to a reddish-orange. The splotches will never be uniform and will be distributed at random over the entire surface of the comb or ornament. Usually there will be at least some of the lighter color in each piece as it was more highly regarded than the darker portions. The back scales of the tortoise are semi-transparent and mottled in red, brown, or blonde shades, whereas the underside plates are a solid color varying from pale blonde to russet and are called blonde tortoise shell. Though there are 22 of these underplates they are smaller and the supply being less than that obtained from the upperplate, they are more esteemed.

PLATE 96. *Figs. 1 & 2:* Top and underside of old Hawksbill turtle shell. Underside clearly shows swirls indicative of this species *(Mercer Museum)*. *Fig 3:* Tortoise shell brushes with silver monogram *(author's collection)*.

FIGURE 1

FIGURE 2

FIGURE 3

American processed or clarified horn from the late 18th and early 19th centuries, also resembles the lighter shades of tortoise when properly processed and dyed. The color will be transparent, yellowish, and in the large back comb will not appear particularly appealing, though it is much more difficult to find a horn comb of this type, or any type for that matter, than a comb of any other material as they were not considered valuable and were discarded indiscriminately over the years.

The sterling silver monogrammed brushes shown on *Plate 96* illustrate tortoise shell to fine advantage. Purchased for a mere three dollars from a dealer in Massachusetts near the town of Leominster, they have a somewhat cloudy appearance but if closely examined the tell-tale swirled watermarks are evident and the random distribution of light and dark shades is marked. The visible straight lines normally characteristic of celluloid are the grooves which hold the bristles and have nothing to do with the material itself.

As with the ivory comb, examples carved in China, (which country incidentally, produced some of the most exquisitely carved combs of all times,) tend to reflect the Chinese culture regardless of the market to which they were to be exported. American tortoise combs, at least early ones, sported patriotic motifs such as the bald eagle, shields, mottoes, entwined oak leaves, initials, baskets of flowers and fruit, full human figures, (often American Indians), such as in the handsome comb from Winterthur Museum, carved profiles in oval medallions and the like. Chinese combs tended to be very large, of natural rather than synthetic materials, and have small, overall lace-like carvings, occasionally framed by a central oblong panel. Winters shows an intriguing comb having only single end teeth and a sculptured bridge wide enough to have contained numerous teeth indicating the comb would have been worn as a coronet or as a frame for a generous chignon.

European tortoise combs preferred such motifs as baskets of flowers and fruits, tiers of wheat sheaves, crowns, orbs and other regalia; the edges of the bridge containing tiny potted flowers, leaves and shells. There is a light feeling about them which is not found in the American tortoise comb. It is entirely possible the shell itself was of thinner stock than their American counterparts.

PLATE 95. Some examples of genuine tortoise shell combs. The wide range of light and dark shades is shown to good advantage here. *Fig. 1:* These were popular during the 1880's *(author's collection)*. *Fig. 2:* A carved Chinese comb *(courtesy Custom House Collection, Dept. of Parks and Recreation, Monterey, California)*.

FIGURE 2

FIGURE 1

Unless One Has dealt with celluloid and tortoise shell for a long period of time it is easy to confuse the two materials. There are, however, some general guidelines which serve as an aid in this area. Few dealers themselves know how to differentiate and may mislead the collector through ignorance rather than malice.

Genuine tortoise is very scarce and is seldom found on today's market so the chances are heavily against the casual purchase being tortoise. Real tortoise will of necessity be costly unless one is fortunate enough to obtain a comb from a relative, a knowledgeable collector who is also generous, at auction where the auctioneer is unimpressed with the lot, from a dealer who considers the item a trivial object among more valuable items obtained in an estate, or some other good fortune.

Depending upon the size and shape of the comb, tortoise is generally lightweight, considerably lighter than a celluloid comb of corresponding size. Tortoise lacks the shine or high luster found in celluloid and if in a dried-out state, it appears lifeless and dull. True tortoise is never found in colors such as green, blue, red, purple, etc., rather it is a rich brown, yellow-mottled or in wavy lines resembling watered silk or taffeta in some instances and in others has lighter blotches of color usually amber or pale reddish-yellow. Sometimes pastel celluloid combs with watery markings resembling tortoise are called ''blue, green, or pink tortoise'', but this is an innacurate term loosely applied.

Tortoise is never marked in evenly spaced diagonal lines from top to bottom, it is the same on both front and back, that is to say the markings do not appear on the front of the comb only, as is the case in poor tortoise imitations. Most tortoise combs were carved in either very simple or highly ornate styles and all without exception were executed by hand which permitted the artisan great flexibility and originality.

Horn, which once was the material most commonly used for combs is seldom seen today, as it was not highly prized as tortoise, ivory or other scarce substances and was not as durable as metals, hard rubber, etc.

Clarified horn which has not been dyed, is a honey color, opaque, very light weight, and probably will have thin, tapered, dagger-sharp teeth. It will be free of mold marks and most likely will be undecorated in any way. Some special combs were painted, such as the one worn by Blanche Bates, an actress at the turn of the century. The early American horn comb was extremely large, curved and was not highly polished when compared to later tortoise shell examples.

Horn combs were dyed mahogany red, dark brown, black and imitation tortoise, both skillfully spotted and otherwise [Plate 97]. Those of solid colors were usally carved in simple patterns of wings, leaves, and florals, though one of the most ambitious shows a small girl feeding a fawn, surrounded by a rabbit and a bird [Figure 3, Plate 97]. It shows skill, imagination beyond the-ordinary and must have been made with a great deal of affection for the recipient. This comb from the author's collection is said to have been brought to the United States from Lithuania in the late 18th century.

Horn combs were frequently hinged in two or more sections held together with horn dowels. The clarified example [Plate 97, Fig. 4] is highly polished, in three sections and is made to fit the chignon, topping it neatly. It is a most exquisite primitive comb dating from about 1830. Combs of raw horn made in the early 19th century tend to be heavier, have shorter and fewer teeth and the teeth are less pointed than 18th century combs of raw horn. Here again, it is very difficult to state absolutely the date of a comb, unless as with the case combs made in Jamaica, the date is an intrinsic part of the design.

The small red, streaked, horn comb at Figure 2 is an early comb which illustrates better than any words can, how simple the early American combs were, how the streaking was applied, and how dissimilar this color is compared to genuine tortoise. All the combs on Plate 97 are horn, clarified and raw; but how different they are as to teeth, color, decoration, size, and style. Each is a fine antique comb in its own right and each is a work of art.

Among The Most exotic materials worthy of consideration which were used in comb manufacture are the following: amber, aluminum, bakelite, baleen, bone, brass, bronze, cut steel, filagrees, glass, iron, lead, mother-of-pearl, rubber, tin, and the woods such as sandalwood, boxwood, ebony, and bamboo.

None of these materials causes more perplexity than amber, an easily imitated material for which there are an abundance of ''tests'' two of which are easily performed; however, since it is unlikely the entire comb will be made of amber, testing with ether is preferable. Amber will not be affected by ether but plastics will soften when touched with this acid. Amber will float in seawater whereas plastics will sink. Amber will be exceedingly light when hefted, but so will other imitators, so this test is inconclusive. There is no such thing as ''new amber'', as it is the pitch from ancient pine trees which under pressure for thousands of years turned into an amber mass and found its way to the Baltic Sea area from whence most amber is recovered. The most common shades are pale yellow, and various hues of brown and oxblood. Those ornaments found on combs will generally be of the yellowish opaque variety and constitute the faceted ball ornaments which surmount the edges of combs made approximately a

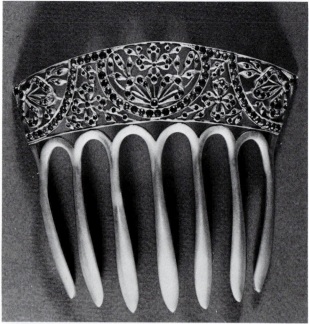

FIGURE 1

FIGURE 2

PLATE 97-A. *Figure 1* shows an aluminum comb, *Figure 2* an early cut steel type.

century ago, or the teeth, seldom ever the entire comb. They are not common, nor are they particularly attractive when compared to the more dazzling rhinestone set celluloids, carved ivories, and tortoise shell combs. The amber usually has become lusterless and the color is washed out on the specimens I have observed.

Aluminum, on the other hand, is an interesting element when considering the comb. It strongly resembles cut steel but was much lighter weight, was brilliant, did not oxidize, was formed into more intricate and delicate patterns; was very costly when first employed (1824–1827) as it was originally thought to be quite rare. Subsequent mining has proven it to be the most plentiful single metallic element on the face of the earth, so it is surprising there are so few old aluminum combs to be found today. The marked differences between the two substances are shown in the two examples found on *Plate 97A.*

Note the wide spoon-handle type of teeth on the aluminum comb and the delicacy of the filagree work which is set with marcasites. Two prong hair pins set with rhinestones were popular in the 1870's [*see Plate 28, Fig. 1*]. They were fanciful, feminine, and quite fragile looking. Cut steel combs were made during the early 1800's and they tend to have hand cut work and pierced designs accentuated with surface engravings of simple lines, circles, and leaves, relatively unsophisticated in nature.

The similarity in patterns is shown in the two steel combs below. One was in the author's collection, the other in the Leominster Historical Society collection which formerly belonged to Mrs. Alice Sawyer of that city. They are nearly identical; each verges in a leftward direction when viewed from front face. They are indicative of the steel comb of the period, almost all having 7–9 long teeth, none are ornamented with other than cut and engraved decoration, and all are created from a single form rather than having teeth attached to the bridge by hinges or pins.

Steel combs will be heavier than the aluminum, will not retain their shape as well as they are less rigid; they are very conventional in design and might be attacked by the elements, though those I have seen have been well preserved.

As bronze combs were a product of the prehistoric age they are only to be found in museums and were discussed in Chapter I, but brass combs are still being manufactured in such countries as India, Pakistan, Turkey and Near Eastern nations famous for their handmade brass objects. They are extremely heavy and are of the utilitarian variety rather than decorative, although some minute examples were used as ornaments.

As PREVIOUSLY NOTED combs made of hard rubber

have a dull finish compared to celluloid, are black color only, are lighter in weight than other materials, are usually unadorned and are not often domestic so they are not encountered as frequently as other materials.

Though celluloid combs far and away outnumber any other type, they were deliberately made to imitate other materials and were so skillfully done it is difficult to tell them apart. Some clues are as follows:

1. Ivory colored celluloid often has uniform lines running parallel to one another so evenly spaced they would not occur naturally.

2. Mold marks may be observed on the reverse side and in poorer examples the rough edges are not entirely removed (called tickling).

3. A far greater range of colors can be observed which do not occur naturally, so a blue comb for instance, could be none other than a synthetic.

4. There is no restriction on mold sizes,

FIGURE 1

FIGURE 2

FIGURE 3

PLATE 97. *Fig. 1:* A dyed European horn comb often mistaken for tortoise *(The Metropolitan Museum of Art, gift of Mrs. Ridgely Hunt in memory of William Cruger Pell).* **Fig. 2:** Early American dyed horn. The bright orange-red color is unnatural *(author's collection).* **Fig. 3:** Light in color, this horn comb is possibly clarified, and was carved in Lithuania in the late 18th Century *(ibid Fig. 2).* **Fig. 4:** Fine example of clarified horn, this chignon-type three section hinged comb employs horn pins for the connections *(ibid Fig. 2).*

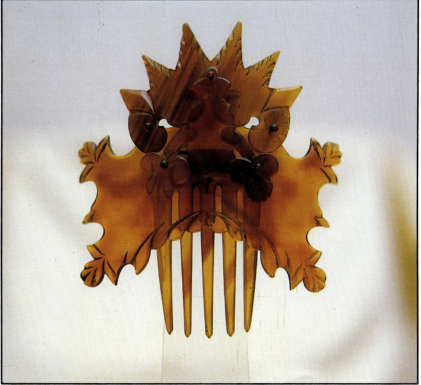

FIGURE 4

146

theoretically celluloid combs could greatly exceed those made of natural materials.

5. Celluloid decomposes rather differently than bone, horn, tortoise etc. It will ultimately turn to powder after crystalizing and crazing, rather than chipping, cracking, or changing color. Nothing can be done to delay this process nor can it be prevented when the combs have been subjected to extremes of temperature or prolonged dampness.

6. If the decoration is applied directly to the surface of the material it *will be* celluloid, or synthetic, not tortoise.

7. Price is a good indicator, though not foolproof; tortoise will be very costly, synthetics far less so.

If none of the above prove conclusive, try eliminating through the other materials and if all fails, take the comb to an expert (lapidary shops are good) for an opinion.

Among the truly rare combs today is the lead comb. As early as the 17th century it was thought lead contained properties which would, like the patent medicines of a later day, achieve such wonders for the user as keep the hair from turning grey, maintain thickness of the hair, prevent headaches, keep the hair looking lustrous and a host of other curatives, which we know today were utter nonsense and indeed may have caused a number of health problems.

Lead combs are seldom found but should the collector happen upon one, lead is extremely heavy weight, the surface is a dull black, not unlike silver which has been allowed to tarnish beyond redemption. The ornamental comb will be of small dimen-sions, and probably etched or inscribed with a simple design. Weight will be the determining factor with lead combs.

Among the combs seen only sporadically are mother-of-pearl and baleen. Baleen was obtained from the lining of the mouth of certain whales, notably the Right Whale and was used in comb manufacture as early as the 18th century. Mother-of-pearl is a common substance and not a dear one, however, one finds very few antique combs made of this substance. It was made from the shell of various mussels, oysters, and abalone, both domestic and from Europe and the Orient. During the 1920–30's various companies made pearlized celluloid imitations which are lighter in weight and have a shiny surface easily recognized when compared to genuine mother-of-pearl. Whole combs of this substance are usually from the Orient featuring florals and simple slightly raised surface carvings. Some imports of modern combs made from this material are available, so care should be exercised in their purchase if one is unsure of the age of the comb.

The two different 2-part pins or hair ornaments shown in *Figure 3, Plate 98* are made of platinum pavé set with rose cut diamonds. In pavé settings, groups of small stones which would not be overly impressive by themselves are fit in recesses in the metal, with the edges then slightly folded over to contain the stones. The many stones give the pavé set object the appearance of a single large stone, and in combination with crenellated edges, visually increase the size. Late in the 19th century platinum was considered the ideal

FIGURE   FIGURE 2   FIGURE 3

PLATE 98. *Fig. 1:* Crook-shaped ornament of tortoise set with French paste stones in low carat silver *(courtesy Augenstein King, Manor House Antiques).* *Fig. 2:* Two prong pin with amethyst color paste stones *(author's collection).* *Fig. 3:* Hair ornaments of platinum, set with diamonds and made in two sections *(ibid Fig. 1).*

precious metal for settings, as its cold white color better reflected diamonds than gold. Further, it did not oxidize like silver, was stronger than gold, and was then a novel element. As diamonds of the period were not generally brilliant cut, they were sometimes foil-backed like the rhinestone is today, increasing their reflective qualities. These pins are interesting because they are uncommon. In use the hair is placed over the convex lower section and the outer case fastened over it, the pointed end is then inserted securely into the chignon. The flower and trellised leaves have the open feeling found in jewelry of this period.

Paste stones such as those found in the shepherd's crook hair pin [*Plate 98, Figure 1*] are neither appreciated nor understood today. Discovered by Josef Strass, paste is a faceted glass substitute for diamonds which is very soft. When placed in a fine setting as done during the 18th century, the resulting jewelry was of exceptional quality and not at all scorned by royalty or people of wealth. Jewelers were exacting in making the paste replicas of the genuine stones, as they were often made simultaneously. Paste was usually set in silver (not base metal) as are the stones in this pin. They are far too large to be genuine diamonds, yet quite superior to the rock crystals known as rhinestones.

I NEVER CEASE to be appalled by the condition of the combs which are purchased from dealers and other sources. Generally they are dirty, grime and dust hide the sparkle of the sets, the prongs are bent, missing, hold the wrong set, sets have been replaced by the wrong size, color, and even stones which have lost their foiling completely. Fortunately combs with missing teeth are seldom offered for sale for their repair is nigh well impossible unless one has the services of an expert lapidary or jeweler who does custom design. Though few people can reattach severed teeth so the joint is undetectable it can be done by a skilled worker.

The first thing to do when acquiring a comb is to gently wash it in warm water with a mild soap scrubbing carefully so the stones are not loosened from their settings. It is positively astonishing what this simple act will accomplish. Sometimes it is enough if the stones are cleaned and carefully dried to avoid removing the foiling. The back foiling allows rhinestones and some non-gem stones to reflect light and sparkle.

If the stones are improperly set, the wrong size for the chaton, chipped, the wrong color or hue, or have lost their foiling so they appear dull, lifeless, or yellowish, as in the case of clear rhinestones, they should be removed and replaced with an appropriate set.

Removing the stones may be a simple or tedious task. Those which have been poorly set may pop out if caught on the outer edge with a sharp instrument such as a penknife or in some cases the fingernail. If the stone resists removal, a sharply pointed icepick inserted with pressure around the base of the stone will pulverize the stone or lift it out. Most of these stones will not be satisfactory for use in other pieces and should be discarded if imperfect in any respect. Use care not to puncture the comb material as it will enlarge the chaton and require a set larger than the surrounding stones or damage the comb irrevocably. One of the most effective and easily used tools is the steel nail file attached to a long handle of celluloid or other material. The point is sufficiently sharp to pry the stone and strong enough to resist buckling under pressure, as do many improvised tools, and the lengthy handle provides needed leverage.

Next clean the recess and with a toothpick, needle, or straight pin insert a small amount of white adhesive such as Elmer's glue, or "tub of tacky". Too much will cause a film to cover the stone necessitating extra cleaning once the glue is dry. Super glue is not recommended as it is dangerous to use and dries instantaneously allowing no chance to alter the position of the stone if need be. Remove the excess glue and allow to dry. White glues will dry without a trace. It is best to allow some time for curing before attempting to use water on the comb.

Filagree metal framing which is attached to the bridge with pins is best repaired by a skilled artisan as it is generally fine, brittle and requires the use of solders. Frequently several materials are used, each reacting differently to heat, which makes soldering difficult if not impossible. Missing sections are easily replaced if made of brass, copper, silver, and infrequently gold. If the comb has sentimental value or great intrinsic value it is well worth the cost of repair as this type of comb is scarce today.

The best rhinestones are imported from Austria and are available from wholesalers. Refer to the phone book under "Beads". They are inexpensive, sold by the dozen or gross and come in a wide range of colors. One firm carries 84 different shades, 48 sizes and 8 different shapes. Since the stones used in combs and hat pins are small, ($\frac{1}{2}$–3 millimeters) they are easily lost and are best kept in separate compartments of the type found in workshop plastic files containing numerous shallow drawers. A card labeled with the colors available and a sample of the color glued to the label is helpful.

It may be possible to use stones from cast off jewelry but the difficulty of removing the stones, finding they are imperfect, the wrong size, color etc., makes their use hardly worth the while. New stones in no way diminish the value of the comb and restore both the beauty and the utility.

Missing stones and imperfect metal decoration

are one thing, but broken teeth are another; so it is best not to purchase combs with broken teeth, as it is an expensive process to repair them and only an expert should attempt to do so.

THE TEETH ARE the weakest part of the comb and care should be taken in handling them. Horn and tortoise combs may have become brittle with age and fracture easily. If the comb is a rare example and merits purchase despite missing teeth or damage to the filagree work or other bridge decoration, it is acceptable in its imperfect state. Museums exhibit numerous examples of such flawed items when the article is otherwise unobtainable in relatively perfect condition. Celluloid, gutta percha, metal, wood, aluminum, bakelite etc., are more pliable and sturdier than tortoise, ivory, or horn.

Especially susceptible to cleavage are the sharply pointed, extremely long narrow teeth found on huge hand worked horn combs and the curved teeth of varying lengths and widths used on high backed tortoise combs. Combs should be handled as infrequently as possible, but when it is necessary to move them, hold them lightly about midpoint in the heading in a section which is not carved.

In this connection, combs may be effectively exhibited in a sheet of styrofoam but the teeth may be permanently damaged by forcing them into the stiff material and leaving them for a prolonged period of time. If great care is taken to insert the properly aligned teeth and the insertion is for a short period, a day or so, styrofoam makes a very serviceable and inexpensive display material.

Combs with metal headings can be made most attractive and the details of the fretwork exposed and enhanced by carefully rubbing them with fine steel wool. Fine steel wool does wonders for all sorts of things from removing the calcium deposit on cut or other glassware to polishing base metals, (do not use, however, on gold or sterling). Once the shine has been restored to the base metals, clear fingernail polish—applied with caution—will prolong the luster. Leave the patina on areas of your choice to highlight the polished areas.

Collections of combs can be shown to best advantage in such receptacles as lighted wall niches, elegant vitrines with plate glass shelving, curio cabinets, breakfronts, commercial display cases, shadow boxes, large glass covered specimen cases, oversized ornate frames, modern strip shelving, large armoires from the 1870's which have had the plate glass mirrors or doors removed or left ajar and fitted with shelving. The latter is currently a smart decorating device as the armoire is a versatile piece of furniture.

Individual pieces are most effective when shown on a clear lucite stand which has a slot in the base into which the teeth are placed while the back rests on a high square support.

Many collectors use their collections to decorate bedroom walls, halls, living rooms or foyers, grouping them in pleasing arrangements on velvet or other fabrics where they may be admired by guests and family alike. If stored they may be loosely wrapped in acid-free tissue paper and placed in shoe boxes which stack neatly and occupy a minimum of space in a convenient closet, never a basement, cellar, or uninsulated attic.

All combs should be stored or exhibited in a dry location which has a fairly even temperature, as they will be affected by extreme changes in temperature over an extended period of time. Heat will warp the teeth and head of a comb and frigid extremes will induce brittleness. Even temperatures can be maintained through the use of lighted cabinets (the light bulbs do not have to exceed 15 watts to be effective) and enclosures with sliding doors.

Contrary to public opinion not tortoise but celluloid is most subject to deterioration as celluloid which has been kept in a damp, hot, or freezing place will decompose. Tortoise will tend to chip along the edges of the bridge or teeth but it will not crumble and disintegrate as does celluloid. Celluloid when exposed to the elements will develop a fine network of cracks which resemble the crazing found in some chinawares and will ultimately turn to a powdery substance, ruining the comb. Celluloid is after all, a chemical substance, whereas tortoise is a form of calcium or skeletal deposit which is quite impervious to decay.

PLASTIC CONTAINERS SUCH as ziplock or baggies are convenient for most things but should never be used to store combs as the circulation of air is prevented and the comb, unable to breathe, will suffer.

Recently a cache of combs which had been stored or forgotten in the basement of a very old comb factory in Leominster, Massachusetts, was examined and unfortunately the tell-tale signs of cracking and fading were evident in some of the finest specimens.

Frequently a handsome tortoise or mock tortoise comb will appear dull and lifeless. Merely rubbing briskly with the fingers will restore some of the shine. Colonial comb makers rubbed combs with a mixture of fine brick dust moistened enough to adhere to a woolen rag, held between the thumb and fingers, and rubbed over the comb until a perfectly smooth surface was obtained. The polishing was done in a like manner but rotten stone, chalk and vinegar were used instead of brick dust or fireplace ashes. Today a little mineral oil or vaseline will have the same effect with half the effort of resorting to such exotic substances.

ANTIQUE PURSES *SECTION II*

Frontispiece: Evalyn Walsh McLean, 1886-1947.

CHAPTER 1
HISTORY OF THE PURSE

As an accessory of dress the purse has been subject to the whims of fashion; indeed the purse as we know it today did not appear on the fashion scene until the early part of the present century. Virtually nothing has been written specifically pertaining to the evolution of the purse and information must be deduced from works of art, early prints, literary passages, ladies' fashion books of the 19th and 20th centuries, catalogues, museum collections, and the like.

For all practical purposes purse collectors will seldom find purses for sale which predate the 19th century although some specimens from the 18th, 17th, and even the 16th centuries may be viewed in museums in the United States and abroad. The term purse or bag will be used throughout this work; however, from an historical point of view, the terms bag, almoner, pouch, pocket, pocketbook, apron, reticule, traveling or carpet bag, handbag, and finally the purse are a reasonably accurate chronological progression.

Prior to the late 18th century purses were not primarily designed for carrying money, a fact which at first thought appears strange, but very few people had any money, as most transactions were conducted by barter; women were rarely permitted the luxury of having money of their own, aside from religious contributions in small coin; wages for the laboring classes were often paid on a yearly basis, farmers owed for their supplies from crop to crop, and few purchases were made in those self sufficient days; there was not the need for money as in an industrialized society. The computer age may again see the end of the purse for monetary uses as the credit card takes over.

Therle Hughes in her book entitled, *English Domestic Needlework,* mentions seal bags dating from early in the 14th century which are still intact. Bags of this sort, which are among the earliest bags and purses, were so called because they were used to carry state papers and were ornamented with the royal seal and thus represented the might of the British crown and its authority. These ancient bags were small in

size, 4–5 inches square or rectangular, flat or box shaped, tassled at the bottom and closed with a draw string, the ends of which formed the carrying loops. Monetary gifts to monarchs, separate from taxes or other levies, were delivered in crudely embroidered silver and gold thread purses. By the end of the 16th century embroideries and trimmings were sophisticated and skillfully executed. Bags used for other than money included "sweet bags" (sachets), work bags to hold embroideries, laces, and sewing of the wealthier class of women, bags for medicines, charms, religious relics, and other small treasures and trifles.

During the Crusades, from the 11th–13th centuries, crusaders were given a leather bag by the parish priest containing gold coins called, "crusados", which were worn on a girdle or belt. These coins were dispensed to the needy as alms, hence the term "almoner," or "almonier." They were also once called "amonieres sarrasnoises" or "saracen almsbags" as the Saracens were the non-Christians from whom the Crusaders endeavoured to wrest control of the Holy Lands.

The practice of wearing an alms pouch by both men and women was continued as a European fashion accent for roughly four centuries until the advent of the men's waistcoat and knee length greatcoat with its numerous and voluminous side pockets which accommodated such articles as keys, medicines, combs, handkerchiefs, snuff, important documents, cutlery, mirrors, and perhaps currency.

THE POUCH WAS rather small, made of a variety of materials, though leather was widely used, and the top terminated in tabs or an ornamental hook which was appended to a narrow girdle or gathered into a ring passed through a simple belted tunic. Some were merely flat rectangles of unadorned materials with long drawstrings in which keys, combs, pincushions, mirrors, beads, pomanders, medicines, religious relics, and other trifles were carried by women.

Among the oldest (if not in fact the oldest) purses

PLATE 1. *The Amourous Old Man.* 15th Century print.

FIGURE 1

in the United States are these two European purses from the XV–XVI centuries made of iron, leather, and velvet [*Plate 3*]. Their massive size (12 inches long by 8¾ inches wide; 9 inches long by 6 inches wide) would indicate they were probably worn by men, and were suspended from the belt by the ring clearly seen on one and the bridge atop the spoke of the other. The detail on each is amazingly graceful consisting of rope twist on each arched iron frame and topped by feudal towers, battlements, and parapets. The leather bag shows the age and wear one would expect of an accessory nearly 500 years old, but the velvet tassled bag with a carefully balanced cut pile design is surprisingly well preserved. Note also that the same methods of attaching the frame to the body of the purse were then used as today: sewing the fabric or other material though a series of holes drilled into the frames, which were very wide. Such superb bags were without question the property of some noble, wealthy merchant or other upperclass man; his wife would have worn an equally fine version on a smaller scale hung from her girdle by long silk or leather cording. (See *Plates 4–8* from Braun and Schneider)

By the 16th century there were guilds of pursemakers in England who produced leather pouches of high quality, as the guilds maintained standards which would make present day trade unions seem ridiculous.

The city of Caen, France, was renowned for its

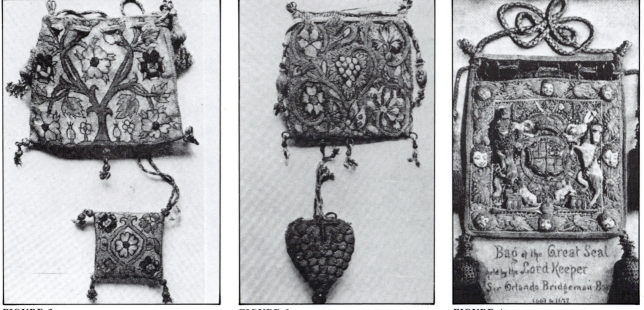

FIGURE 2 **FIGURE 3** **FIGURE 4**

PLATE 2. Fig. 1: Embroidered bag, English, early 17th Century *(The Metropolitan Museum of Art, Rogers Fund)*. **Fig. 2:** Bag and pincushion, early 17th Century *(Victoria and Albert Museum, London)*. **Fig. 3:** Bag and purse with purse shaped like bunch of grapes, early 17th Century *(Victoria and Albert Museum, London)*. **Fig. 4:** Bag of the Great Seal, 14th Century *(Guildhall, London)*.

FIGURE 1

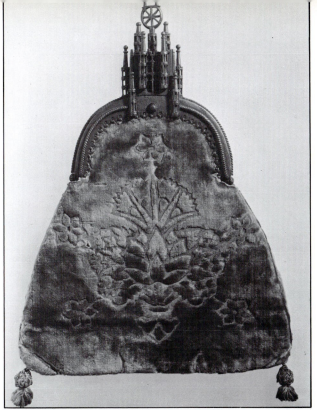

FIGURE 2

FIGURE 3

FIGURE 4

PLATE 3. *Fig. 1:* Iron and velvet purse, European, 15th-16th Century *(Metropolitan Museum of Art, Cloisters Collection).* *Fig. 2:* Iron and leather purse, European, 15th-16th Century, *(Metropolitan Museum of Art, Cloisters Collection). Fig. 3.* Bag, embroidered green satin, Italian, 17th Century *(Metropolitan Museum of Art, Rogers Fund). Fig. 4:* Game bag of iron, velvet and silk, European, 15th-16th Century *(Metropolitan Museum of Art, Cloisters Collection).*

FIGURE 2

FIGURE 3

PLATE 4. *Fig. 1:* 12th Century, Knights Templar. *Fig. 2:* 14th Century, England. *Fig. 3:* 14th Century, German chatelaine. *Fig. 4:* 14th Century, German partricians. *(All from "Historic Costume In Pictures" by Braun & Schneider, Dover Publications, New York, NY, 1975.)*

FIGURE 1

FIGURE 4

pouches as Charles De Bourgueville relates in *Recherches de Antiquities sur le Ville Caen,* "As for Caen pouches, none made in other towns can compare with them for choiceness, character, and excellent materials, such as velvets of all colors, gold, silver and other threads, or in suitability for the use of nobles, justices, ladies and maidens, so that it is a common proverb to speak of 'Caen pouches' above all others."

In 1430 Henry VI is known to have worn a bright red girdle from which was suspended a small gold purse.

At Traquais House, Peebleshire, Scotland, is a purse attributed to Mary Queen of Scots (1542-1567). Made of cloth of silver with beaded tassel ends and delicate embroidery, it has such a modern appearance it may be one of the doubtful items ascribed to Queen Mary, who unlike her cousin Elizabeth I, was a needlewoman of some stature.

Late in the 14th century elongated tasseled bags were suspended by a pair of tabs over wide leather belts as a fashion accent worn by upper class youths. An illustration for the epic poem, *The Romance of the Rose,* entitled, "Dance of Mirth in a Garden", shows four young men in various styles of clothing being serenaded by musicians as they frolicked behind a turreted wall with a group of maidens. The young women's costumes are plain and drab compared to the magnificent outfits sported by these young dandies, though one of them appears to be wearing a form of purse on an elaborate chain reaching from her waist to her knees, a style which was fashionable in Europe for more than a century and is frequently seen in court paintings. Though the men's purses are individualized through unique embroideries, each is finished with three tassles (which dwarf the purse), combining their decorative importance with the utility of the purse.

FIGURE 1

FIGURE 2

PLATE 5. *Fig. 1:* 14th Century. *Fig. 2:* 15th Century, French noblemen. *Fig. 3:* 15th Century, French. *Fig. 4:* 15th Century, German noblewomen *(ibid Plate 4).*

FIGURE 3

FIGURE 4

In the *Canterbury Tales,* Chaucer tells of the purse of the young wife in the Miller's Tale,

"And by hire girdel hung a purs of lether
T'assled with grene and perled with latoun."

Fynes Moryson in his Itinerary of 1591 tells us of the Dutch,

"Citizens wives put off their ruffes when they goe out of the house, covering their necks and mouthes with a linen cloth for feare of cold and they weare great heavy purses by their sides with great bunches of keyes hanging by chaines of brasses or silver."

Aside from the meager references to the purse as above in literature, histories, letters, wills, account ledgers, newspaper advertisements, costume and decorative art texts, the only reliable sources of information are etchings, paintings, wood cuts and other art forms which depict the attire of the various social classes.

MEDIEVAL AND RENAISSANCE artists depended upon art patrons for their support as only the feudal lords and noblemen were wealthy enough to maintain an artist or purchase his creations. Techniques varied with the individual craftsman but the subject matter never deviated from the classical portrait of the noble and his family, bejeweled and clothed in their finest and latest fashions, or religious subject matter generally concerned with the saints, some Biblical allegory, or the life of the Holy Family. These Christian art patrons were less concerned with advancing art as a form than with courting favor with the clergy and indirectly with the Diety beyond this mundane existence, so the great bulk of art work is ecclesiastical in nature and only indirectly reflects the costume of a particular day.

In 1550 the great Flemish painter Antonio Moro, painted a full length portrait of Maximilian II in his

PLATE 6. *Fig. 1:* 15th Century, English. *Fig. 2:* 15th Century, German townspeople. *Fig. 3:* 16th Century, English. *Fig. 4:* 16th Century, German soldiers. *(ibid Plate 4).*

FIGURE 1

FIGURE 2

FIGURE 3

FIGURE 4

PLATE 4-A.
Maximillian II

slashed garnet colored melon trunks showing the gathered satin beneath the slashes, long silk hose, bear shoes of white satin, a long jerkin or shirt with a high standing collar, a belted sword and magnificent embroidered purse hooked to a second jeweled girdle. Because of the importance of the subject, accurate dating, and the size of the portrait, this may well be the finest instance of the girdled pouch to be found in portrait art.

An amusing sidelight to royal wardrobes and their munificent owners was the custom of renting out their finery to citizens in need of elegant clothing for a limited period of time, similar to our present day custom of renting men's formal wear, so a person sitting for a portrait might be wearing one of the 1600 gowns of Elizabeth I or the finery of the fop, Sir Walter Raleigh. This custom applied to jewels as well, so many a lady was painted wearing the same rope of

PLATE 7. *Fig. 1:* 16th Century, German townspeople. *Fig. 2:* 17th Century, noblemen and officer. *Fig. 3:* 17th Century, Switzerland. *Fig. 4:* 17th Century, Denmark *(ibid Plate 4).*

FIGURE 1

FIGURE 2

FIGURE 3

FIGURE 4

159

FIGURE 1

Spring dress, 1794.   Winter dress, 1795.

FIGURE 2

1818

FIGURE 3

FIGURE 4

PLATE 8. *Fig. 1:* 18th Century, Germany. *Fig. 2:* 18th Century, Germany. *Fig. 3:* 19th Century, France. *Fig. 4:* 19th Century, France *(ibid Plate 4).*

pearls and sparkling jeweled tiara and many a gentleman sported the same sword or other gems, which incidentally were more liberally worn by men than women in the 16th century.

This five inch square alms bag ·or almonier [*Plate 3A*] from The Boston Museum of Fine Arts has to be one of the most intriguing in the book, and despite its great age (1630–1650) it is in remarkably good condition. The message *Remember The Poor* done in white beads against a dark mesh background, speaks well for the sensibilities of the 17th century person of means and indicates the country of origin beyond a shadow of a doubt. Here ''poor'' is spelled ''poore'' but on other examples it reads ''pore'' phonetically. A sense of humor is plain in the same type of purse which contained the motto, ''Heare et is Hit or Miss.'' in yellow and green beads on a purplish background, threaded on brown silk. Hardly an appealing color scheme!

The trim above the drawstring is ornamented further with drilled bits of metal resembling sequins, though they are somewhat dull. The drawstring is made of flat braided metal thread and the decoration is of small metal rings arranged in half circles and tacked to the fabric, which looks like hand loomed linen. The design features a bird in side view and some primitive florals and acorns, repeated in a simple fashion on the tasselled ends of the drawstrings. The different shades of silk used in beading the pattern are likewise visible in the tassell.

SOME VERY INTERESTING information can be gleaned from this Dutch engraving [*Plate 3B*] done about 1600 entitled, ''Fleshy Disguises''. The servants who are busily tieing sausage-shaped bolsters around the waists of their fashionable mistresses (called rolled farthingales) are wearing the older type of buttoned pouch purse which is exposed to full view. The hanging tasselled purse worn by the upper class lady will be hidden under her voluminous skirts, though they were not always so worn as the Braun and Schneider plates show. The long corded and tasselled purse was quite the fashion accent and was made of rich materials and trimmings. The size of the ruffs (a form of collar) worn by the servants is an aid in determining their station as the lower classes were not permitted the wider and costlier ruffs.

They are, however, wearing the masks which were then popular for outdoor wear as a protection against the elements. These masks of animals and grotesques were worn at carnivals, balls, and dramas. Van Meteren said in 1575, ''Ladies of distinction have lately learned to cover their faces with silken masks or visards and feathers.'' Surely these must have been the most absurdly uncomfortable clothes of all times!

Dover Publications has compiled a set of historic

PLATE 3-A. Front and back sides of bag reading "Remember the poor", English, c. 1630-1650 *(Museum of Fine Arts, Boston, gift of Philip Lehman in memory of his wife, Carrie L. Lehman).*

PLATE 3-B. 17th Century Dutch engraving titled "Fleshy Disguises" and showing the buttoned pouch purse.

costume plates several of which have been included with their kind permission. Drawn by various German etchers and published originally by Braun and Schneider in Munich between 1861–1890, they faithfully depict the costumes of European, Asian and Near Eastern societies from antiquity through the 19th centuries in characteristically everyday settings.

Particularly significant are the following observations:

1. For several centuries both men and women wore the almonier in connection with a sheathed knife which was used for a variety of purposes, from eating utensil to weapon.

2. The 14th century chatelaine is plainly shown with a group of keys gracefully suspended from a girdle which also served to lift the outer skirt from the mire of the unpaved paths.

3. Though the almonier was generally worn to the side, it was also worn by men, much as the Scottish Highlander's kilt purse called the "sporran" of the present day, low on the abdomen.

PLATE 9. (BELOW) Three silk purses decorated with gold and silver thread, made in Limoges, France at the end of the 17th century. Thought to have been wedding gifts from the groom to the bride during the course of the ceremony as a symbol of the groom's affluence. Enameled portraits of the couple appear on opposite sides of the purse, perhaps in their wedding finery. Note the holes through which the connecting cord was drawn on these fine examples *(Museum of Fine Arts, Boston, Elizabeth Day McCormick Collection).*

FIGURE 1

FIGURE 2

PLATE 10. (ABOVE) *Fig. 1:* Drawstring bag with silk embroidery, c. 1800–15, France. *Fig. 2:* Double pocketbook with silk embroidery, c. 1780–95, France. The saying reads ''May it be the guardian of the feelings of a heart who knows how to love…It is not a thing which a friend would want to be silent about…It is conveying more than words can say.'' *(Both figures courtesy Museum of Fine Arts, Boston, The Elizabeth Day McCormick Collection).*

163

FIGURE 2

FIGURE 3

FIGURE 1

FIGURE 5

FIGURE 4

FIGURE 6

PLATE 11. *Fig. 1:* Fine bead drawstring bag showing crown of Maria Theresa of Austria, c. 1740–80, France *(Museum of Fine Arts, Boston, Elizabeth Day McCormick Collection).* *Fig. 2:* Fine bead drawstring bag showing portrait of Pilatre de Rozier and balloon, 1783, France. Balloon ascension was November 21, 1783 *(ibid Fig. 1).* *Fig. 3:* Envelope pocketbook of silk and silver tapestry weaving *(ibid Fig. 1).* *Fig. 4:* Escutcheon-shaped purse of white satin and silk thread *(Costume Institute of the Metropolitan Museum of Art, gift of Miss Catherine Oglesby).* *Fig. 5:* Gold tissue handbag embroidered with pearls, beads, and metal threads. Date and origin unknown *(Metropolitan Museum of Art, gift of Mrs. James Orme).* *Fig. 6:* Circular purse of embroidered silk and paper. Iron frame with belt loops. Either pattern or frame is upside down. Early 17th Century *(ibid Fig. 4).*

FIGURE 1

FIGURE 2

FIGURE 4

FIGURE 5

FIGURE 6

FIGURE 3

PLATE 12. *Fig. 1:* Envelope pocketbook of fine beadwork, Louis XIV, 1805, France. *Fig. 2:* Envelope pocketbook of fine beadwork, Louis XIV, 1715, France. *Fig. 3:* Fine beadwork, c. 1750–90, France. *Fig. 4:* Envelope pocketbook, c. 1700–50, France. *Fig. 5:* Souvenir envelope pocketbook of silk and metallic yarns, 1755, Turkey. *Fig. 6:* Miniature envelope pocketbook of fine beadwork, France (*All courtesy Museum of Fine Arts, Boston, Elizabeth Day McCormick Collection*).

4. The purses worn by middle and upper class men were fashion accents as well as utilitarian in nature.

5. Ladies' bags of the 14th century, though less elaborate than the mens; were worn on long cords or straps reaching nearly to the ankles.

6. In a given century the general shape and design of the purse appears constant regardless of the country of origin.

7. By the late 16th century the popularity of the hoop and farthingale among the upper classes caused the bag to disappear from view and remain hidden as pockets for three centuries.

8. The small pouch used by the military of all nations became a huge double saddle bag by the 18th century.

9. *Plate 8, Fig. 2* showing a lady carrying a large basket type of reticule with a gathered fabric top called a "bird cage", reveals the Germans were the avant-garde by a full generation in respect to this type of

165

purse rather than the French who are usually considered the pace setters of fashion.

IT IS NOT known for certain whether tambour work originated in India and migrated to China or took the reverse course, but it is known that it was not used in Europe until the 18th century. Tambouring is a method of embroidering using a hook which produces a tiny chain-stitch. The fabric is stretched on a frame or drum and the hook is threaded below the material where the pattern is not visible so the operator must be skilled in its use. In China this incredibly tight fine chain-stitch became known as the "forbidden stitch" as the embroiderer's eyesight was so strained that blindness frequently resulted and tambour work was eventually decreed illegal in China. Chinese tambour work solidly filled specified areas of the pattern, whereas in the 18th century the French (who became masters of the art) tended to produce patterns of a

PLATE 15. Drawstring bag, c. 1800–30, United States *(Museum of Fine Arts, Boston).*

FIGURE 1

FIGURE 2

FIGURE 3

PLATE 13. *Fig. 1:* Front view of silk and metal pouch, 17th Century, Northern Europe. *Fig. 2:* Back view. *Fig. 3:* Woven silk and metal reticule, 18th Century European. *Fig. 4:* Envelope-type pocketbook of silk shot with metal thread, 17th–18th Century, France *(All courtesy Cooper-Hewitt Museum, The Smithsonian Institute's National Museum of Design).*

FIGURE 4

166

FIGURE 1

FIGURE 5

FIGURE 2

FIGURE 3

FIGURE 6

PLATE 14. *Fig. 1:* Envelope pocketbook of silk embroidered with silk and metallic yarns, c. 1675–1725, Italy *(Museum of Fine Arts, Boston, Elizabeth Day McCormick Collection). Fig. 2:* Drawstring bag of beadwork and silk, c. 1760–80, France *(ibid Fig. 1). Fig. 3:* Drawstring bag of cotton twill with very fine beading, c. 1822–25, Western Europe *(ibid Fig. 1). Fig. 4:* Drawstring bag of extremely fine beads showing Venetian street scene, c. 1820–50, Italy *(ibid Fig. 1). Fig. 5:* Pocketbook with crewel embroidery made for Lemeul Hayward of Boston by his mother, 1768 *(Museum of Fine Arts, Boston, gift of Mrs. Henry K. Metcalf). Fig. 6:* Reticule of silk satin with embroidered flowers *(Costume Institute of The Metropolitan Museum of Art, gift of Mrs. Stewart Waller).*

light open character preferring sentimental verses, flowers, trailing vines, hearts and doves, and domestic animals with strangely human characteristics. In comparing the tambour work done by the two cultures it would appear the hook employed by the Chinese must itself have been finer, producing a nearly microscopic stitch.

Dr. Joan Edwards, in her book, *Bead Embroidery,* gives a detailed explanation of how tambouring, and particularly bead work using the tambour needle, is accomplished.

PLATE 17. Fig. 1: Cotton-linen pocket embroidered with wool having monogram ''M W,'' c. 1750–1800, England *(Museum of Fine Arts, Boston, bequest of Maxim Karolik, M & M Karolik Collection).* **Fig. 2:** Linen pocket with monogram ''LB,'' 1801, England *(Museum of Fine Arts, Boston, Special Textile Fund).*

Plate 10 shows (18th century French tambour work), an elegant pocketbook which was doubtless intended as a gift from a lady of quality to a gentleman admirer. Vanda Foster *(Beads and Purses)* relates, ''. . . by the late eighteenth century the giving of purses was so common that Lord Bessorough was forced to turn down such a gift from Sarah Ponsonby, saying 'I desire the favour of you not to send me the Purse you mention for I have, I believe, twenty by me which are not of any use. It has been the fashion of ladies to make purses and they have been so obliging as to give me a great many.'''

From the early 1600's dresses had contained a slit sewn into the hip side seams allowing the wearer to reach into a pocket-bag held by tapes to the girdle or corset and hidden from view under several petticoats and billowing skirts.

These pockets were most often worn in pairs and were more generous in proportion than any of the

168

preceding types of bags, some being more than a foot square while others were rounded at the bottom. They were gathered to a tape and worn suspended under the skirts attached to the hoops, farthingale, corset, or whatever foundation garment was in fashion at the time. The width of the skirt was the determining factor to the design of the foundation. Some skirts extended from the sides like shelves adjacent to a pillar, some were complete spheres, some were intended to create a bustle effect and extended the hips to absurd dimensions while the waist was nipped to a mere 12–14 inches. The pockets were worn under the full hooped skirt as early as the 16th century and continued as the fashions allowed until the reticule came into being at the end of the 18th century.

As they were hidden from view the pockets did not need to be made of choice materials and were very simple in design often unadorned and could be considered functional rather than decorative. They were made of linen, calico, dimity, chintz, cotton twill, canvas, flannel, and other sturdy materials. The opening was merely a slit, extending halfway down the front of the top side of the flat bag, and in those which were decorated, embroideries often of the crewel type were done around this opening which matched the slit in the side of the skirt so the wearer could deposit or retrieve articles easily. Since they were not costly and could be individualized, pockets were often given as gifts to their elders by small children learning to embroider. The will of a New England woman reveals what was kept in these pockets for she left a friend an ''embroidered dimity pocket with a pocket-glass, comforter and strong-water-bottle kept within it.'' The pocket-glass was a small mirror, the comforter a hand warmer, and the strong-water-bottle a container for rum or other strong liquor.

Washington Irving, writing about 1660, tells us of the Dutch housewives in New Amsterdam, ''Those were the honest days in which every woman stayed at home, read the Bible, and wore pockets, ay, and that, too, of a goodly size, fashioned with patchwork into many curious devices, and ostentatiously worn on the outside. These, in fact, were convenient receptacles where all good housewives carefully stored away such things as they wished to have at hand; by which means they often came to be incredibly crammed.''

A GROUP OF pockets on display at Old Sturbridge Village, Sturbridge, Massachusetts, includes some of these patchwork pockets which resemble the exotic crazy quilts of a later day, though they are of cotton patches rather than silks and velvets.

For nearly four centuries an important item of dress, seldom seen in use today, was the apron. Not the colorful gaily patterned calicos, the gaudy cottons, bold ginghams, the pristine cambrics of recent memory, but aprons of the finest silk, lace, lawn, satin, velvet, linen, filmy muslin, and other costly and delicate fabrics were worn by ladies of wealth and royal status aping those cruder and more functional ones worn by the working classes.

Not all pockets were hidden from view nor were they all made of inexpensive materials as this request from Eleanor Wortley of Yorkshire reveals, ''If you woulde plese to employ somebody to chuse me out a lase that hath but very littell silver in itt, and not above a spangell or two to a peke I think would do well; I would not have it too hevy a lase; about the breth of a three-penny ribinge, very littell broder will bee enofe; and desier Mrs. Verney I pray you to chuse mee out some ribinge to make stringes; six yardes will be enofe; some shadoed sattin ribinge will be the best of fourpenny breth; and I would fain have some littell eginge lase as slite as may be to ege the strings and but littell silver in it; ten yards will be enofe.''

PLATE 16. This 18th Century print depicts servants helping a lady into her corset.

This perfumed pocket would have been worthy of display outside the skirt with its laces, satin ribbons, and spangles.

An engraving by John Collett, circa 1770–1780, [*Plate 16*] humorously portrays a fashionable French lady being laced into her whalebone corset with the assistance of her footman, personal maid and messenger boy. Her pet monkey points to a text which warns the lady against becoming a victim of Satan, (much like the warning in the 13th century etching [*Plate 6, Comb Section*]) through vanity. Everyone *but* the suffering lady is enjoying the situation. Seen beneath the corset points is a simple pocket, partially filled.

Eighteenth century engravings ridiculed women's fashions in both the dressed and undressed states, and afforded much humor for the magazines of the day.

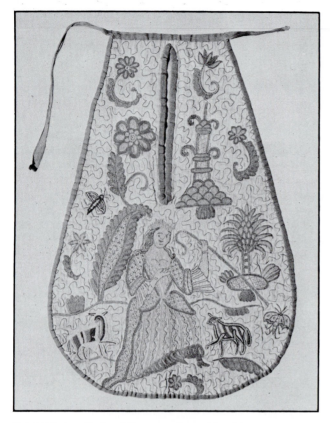

PLATE 18. Quilted linen pocket embroidered with silk, c. 1700–50, England *(Museum of Fine Arts, Boston).*

Society restricted women to the home where they were unable to demonstrate any but a false image of vain ineptitude, while bolstering the male ego; a fact which seems to have entirely escaped most men. Women wore the corsets designed by men, but they certainly did not hunt the whale to near extinction, nor engage in the profitable commerce such industry produced.

CONCURRENT WITH THE pocket was the pocketbook, a flat envelope shaped container with a fold-over flap, for the valuables which a lady or gentleman wished to carry on her or his person. The stuffed pocketbook was deposited in the pocket. Newspaper ads for lost articles reveal the following strange items of sufficient consequence to offer a reward for their return: mirrors, combs, sachets, knives, smelling salts, toothpicks, fine materials, sewing implements, legal documents, fans, snuff, handkerchiefs, powder puffs, keys, poker counters, literally any trifle, but seldom ever currency. Then as now little hope was held out for recovering lost funds and appeals were for personal papers and objects of sentimental value.

These notices are immensely significant to researchers as they indicate without a doubt what the pocketbooks contained and what their owners considered valuable to them.

Embroidered pocketbooks were of the canvas type done in crewel yarns and silks, the classic flamestitch, rice, Irish, cross, Queen's, tent, diamond-within-a-diamond, and other patterns in cheerfully bright colors, showed a marked contrast to the drab solid colored materials used in clothing which was considered ''proper.'' The most popular stitch was Bargello used in the 19th century pocketbooks worked by ladies for their fiances, husbands, or other family members as gifts. As they lacked fasteners, the tape which was used to bind off the edges was extended to form long strings which were wrapped securely around the pocketbook and tied. Pocketbooks were lined with colorful materials, occasionally were dated and signed, and were held in great esteem not only by the makers but by succeeding generations.

Pocketbooks were also made of leather, parchment, brocade, linen and other materials in addition to decorated ones, but they all appear to have been hand made in the home. Susan Swan stresses the point that early in American history women of all classes were expected to be accomplished in needlework. Those fortunate few who did not have to work as servants, in factories, or on the farms and had the opportunity to obtain some schooling, however brief, often found their curriculum composed of sewing and embroidery lessons or ''fancy work'', as opposed to the ''plain sewing'' done by the great mass of women. As is so often the case, it was a matter of convention mixed with Biblical admonition against allowing the Devil to make use of idle hands, that found the proper lady never without the tools for her fancy work and/or sewing, as well as the objects themselves. A practical sewing machine was not in general use before 1846, so all articles of clothing and linens were hand sewn in the home, the wealthy alone availing themselves of the services of seamstresses or tailors. Among the items made by these women and girls were the apron, the pocket, the pocketbook and finally the reticule.

The word apron or napron came from the French word ''nappe'' meaning cloth; in English the word is used to designate a table napkin. It is easy to see the extension of the word to include ''pinners'', or ''pinafore'', aprons with a bib which was pinned to the shirt or dress top. Table ''pinners'' were required of Harvard University students in 1677 and all children wore ''pinners'' or aprons of serviceable materials.

The apron seemed to have 200 year cycles of popularity as it was known to have been used as early as 1300, revived again in 1500, and enjoyed its greatest acceptance in the 1700's. Initially it was intended to protect the outer dress or skirt, but with the introduc-

170

FIGURE 1

FIGURE 2

FIGURE 3

FIGURE 4

PLATE 19. *Fig. 1:* Crewel embroidery pocketbook, c. 1725–75, New England *(Museum of Fine Arts, Boston, gift of Mr. and Mrs. S.A. Biggin). Fig. 2:* Crewel-work ''flame stitch'' pocketbook, 18th Century, New England. The flame stitch contains a diamond-shaped cone in the midst of a zigzag section resembling a candle flame. The flames were black, green, blue or any color which caught the embroiderer's fancy *(Museum of Fine Arts, Boston, gift of Mrs. Luke V. Lockwood). Fig. 3:* Crewel-work flame stitch pocketbook, made by Abigail Lee, pre-1786, Providence, Rhode Island *(Museum of Fine Arts, Boston, gift of Mrs. Marcus Morton). Fig. 4:* Crewel-work pocketbook made for William Cusing, 1779, Waltham, Massachusetts *(Museum of Fine Arts, Boston, gift of Eleanor E. Barry).*

tion of elegant embroideries from China it became a favorite accessory worn by wealthy women for over a century.

Distinction was drawn between the classes by the richness of the apron; the more affluent lady wearing long or short aprons of plush, lace, cutwork, needlepoint lace, fine white lawn embroidered with white thread, swansdown, and other delicate fabrics. Working, lower class women, and domestics wore long plain aprons of wool, linen, hemp, even leather, which bore little resemblance to those pretty appendages which their pampered mistresses wore to show their social station. Wealthy women were known to have spent as much as 10% of their clothing budget for aprons and those who could not afford to have them custom made, sewed and embroidered them themselves, as the fashion magazines of the day carried patterns and full instructions for their creation.

Some aprons were of generous proportions while others were more like shams, being decorative rather than useful. They were embroidered, trimmed with the finest laces, decorated with cut work, dyed to match favorite gowns, were made in long, short and bib lengths, were bowed and beribboned, appliqued

with filled designs, and most importantly, they were fitted with large pockets which substituted for the indispensible reticule to follow.

ELIZABETH I Is said to have owned no fewer than 18 of these not so lowly articles of attire. Mary Tudor paid 17£ for one, and every major portrait painter from Gainsborough to Singleton elected to pose his subject with an elaborate apron. George Washington, fashion conscious himself—as were plantation owners of his day—ordered all the clothing needs for his family from abroad including: ''A fashionable cap or fillet with bib apron'', and, ''Tuckers, bibs, and aprons if they are fashionable.''

The preoccupation with proprieties of dress seems amusing to us today, but Alice Earl relates in the interest of modesty, women members of the Society of Friends were required in 1695 to wear aprons of the plain white variety in Burlington, New Jersey, but other groups of Quakeresses wore aprons of green or blue as in a 1721 meeting it was decided that, ''Green aprons are Decent and Becoming to us as a People. Let none want aprons at all and that either green or blue or other grave colors, not white upon the street or in public at all, not any spangled or speckled silver or cloth or any silk aprons at all.'' When Rachel Budd married in May, 1771, she donned, on her return from the ceremony, ''a thin white apron of ample dimensions, tied in front with a large blue bow.'' In 1668, an inventory of Jane Humphreys of Dorchester, Massachusetts, contained: ''2 Bleu aprons, a White Holland Apron with a Small Lace at the bottom. A white Holland apron with 2 breathes in it, My best white apron. My greene apron.'' In case the reader should wonder about the strange spellings, there was a general lack of education and more importantly, there was no standard dictionary to establish widely accepted spelling rules until 1783 when Noah Webster published his spelling book and 1828 when his dictionary, which was hand written and entirely his own effort, appeared in New England.

From the wardrobe inventory of a wealthy woman settler of New Amsterdam in 1650 we find, ''an embroidered purse with silver bugle and chain to the girdle and silver hook and eye valued at 14 shillings.'' A certain Madame Cornaile de Vis had a ''green cloth petticoat, a red and blue waistcoat, a pair of red and yellow sleeves, a white cornet cap, green stockings with crimson clocks, and a purple 'Pooysee apron'.'' The Dutch were fond of bright colors and would have been most unhappy had they had to live with the somber Puritans with their black, browns and greys.

The rich silk embroidered aprons have survived in museum collections for the beauty of their embroideries, while those everyday versions have long since been discarded to the dust cloth bag. The pockets on these aprons were the vertical slit types and later, by 1830, they were small and gathered puffy affairs on silk or satin trimmed with lace and jet (1880) along with light colored crewel embroidered versions. Designs for these aprons were invariably florals, scrolls, vines, sprigs of buds, and birds slightly Oriental in feeling. Some were done in white embroidery on sheer white muslins such as would be admired on infants' christening gowns.

FIGURE 1

FIGURE 2

PLATE 20. *Fig. 1:* Black silk apron from ''Lady Godey,'' 1859. *Fig. 2:* 18th Century pocketbook of wool petit point with metal clasp (*The Metropolitan Museum of Art, Rogers Fund*).

172

Stephen Grosson tells something of the cost of these aprons in his *Pleasant Quippes for Upstart New Fangled Gentlewomen* in 1596:

"These aprons white of choicest thred,
So choicely tied, so dearly bought,
So finely fringed, so nicely spred,
So quaintly cut, so richlie wrought;
Were they in work to save thier coates,
They need not cost so many grotes."

(A grote was an English silver coin worth 4 pence issued from the time of Edward III to Charles II and later known as Maundy money.)

Aprons were equally popular in France as Challomel in his *History of Fashion in France* wrote,
"Furl off your lawn apron in flounces and rows,
Puff and pucker up knots in your arms and your toes;
Make your petticoat short, that a hoop eight yards wide
May decently show how your garters are ty'd"

Today the apron has all but vanished, but the purse in all its various forms from practical to absurd is firmly entrenched, probably forever.

After the fall of the monarchy in France, a revival of classical Greek and Roman costume which advocated simplicity of garment and material, became fashionable on the continent and in the newly created United States of America. Dresses made of fine white linen, gauze, muslin, and voile were embroidered with laurel wreaths, key designs, and extremely simple decorations around the skirt bottom and sleeve, in earthy tones of red, green, blue and yellow. Some dresses were devoid of any decoration at all. Waist lines were raised to just under the bust and scooped necklines were startlingly low. Laced sandals and thongs were worn over white hose or bare feet. Elaborate jewelry was considered an ostentatious remnant of the hated upper classes and nobility, thus fell

PLATE 21. Woman wearing Roman costume with long reticule. From "Costume Parisien," 1798.

FIGURE 1 FIGURE 2

PLATE 22. Series of costume drawings c. 1820–1840 showing early reticules.

PLATE 23. Martha Custis Washington with purse she made *(Smithsonian Institute)*.

174

from favor. Corsets, hooped skirts, padding, etc., were discarded entirely for a natural straight line and it is said little or no underclothing was worn. The mystery of what was worn under those sheer dresses which spelled the demise of the pocket and established the reticule and its successors forever is solved in the following ad which appeared in 1808, "Invisible dresses-drawers, petticoats and waistcoats made of real Spanish lamb's wool. Mrs. Morris, late Mrs. Robert Shaw, informs Ladies she has now ready for their inspection an entire fresh and extensive assortment of her patent elastic Spanish lamb's wool petticoats, drawers and waistcoats, all in one, and separate. Articles much approved of for their pleasant elasticity, warmth and delicate colour, will add less to size than a cambric muslin, warranted never to shrink in the wash. . . ." These undergarments fit closely enough to insure the scanty Empire dress lines would not be ruined by unsightly bulk.

In The Same year a Philadelphia magazine maintained, "No lady of fashion now appears in public without a riticule which contains her handkerchief, fan, card-money, and essence bottle. They are at this season usually made of rich figured sarsnet, plain satin or silver tissue, with strings and tassels, their colors appropriate to the robes with which they are worn."

Out of this neo-classical fashion came the beginnings of the modern bag worn outside the skirt and of such elaborate styles and huge proportions that it is the predominant feature of dress in some French fashion plates of the 1790's. One such plate shows an elongated pocket bag, betasseled and fringed suspended by a series of cords from the waist which was belted in matching material. The bag is embroidered with the wearer's monogram, a tasseled bow and olive wreaths, bordered by what appears to be fine braid. Since the bag reaches from the wearer's thigh nearly to the ground, it is impressive indeed!

From *Costume Parisien 1798* comes this drawing [*Plate 21*] which is not a fashion plate but an exaggeration of the prevailing costume. The short curly hair mocks the practice of marking those bound for the guillotine by shearing their hair. The elongated torso, bare feet, and ridiculous laced sandals are not our interest, only the pocket bag, which reaches nearly to the ground on absurdly long cords. The pockets so carefully concealed for centuries now appear as an exterior accessory of dress and soon convert to the hand held reticule of great, great grandmother's day.

British novelist Jane Austen, in 1798 ordered seven yards of materials for a new dress, inquiring of her seamstress if this was sufficient. This does not square well with the claims of some outraged clergymen that the dresses were so transparent they were certain there was no chemise underneath. Actually there were several petticoats in addition to the supposedly absent chemise! [From Lady Louisa Stuart, "Gleanings from an Old Portfolio" quoted by Noah Waugh in, "The Cut of Women's Clothes", London, 1968.]

The Practice Of stuffing the pocketbook into the pocket caused the feminine figure to bulge awkwardly and prevented a graceful carriage, and gracefulness was the one virtue ladies strove mightily to attain in the Empire fashion just described, so the stage was set for the reticule.

The term reticule (indispensable, ridicule) was loosely applied to early purses somewhat incorrectly as the term applies to network, and prior to the early 19th century purses were made of leather, satin, cloth of gold, linen, wool, canvas, ivory, furs, mesh metallics, embroideries, and various other fabrics, but they were not necessarily network. Though they varied as to decoration, shape and materials, they were invariably closed by long drawstrings shirred through the top, strung through a series of small bone, metal or hand-whipped rings, and were charmingly feminine. Held in the hand or dangled from the wrist, they were so universally adopted that men humorously referred to them as "ridicules" or "indispensables".

The reticule or indispensable took simple shapes such as oblong sacks with drawstrings run through gathered tops, U-shaped sides with the materials pulled together so as to form a fringe, diamond pointed bottoms and sides finished by small tassles, embroidered smallish purses (not more than 3 x 4 inches); and most appealing, those decorated with verses and dated, similar to the Colonial samplers which young girls of the upper classes were required to complete to demonstrate their proficiency with the needle.

In the *Woman in Fashion*, Doris Langley Moore shows some marvellous fashion plates of her extensive collection of dress and accessories from 1800–1940, and we are able to note her comments on three reticules. She dates the reticule from the year 1800, as a result of the diaphanous muslins which came into prominence in the Empire Period in France, the undisputed center of haute couture for roughly 200 years. There is little dispute among authorities that this style resulted in the reticule bridging the gap between the apron pocket and the modern handbag. Two of the purses she exhibits exemplify the concept of the reticule as having a drawstring with long slender carrying tapes and various types of decoration, but they are straight across the bottom rather than shaped, and one has a metal frame and chain and is so large and square she mentions this fact as being "the latest style" (1820). Its interest is indeed more than merely fashionable and unusual; as she recounts it was one of a number which were sold by an organization of

FIGURE 1

FIGURE 3

FIGURE 2

ladies opposed to the slave trade which was then in its heydey. These satin embroidered purses showed a black mother sitting under a palm tree holding an infant, and on the opposite side an impassioned plea for the abolition of enslavement of human beings. It is the only fashionable object which she feels has been directly associated with philanthropic movements.

One of the most appealing paintings in the American primitive school of protrait painting was done in 1815 by Ammi Phillips of Harriet Leavens from Lainsingburg, New York. From the standpoint of costume it is a masterpiece, for it shows a youthful Miss Leavens in a pink Empire style gown of the simplest lines, prominently displaying in her left hand, which was ornamented with a large ring on her index finger, a plain black and crimson reticule of generous size. Of course one notices the combs, one of which is placed oddly enough in the middle of her forehead at a vertical slant. Either Miss Leavens was very diminutive, or the umbrella she is holding was enormous, and it is obvious from her half smile that she was proud of her clothes and accessories [*Plate 24, Comb section*].

The First Ladies Hall in the Smithsonian National Museum of History and Technology contains another historic purse which may be classified as a reticule. Made by the *first* First Lady, Martha Custis Washington, it is modeled by a mannequin wearing a dress of salmon pink faille handpainted with a design of native North American wildflowers in the larger medallion spaces and insects in the smaller ones.

PLATE 24. *Fig. 1:* Printed leather bag, 1840, Western Europe *(Museum of Fine Arts, Boston, gift of Maxim Karolik).* *Fig. 2:* Slipper-shaped bag of beadwork and leather, c. 1830–50, Western Europe *(Museum of Fine Arts, Boston, Elizabeth Day McCormick Collection).* *Fig. 3:* Silk bag with metal thread, sequins and pearls, 19th Century, France *(The Metropolitan Museum of Art, gift of Mrs. William Guggenheim in memory of her son, William Guggenheim, Jr.).*

176

The dress was probably made in England, as records in George Washington's own hand reveal he ordered all the fine clothing worn by members of his family from that country. This reticule was made entirely by Martha Washington herself, though it is questionable that it was carried by her at the first inaugural. It is made of brown satin and embroidered in ribbon work with the odd inscription: "Worn by Genl.G.& Mrs.Washington". Only Mrs. Eisenhower, Mrs. Kennedy and Mrs. Nixon are shown carrying any form of purse in this display, and they are of the evening bag variety, which highlights the difficulty of finding photographs of historically significant purses. Ladies are shown carrying fans, gloves, card cases, animals, infants, dolls, musical instruments, flowers, baskets, art objects, books, skirt trains, photographs, opera glasses, handkerchiefs, shawls, laces—just about anything *but* purses.

IN 1759 WASHINGTON ordered from England, "A salmon colored tabby made with a saque and coat" for his wife and a "cap, handkerchief and ruffles of Brussels or Point lace to be worn with the above negligee, to cost 20£." Could this be the gown she is wearing in the display? The rest of the order is amusing as well as revealing much about the character and habits of our first president:

> "Two fine flowered aprons
> Four pairs of thread hose
> Six pairs of women's fine cotton hose
> One pair of black satin shoes
> One pair of white satin shoes of smallest 5's
> Four pairs of calamanco shoes
> One fashionable hat or bonnet
> Six pairs of women's best kid gloves
> Eight pairs of women's best mits
> One dozen round silk laces
> One black mask
> One dozen most fashionable pocket handkerchiefs
> One piece of narrow white satin ribbon with pearl edge
> Four pieces of binding tape
> Six thousand miniken pins, six thousand short whites, six thousand corking pins
> One thousand hair pins"

Washington appears to have been a devoted and considerate husband who wanted the most fashionable garments for his wife, and all those curling pins for a lady seldom seen without her mob cap is pure indulgence!

The reticule continued to be fashionable for over a century and a number of them are shown in the colorful plates; though their simplicity makes them less attractive to collectors than beaded purses, they are interesting and predate the typical beaded purse by 50 or more years.

FIGURE 1

FIGURE 2

SAC DE VOYAGE.
Modèle de chez M. Nunheim, rue Ste-Opportune, 2.

FIGURE 3

FIGURE 4

PLATE 25. Fashions from "La Mode Illustré," 1875.

The development of the railroads in Europe and the United States permitted an ease of travel previously unknown. Women and children, as well as men, no longer had to endure the hardships of travel by stagecoach or covered wagon and by the second half of the 19th century were encouraged to travel by train from coast to coast. Along with the steamer and carriage trunk, the gladstone, canvas satchel, and various other types of traveling bags came the carpet bag, made infamous by its association with corrupt Southern reconstruction governments following the Civil War. (1865). These scalawags carried all their ill-gotten gains and bribes in bright colored bags made of carpeting, thus the term carpetbaggers came into use.

Among the most difficult authentic antique bags to find today are the carpetbags and leather traveling cases which were the only bags shown in early fashion magazines, possibly because all other types of reticules could be and were constructed in the home and were in a sense, examples of fine needle and beadwork. There are two or three well preserved samples of the carpetbag in the Metropolitan Museum, their vivid blues, reds, pinks, and olive green patterns in huge roses and scrolls as fresh as the day they were loomed. One has leather end pieces with cotton cord handles, the other is entirely made of carpet. Both are approximately 15 × 18¼ inches, fitted with a brass lock and key which have been nickel plated as was then customary with all brass objects. This confuses collectors who often think the material is silver plated. At first glance these large bags seem less like purses than overnight cases, but in 1864 Lady Godey recommended them as "graceful and very convenient to hold the numberless small articles which a lady always wishes to have by her during a journey." Directions for a huge traveling bag or "poche pompadour", as they called it, required 2½ yards of violet rep, (a combination of silk and wool with a transversely corded or ribbed surface), 2½ yards of silk fringe, 2½ yards

FIGURE 1

FIGURE 2

FIGURE 3

PLATE 26. *Fig. 1:* Wool and bead on leather bag. Date and origin unknown *(Costume Institute of the Metropolitan Museum of Art, gift of Mr. Lee Simonson). Fig. 2:* Plush wool and cotton carpet bag, c. 1850–90, United States *(Costume Institute of The Metropolitan Museum of Art, gift of Mrs. Lyall Dean). Fig. 3:* Carpet bag, mid-19th Century, United States *(Metropolitan Museum of Art, gift of Mrs. Donald Ferguson). Fig. 4:* Traveling bag, "Lady Godey," 1858. *Fig. 5:* Beaded velvet traveling bag *(Collection of Michaela Bennett).*

178

FIGURE 5

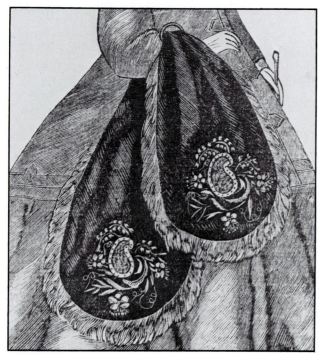

FIGURE 4

of white calico lining material, five skeins of white embroidery silk for the trimming, two ivory rings, and some pearl buttons. It really was nothing more than a gigantic miser's purse and was constructed in like manner. It is interesting to compare this bag with the one found on *Plate 26, Fig. 4.* Made in rich brown velvet and trimmed in cut steel beading and fringing, it is of the same generous proportions and could well have been a traveling purse of the same genre.

THE CARPET BAG was also made of vivid colored plush, velour, and wool as well as carpeting. The patterns were all-over designs somewhat Oriental in feeling, often with a leather carrying handle and leather edging. The rolled and shoulder strapped versions freed the hands; the model with a top grip appears somewhat more commodious than the others. The travelling bag constructed entirely of leather was a commercial product and lacked decoration of any sort, as evidenced by the two Canadian examples from the Metropolitan Museum [*Plate 26*].

Though the reticule continued to be used for twenty or more years, the handbag made its appearance about 1900 and has remained popular throughout this century. Since then changes in fashion have been radical and numerous, but not nearly as startling as the technological, industrial, sociological, and economic revolutions which guarantee the manufactured purse has, for all practical purposes, replaced the handmade purse. Working women who comprise an ever increasing percentage of the total labor force have neither the free time, the inclination, the energy, nor the skills requisite to handcrafted purses.

Since 1907 with the advent of protective tariffs and the need to establish some arbitrary date which might constitute the line between the antique and the modern, the United States Customs Department declared an article 100 years old or older to be a bona fide antique. Though it is not always possible to adhere rigidly to such classifications, it seems advisable to confine the present coverage of purses to an era no later than the Art Deco Period or roughly 1930. The handbag therefore will be the final purse considered.

The handbag, as its name suggests, differed from previous purses chiefly in that it was to be carried in the hand exclusively, unlike the chatelaine, the miser's bag, even the reticule, which was still occasionally worn suspended from the belt or hook. It also became larger and larger as by 1907 the emancipated 20th century woman added substantially to its contents, skirts became narrower, jackets were fitted, pockets disappeared and handbags resembling briefcases were universally adopted. Handbags came to include such hitherto unknown or "prohibited" things as cosmetics, cigarette cases, checkbooks, writing equipment, prescription glasses, perfumes and ointments, manicuring

FIGURE 1

FIGURE 2

FIGURE 3

FIGURE 4

PLATE 27. *Fig. 1:* This traveling reticule featured by ''Lady Godey'' in 1864 is a strange combination of apron and aumoniere, clearly intended to be worn outside the skirt. It is also reminiscent of the chatelaine which became so popular between 1880-1905. The decoration might be soutache braid; note that the belt is similarly decorated. *Fig. 2:* This aumoniere girdle from ''Lady Godey'' in 1858 presents a novel ''button on'' purse. The terms aumoniere and reticule are applied to nearly identical items here. *Fig. 3:* Woman wearing a traveling reticule, 1858. *Fig. 4:* Typical carpet and traveling bags from ''Lady Godey,'' 1859.

tools, billfolds to hold papers and licenses, and an endless variety of other items. Some were chained to the purse for safekeeping.

The handbag from 1900–1910 was more often than not suspended from the shoulder on extremely long thin straps made of leather, cord, or chain; handbags were made of calf leather, steer hide, crocodile, alligator, seal skin, cape goat, walrus, pig skin, lizard and a great many imitation leathers, grained to resemble ''genuine skins.''

One of the most popular styles was the shopping bag, which was advertised in all the catalogues and ladies' magazines from the most commonplace to those catering to the wealthy. In a sense it was a combination of the reticule and more modern handbag in that it wrapped a section of leather or leatherette U fashion about a sateen drawstring pouch, the shell being fit-

ted with sturdy rolled leather carrying handles. These handbags had pairs of outside pockets, one held a small coin purse with nickel plated closing, the other single pocket, much larger in size, was snap closed. They ranged from 10–14 inches wide and 7–10 inches long, substantially larger and sturdier than the dressy beaded purse used for afternoon and evening functions. Another version of the shopping bag was merely a pouch with either drawstring or gatetop closing made of moire silk or calf skin, sometimes called an opera shopping bag.

These turn of the century handbags retailed for as modest a sum as 43¢ and even the more expensive versions were sold by both Sears and Montgomery Ward for $1.25. Sol Mutterperl Company of Fifth Avenue sold his genuine calf leather handbags for only a dollar each in 1901.

CHAPTER 2
TYPES OF PURSES

Although The Reticule continued to be used until World War I, early 20th century women's magazines indicate a subtle but definite trend away from the reticule to a more sophisticated, sleek, commercial type of purse and the handsome colored fashion plates dating from 1911 were illustrated by mannequins carrying various kinds of purses which had not previously been shown. The sudden diversity of shapes, sizes, materials, and carrying mechanisms is surprising.

For a number of years the most striking purse was hardly a purse at all as it was a huge fur muff approximately 20 × 14 inches, padded and squarish in shape. In the December, 1911, *Delineator* a popular magazine of the day, Perry Dome and Company of West 23rd Street, New York City advertised a muff, stole and hat trio which they described as, "lusterous, beautiful and durable made of French coney". Coney is nothing more than rabbit fur dyed black to imitate seal, and the famous Hudson Seal coat which great grandmothers of a century ago prized so highly, was not a seal at all but dyed muskrat, (which is amazingly durable) and when shirred and dyed, made a soft and dramatic muff.

That not all muffs were of the above quality is strikingly borne out by the beauteously photogenic Evalyn Walsh McLean shown on *Frontispiece* wearing her sables and muff. Lillian Russell, the handsome and beloved actress, is shown wearing a costume similar to the one just described, though the chances are good that her outfit is the finest grade of fur. Note she is also carrying a satin shirred purse in her left hand in addition to her muff and her hat is one of those magnificent creations, which drove those who could only admire from a distance, to madness! [*Plate 30*].

As we have seen, some ladies carried both a muff and a purse, though the commodious muff was fitted to accommodate whatever small articles would have been carried at this time.

Furriers of the day "made over" muffs, possibly of more substantial and expensive furs, and the housewife who concerned herself with fashion (and this was a universal passion among the upper and middle classes) was encouraged by the helpful hints columnist to rescue any furs which might be thus used. Small sized muffs were also made of velvets and plush materials, gathered and shirred so even today they have both a romantic and utilitarian feeling about them.

Between 1911–1914 large leather envelope bags with long strap handles suspended from the shoulder were modish, as were heavy mesh, German silver kid-lined bags with strong, plain frames costing $5.00; sterling ones with elaborately embossed frames and a fine softer mesh than the German silver; small, gilt and silver colored fine mesh and fringe; monogrammed linen envelopes sparingly decorated with cut work and cord handled; suede leather decorated with beads, though not as profusely nor as elaborately as those beaded purses to come in the 1920's; all accompanied the ubiquitous hand made reticule. Paris fashions decreed the skirt and shirtwaist, dresses with straight sides falling to the ankle, rows and rows of buttons, and softly draped natural shoulders, to be chic.

Year after year the editors of *Ladies Home Journal* devoted a page in their December issue to the hand-made purse as the ideal Christmas gift from one homemaker to another. The 1911 issue contained a full color page of these suggested presents, the distinguishing characteristics of which are here listed in order to help collectors assign approximate dates to the items in their possession:

1. Embroidery hoops were used for handles, covers, and frames.

2. Cretonne was all the rage (unglazed cotton).

3. Jade bracelets were used as handles for reticules.

4. Irish crocheted bags with silk linings to show the lacework were just being introduced.

5. The attempt toward novelty was so marked

PLATE 30. Lillian Russell in muff, furs and satin beaded purse *(Library of Congress)*.

PLATE 29. The Walshes and their friends, the McLeans *(from the Collection of the Library of Congress)*.

that even a straw hat lined in China silk was used as a purse.

6. Oriental was "in" so all sorts of things were called Japanese which were not.

7. Cut work and monograms on linen were highly regarded.

8. Whalebone was used as a brace.

9. Purses with matching card cases and other fittings were favored.

10. So many bags were made for every conceivable purpose that purses may be confused with containers intended for other uses.

A PERENNIAL FAVORITE among purses for at least a century is the petit point, needle point, tapestry, and wool embroidered type from France, Austria, and Hungary.

There is a tendency to call all such purses petit point when in reality the petit point purse is a rare commodity. To distinguish between the categories requires a sharp eye, a ruler, and the patience to count one square inch of stitches. A fine petit point (French for small stitch done with a needle, as opposed to laces made on a pillow with bobbins) will contain some 900 stitches to the square inch, whereas a nicely executed

needlepoint will have only 440 or less than half that number. Some coarser yarns will be in the 360 range or as few as 250 stitches per square inch. The stitch used is the tent stitch which diagonally fills each square of the canvas. The process is a tedious and time consuming one, the end product depending upon the fineness of the canvas, the skill of the needle worker, and the beauty of the patttern. The patterns are floral, pastorals, garden scenes, French courting scenes, mythological representations, and the like, and almost without exception done on a field of beige, ivory, pale yellow or some neutral shade which allows the patterns to stand nicely away from the background. The exceedingly fine wools are pastels and vivid colors which are shaded and variegated to add dimension and interest. There is hardly a color which is not blended to perfection, the finer the canvas the wider the choice of subtle and brilliant colorings.

The background of the circular section forming the pouch is frequently black, though some of the more expensive purses are done in pale lavenders and golds. Both the needlepoint and petit point canvas bags have rounded bottoms, ornately impressed designs on brass frames, occasionally sterling or gold, which are often set with jet, marcasites, rhinestones and precious

stones, and chain handles approximately a foot long. The clasps are of the twist type, though the more costly versions have a large glass or polished cabochon stone set in a plunger closing and jeweled tab. The frames or some part of the lining are marked with the country of origin, linings are of faille, silk, rayon, or moiré.

Commonly they measure 6½ × 5½ inches and they can be used, as they are as smart today as they were 75 years ago.

Tapestry will in most cases be machine made as true tapestry work is seldom found outside museums. The handmade example [*Plate 78, Fig. 4*] is beyond

FIGURE 1

FIGURE 2

FIGURE 3 **FIGURE 4** **FIGURE 5** **FIGURE 6**

PLATE 31. *Figs. 1–4:* Miser's purses as shown in ''Lady Godey,'' ''La Mode Illustré,'' and ''Priscilla Needlebook.'' *Fig. 5:* Silk knit miser's purse, 1812, Italy (*Museum of Fine Arts, Boston, gift of Mrs. H. deForest Lockwood*). *Fig. 6:* Silk knit miser's purse, c. 1780–1800, Spain (*Museum of Fine Arts, Boston, Elizabeth Day McCormick Collection*).

belief in complexity of pattern, color range, technical skill, and the quality of materials, though it has suffered some damage over the years and repair appears virtually impossible. The machined tapestry purse imitates the finer hand made types and has a more complicated flawlessly executed pattern, is lighter in weight, the colors are somewhat faded in appearance and lack the sharpness and crispness of the hand done purse. The sterling pastoral example [*Plate 78, Fig. 3*] is worn at the sides and bottom but is also executed in a fine wool-silk mixture and is beautifully shaded by hand.

Far less valuable than the hand done purse, the machined tapestry purse is interesting because the ground containing the pattern is left unfilled and the warp and woof threads are clearly visible.

Wool embroidered purses are infrequently seen and are therefore appealing though simple personal expressions, which lack the refinement of any of the aforementioned purses.

THE LONG PURSE, miser's purse, ring purse, stocking purse, and string purse are all one and the same. Coming into favor in the 1780's they differed from all previous containers as they were primarily intended to hold coins and currency. This bag was a long tube-shaped affair which was beaded, made of fabric, meshed silk, knitted, crocheted, or netted, the ends of which may have been identical in shape or quite different. The decoration was simple beaded work, embroidery, tassele, fringe, or ended with a small metal decorative ornament. But in these respects they were identical: One, they all have a slit through the middle for the insertion of money which fell into one of the toes or ends when tilted. Two, they all contain two rings, generally of steel, though gold and silver were used, which slide down to the ends and prevent the coin or currency deposited therein from moving past the ring and being lost. Three, they could all be worn over the belt, the ends hanging downward allowing the hands to be unencumbered. Four, they were worn by men and women alike, there being no distinction drawn between purses on the basis of sex.

The ends were basically of two shapes: both ends round, pointed or finished with a tassel at each end, or a flat end with bead fringe and one round end with a tassel. Often they were radically different in size and shape for an interesting reason. Lighting was poor or nonexistent prior to the 20th century and when it was necessary to pay a coin to a coachman, waiter, or some other tradesman, the correct coin could be withdrawn by feeling the end of the purse. The straight flat end with a fringe might contain the silver coins and the diamond, round, gathered or tasseled end might contain the gold coins. The bead ornamentation or embroidered pattern was frequently of gilt for the gold

coins and silver for the sterling. In the 19th century these purses were made in black cotton or silk but they were also found in forest green (the most popular color in the 18th and early 19th centuries), crimson, royal blue, opal, garnet and the example from an 1859 *Lady Godey* shows a fine enlarged misers which is worked

PLATE 32. This miser's purse was probably intended for a man, and has identically shaped ends but with different patterns. It is 26 1/2″ long. *(author's collection).*

in two colors, crimson and deep maize, blue and deep maize, light and dark green, blue and scarlet, and scarlet and gold, though they warn the gold has a tendency to tarnish and suffer from ill use.

The miser's purse continued to be popular for nearly 150 years as a publication from 1925 included a miser's purse the directions for which are included on *Plate 45a*. Patterns for these purses tended to be limited to 50 or more rows of geometric bands, depending of course on the length of the purse and the ornateness of the pattern, located at either end of the

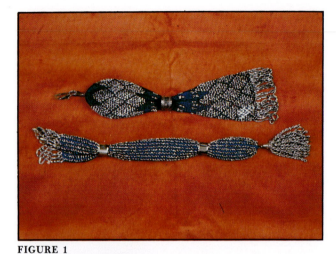

FIGURE 1

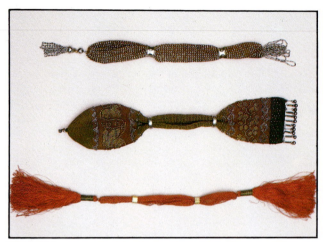

FIGURE 2

FIGURE 3

FIGURE 3

FIGURE 4   FIGURE 5

PLATE 33. Miser's purses. *Fig. 1: (courtesy The Venerable Bead, Berkeley, California).* *Fig. 2:* Three purses from the author's collection. *Fig. 3: (Collection of Bonnie Stone).* *Fig. 4: (Collection of Penelope More).* *Fig. 5:* Silk and cut steel, c. 1830–80, France *(Museum of Fine Arts, Boston, Collection of Mrs. Edward M. Herzog).*

FIGURE 1

FIGURE 4

FIGURE 3

purses approximately 7 inches to 2 feet in length were more completely decorated on the outer side only, with fine steel cut beads either crocheted or knitted into the body.

There is an outstanding collection of miser's purses in the Boston Museum of Fine Arts which includes a large number of pale pink, aquamarine, coral, amethyst, and other utterly feminine pastel shades, heavily studded with sterling and gold beading and containing finely enameled slides, some of which are complemented with precious and semi-precious stones. With a few exceptions they are tiny with the extra fine beading in delicate, subtle patterns characteristic of French handicrafts in the early 19th century. Those from the 18th century tend toward darker more intense colors, bolder patterns, and are from two to five times the size of the later versions. One of the largest exceeds two feet in length, is similarly shaped on either end and finished with pompom tassels [*Fig. 5, Plate 31*]. One end is dated 1812 and the other contains the carefully worked name. Compared to the lacy creations resembling miniature bar-bells—comprising the major portion of this grouping—it is difficult to imagine the latter purse belonging to other than a gentleman, though we are assured they were carried by both sexes.

AMONG HANDBAG COLLECTORS the term "Dorothy Bag" is frequently heard but the variety of opinions as to exactly how the Dorothy Bag differs from other handbags appears to hinge on a relatively minor detail.

Vanda Foster tells us the Dorothy Purse was a "soft leather drawstring", a long rectangle of fabric

purse. The narrower part contained the opening and was left plain. Smaller purses ranged from 4–6 inches in length and 2–3 inches in width, like the one shown on *Plate 33, Fig. 2* which is nicely decorated on both sides with a combination of steelcut, gilt, seed, and colored glass beads in a floral and leaf design which appears rather large for the size of the purse. Larger

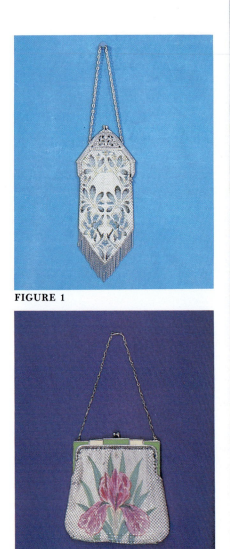

FIGURE 1

FIGURE 2

FIGURE 3

PLATE 35. Enameled mesh purses. *Fig. 1:* Mandalian. *Fig. 2:* Mandalian *(Collection of Michaela Bennett). Fig. 3:* Mandalian *(Collection of Penelope More). Fig. 4:* Jeweled set and enameled frame *(author's collection). Fig. 5:* Mandalian *(Collection of Sharon Peterson). Fig. 6:* Mandalian (5″ × 8 1/4″) with Vandyke edge

with a drawstring ribbon usually set a little below the top to form a frill. It was easily constructed, light to carry and could be made of the same fabric as the dress.''

The name Dorothy was drawn from a play by A.J. Munby in 1880, whose heroine was skilled with

the needle and also made embroidered bags to match favorite gowns.

The criteria appears to be that the Dorothy Bag was constructed with a fold over portion of the top of the purse, which was beaded as the rest of the body, or in the case of a mesh purse, a folded mesh portion or skirt below the drawstrings. It is possible the term and the bag itself were peculiar to England as only a few have been observed in the United States. They were popular around 1907–1920. Vanda Foster includes two examples in her *Bags and Purses,* unfortunately none was available for this edition.

Among the unique hand made purses of the early 1900's were the Irish crochet purses. Crochet cotton-filled ornamentation literally dripped from their sides, corners, bottoms and every other place to which they could be attached. Though they were made of silk,

FIGURE 4

FIGURE 5

FIGURE 6

cotton, linen, and combinations of various fibers, they were usually of one color, beige or off-white, and the patterns tend to have a strong resemblance, which was relieved somewhat by the colorful silk linings which were intentionally visible through the lacy patterns. They were closed by a drawstring doubling as a handle, or on occasion a fold over flap closing and had a limp appearance which suggests they were chiefly used for informal occasions.

Heavy, Irish crochet purses are rather plentiful as the crochet patterns were not exceedingly fine nor difficult, the texture heavy and the materials were durable and could be laundered (save for the applied decorative balls which appear to have replaced the inevitable fringing materials). They were inexpensive to make, and a skilled needleworker could have made one in a relatively short period of time. They were

a pleasant and appropriate accompaniment to the simple lawn and chiffon dresses which were then in vogue. They were representative of a fad utilitarian purse which was very suitable for its time.

SOME OF THE most beautiful purses found today are the tambour worked ones; surely some of the most colorful. Tambour was originally done by hand using a small hook and embroidery frame to make a series of tiny chains working from the underside of the material to create intricate, flamboyant designs. In the Flapper Era whole dresses were beaded using this method in which neither the bead nor the thread were visible to the worker. Needless to say, few people are capable of doing this type of decoration today and even could they, the cost would be prohibitive.

Done on black faille or watered silk backgrounds,

189

FIGURE 1

FIGURE 4

FIGURE 3

FIGURE 6

PLATE 36. *Fig. 1:* Mandalian with teardrops of enameled brass *(author's collection).* **Figs. 2 & 3:** Mandalian purses with elaborate frames *(courtesy "Ladyfingers," Carmel, California).* **Fig. 4:** Unusual fine sterling mesh with sterling fold-over flap *(Collection of Sharon Peterson).* **Fig. 5:** Rare skirted red enamel Whiting Davis purse *(ibid Fig. 4).* **Fig. 6:** Similar to Fig. 1 but with jeweled frame *(ibid Fig. 1).*

tambour work—pronounced tam'pour—is shirred into handsome brass frames, one is known to be set with turquoise, pinks, and lavenders predominant. These purses were handmade even to the linings, which read, "Real Hand Maid Point. . . .Made in France." They were fitted with a pocket and mirror and measure approximately 9 × 10 inches. They do require rather delicate handling as the silk is very fine and the ends must be tightly secured to prevent raveling.

Among the most elegant and costly purses found today are the solid gold meshes as pictured on *Plate 34* which were graciously lent by various collectors who wish to remain anonymous. *Figures 1* and *4* are approximately the same dimensions and each is terminated by natural pearls on the tassels. The small slide allowed the strap to adjust to fit the wrist, or the larger loop could be used to slip over the hand for additional security. Though not always, they are most often of the wrist type, popular about 1915. The first purse has a mirror beneath the monogrammed exterior flap, whereas number four has the mirror to the outside

merely for illustrative purposes. Some costly versions contained a watch set into the frame surrounded by ornamental raised patterns. The watch was, in addition to the wedding ring, becoming the second essential jewelry item for every lady, so this novelty seemed appropriate. These purses were not made in abundance and command at least one hundred or more dollars over a corresponding purse, of like metals, without an inset watch.

Long and narrow in shape, the gold content made these purses relatively heavy. The purse shown at *Fig. 2* is of the same era, a vermeil (gold over sterling) with a beautifully embossed frame and delicate fringe. It would not have the same value as the solid gold purse, but is equally attractive.

The third purse is square shaped, 14 karat, weighs 7 ounces, was made in 1920, and has 7 emeralds and 22 diamonds set in the frame. The difference in color is due more to the film and lighting conditions than to the gold itself, although the hardening agent used to alloy the pure gold accounts for the tints which

190

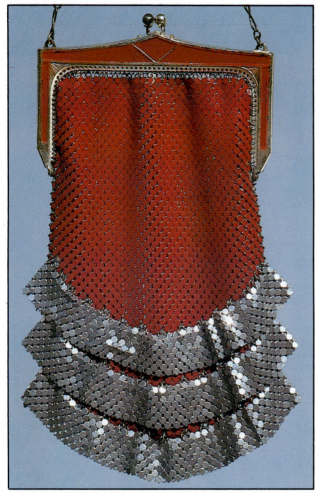

FIGURE 5

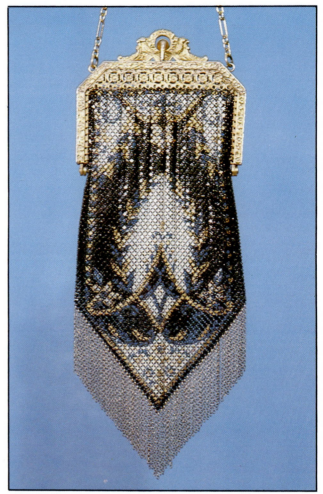

FIGURE 2

range though rose, white, green and yellow.

ONE OF THE earliest firms to manufacture handbags and decorative accessories in America and still in continuous operation is Whiting-Davis of Plainville, Massachusetts. Since 1876, when it was known as Wade, Davis and Company (Whiting joined the firm in July, 1880) they have produced a mesh purse of outstanding quality.

Prior to 1892, ring mesh was hand made by goldsmiths who wound, split and joined each interlocking gold ring to form a flexible material. Attached to a metal frame by a series of rings and carrying chain, the mesh bag frequently attached to a belt or chatelaine. The frame was embossed with floral and sentimental designs and across the squared bottom were often suspended a series of small metallic balls which added a decorative touch. When a mesh making machine was invented in 1909 by A.C. Pratt, white or pot metal chain was usually used, but other metals such as German silver and sterling were also used.

Usually the frame and mesh are made of a silver colored inexpensive wire metal but custom purses were entirely made of sterling or gold, with the owner's name and home town often engraved on alternate sides of the frame in elaborate script. Though not a Whiting Davis purse, *Fig. 6, Plate 37,* is an interesting one. Patented December 10, 1912, it combined a nicely embossed, rigid handle frame which swivels open. It could be slipped over the wrist but most likely was carried in the hand. The mesh is of medium fineness and it was probably finished with a chain tassel. It is unfortunately not marked by the manufacturer.

By 1900 the chain mail or interlocking rings were supplanted by a flat topped piece of silver or gilt colored metal with four teeth on the reverse side which interlocked with every other ring in four places, then the teeth were flattened securely forming an interlayer. The exterior was smooth and free of any sharp points or breaks in the links such as are found in older types of rings. The 1901 purse clearly shows a somewhat enlarged chatelaine purse with beautiful repousse

191

FIGURE 1

FIGURE 2

FIGURE 3

FIGURE 4

PLATE 35-A. *Figs. 1 & 4:* Sometimes termed "hard enamel" purses. These are Mandalian patterns in the brilliant colors popular in the 1920's, with chain fringes. They are 4″ × 7″ in size and were originally offered at $11.50 and $21 respectively. *Figs. 2 & 3:* "Dresden" purses by Whiting Davis; expensive in their day 60 years ago, costing an average of $40. They are quite beautiful compared to other examples. *Fig. 3* has a black enamel frame set with marcasites and black onyx. *Fig. 2* is unusual in that it has a chain fringe, seldom found on Whiting Davis purses. This style was called a "Costume Bag" and the catalog listed some as being lined and containing a mirror and other fittings. It is 5″ × 9″ in size *(Collection of Dr. Paul and Anna Curtis). Fig. 5:* Another handsome example of a Mandalian purse.

FIGURE 5

frame and the new type of mesh [*Plate 37, Fig. 3*].

Between 1900–1926, technical progress allowed the manufacture of so fine a mesh that its texture resembled fabric. Solid gold and sterling mesh created for the affluent little jewels of purses which their fortunate owners today keep in safe deposit boxes. Examples of these fine purses are shown on *Plate 34*. In January, 1926, *Women's Wear* carried a news item stating, "To match gold and silver frocks mesh handbags are being shown by the majority of retail departments here." Entire garments were woven for Hollywood productions such as El Cid, The Crusades, Joan of Arc, and a host of others during this romantic era of the films which required simulated suits of chain mail for both man and beast. Skillful advertising had transformed mesh from a luxury style item to a necessity for fashion conscious women. Presently this glittering material is made into such accessories as cigarette cases, belts, eyeglass cases, bracelets, clutches, credit card cases, key cases and the like.

The Flapper Era saw the popularization of the enameled purse which ran the gamut from slender, extremely fine, rectangular bags which dangled from the wrist on a short strap handle—which could be adjusted by sliding a buckle to the desired snugness—to huge bags which approached the size of shopping satchels! The enamels of the earlier period were done in delicate pastel florals with gold and silver accents and motifs drawn from nature. Those done in the 1930's were typically Art Deco; the tone was brilliantly harsh reds, oranges, blues, black and white in geometric, angular, straight-line stark patterns. Art Deco created a revolution against anything flowing or sentimental in feeling; boldness was the order of the day and the enameled mesh purse reflected the discordant colors and zig-zag lines.

Although early Whiting Davis purses were lined with silk or rayon material and contained a small mirror, it is rare to find a lined and fitted example today. The fabric was not durable and the mesh was a sufficiently close enough weave so the lining was not considered essential as it would have been in other constructions. These handbags were carried to afternoon and evening functions and ladies of fashion owned an assortment to accent the ensembles in their wardrobes; the mix and match allowed today would have caused a stylish woman of the '20's–30's to shudder.

The solid colored gold and silver oval, triangle, and octagon mesh for which Whiting-Davis is now so famous, came into prominence with the sophisticated use of lamé, Baby Louis heels, fox fur scarfs, and the runabout sports car complete with rumble seat.

In 1929, The wholesale jewelry firm of Richter and Phillips, of Cincinnati, Ohio, included in their supplemental catalogue an insert of Whiting-Davis bags in full color, (which must have been horrendously expensive,) and sepia, which adds greatly to our accurate knowledge of the colors used in mesh enameled purses.

These mesh handbags were extremely expensive for the era, ranging in price from $4.00 to $45.00 for a soldered mesh which was so fine it resembled spun gold or sterling. It was an age when ladies were willing to pay for the "latest thing." However, it was the patterns which were so markedly different from those of the previous decade. They were called "Dresden" enamels and were impresisonistic and indistinct in nature, perhaps to imitate the delicate patterns used in Dresden, German porcelains. The colors were very subdued with pink, green, pale blue and touches of yellow predominating in the floral designs. Two fine examples are found on *Plate 35A, Figs. 2–3.*

The frames were occasionally 24k gold finished, the handles were chain links and snake chain; a flexible closely coiled material. They show a definite trend toward the Art Deco influence (1925–1940) which was a mere season or two in the offing, but as with all movements in style and art, it is difficult to assign a definite date as one did not die instantly and another take its place.

One of the surest ways to assign a date to a mesh purse is to observe the way the bottom is finished. If it terminates in elongated points, in decreasing widths resembling steps, in twisted rope chain from a fine mesh body, in a gathered skirt-like effect of fine mesh, rarely in enameled tips suspended by rings from a diamond shaped mesh end, or a skirt extending beyond the body for an inch or two, it can be dated from the late 1920's–1930's. Earlier purses had tassels, lacy open work, scallops, shirrs, and metallic fringes across the bottom.

The factors which determined the price appear to have been size; the wider and longer purses costing approximately twice as much as the smaller bags.

In 1976 for their centennial celebration, Whiting Davis used their early hand crafted sterling patterns and frames to make a limited edition of 300 sterling silver bags. With the advent of disco dancing they recently revived the tiny purse, which the British in Victorian times called the shilling purse. These pursettes, hung on a 30 inch chain about the neck, are a mere fraction over 2 inches square and have a solid ball trim at the base, surely more of an ornamental accessory than a utilitarian device, but no doubt useful to disco devotees.

Most intriguing to the purse collector were the replicas of the gatetop purses which were so popular in the 1880's. This pouch is so-called because of the expanding metal necked top which permits an opening of 5–6 inches and then contracts to fit into a cap the size of a silver dollar. Though the modern change

193

FIGURE 1   FIGURE 2   FIGURE 3

FIGURE 6   FIGURE 7   FIGURE 4   FIGURE 5

PLATE 37. *Figs. 1, 3, 4 & 5:* Mesh purses from 1901 to 1960 *(courtesy Whiting Davis, Plainville, Massachusetts).* **Fig. 2:** Sterling mesh wrist purse with compact, c. 1918, United States *(Metropolitan Museum of Art, gift of E.K. Bramson).* **Fig. 6:** Plated mesh with patented handle *(author's collection).*

purse version is only 3 × 2¼ inches, the originals were at least double these dimensions.

Whiting Davis bags are always stamped "Whiting Davis Co. Mesh Bags, Registered U.S. and Canada" either on the metal frame (inside the purse) or they bear a small metal tag with the same signature attached to the mesh. This is a distinct aid to the collector for the immediate identification of the maker and an unrivaled symbol of integrity and quality.

Contemporary with Whiting Davis was a manufacturer of mesh purses named Mandalian Company from Attleboro, Massachusetts, whose products were so distinctively decorated that they are immediately recognized even though they closely parallel those of Whiting Davis in size, shape, and materials. The Art Nouveau patterns tended toward delicate pastel florals

FIGURE 1

FIGURE 2

FIGURE 3

FIGURE 4

PLATE 38. Whiting Davis mesh accessories. Una Merkel is shown in *Fig. 3* and Gertrude Nissen in *Fig. 4.*

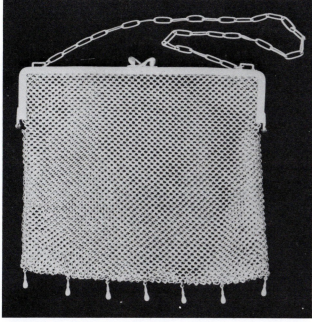

FIGURE 1

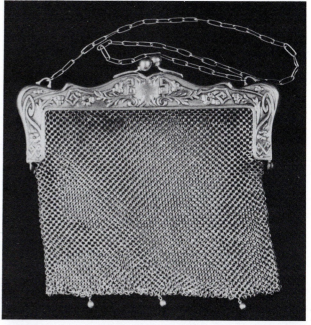

FIGURE 2

FIGURE 3

FIGURE 4

PLATE 39. Four German silver mesh purses.

and nicely balanced, almost monochromatic bolder, color schemes. They were fitted with curved embossed frames set with enameled or jeweled decor and are so delightful and charming in nature they are unforgettable once their general appearance is fixed in the mind. Their Art Deco designs are often found in those combinations of striking colors seen on *Plates 35–36* along with the single strand of metal fringe and the more elaborate frame characteristic of this jewelry firm. Carefully tucked into the folds of one bag was a small cardboard card which proclaimed the superiority of the Mandalian purse as follows: *"Color Vision Bag* Trade Mark Process Patent Pending New method of blending and shading of colors *Enamel* guaranteed   Dampness or Salt Water will not effect the gloss or smoothness of this bag. Please tell your friends about it. Beware of imitations. None genuine unless stamped *'Mandalian'* Originators." Although the impresison is rather small, the single word *Mandalian* or Mandalian Mfg. Co. can always be found in the inside frame.

Despite their high quality enamel work, superior designs and appealing color schemes, they apparently met with financial reverses and were acquired by Whiting Davis in the mid 1930's. Relatively few Mandalian purses have survived and as many have elegantly decorated frames and lovely patterns, they are a fine addition to any collection.

VANITY PURSES ARE distinguished by the use of a cord which was attached to the top of the celluloid case or a grosgrain ribbon which ran through tab ends much like a watch strap, tasseled on the bottom. These vanities were also made of metals, enameled metal, meshes, and other substances and feature bold Art Deco designs. Some had applied rhinestone decorations, some enameled centers featuring baskets of flowers or florals in delicate pastel shades, some were monogrammed, and others used the traditional patterns of their standard sized cousins done to scale, as the vanities were just large enough to hold a mirror, powder, and rouge. They are novelties rather than conveniences.

A common substitute for sterling silver was German silver, extensively used in the manufacture of inexpensive purses which masqueraded for their valuable counterpart. Indeed German silver contains no silver whatsoever, being an alloy of zinc, copper, and nickel. It is easily detected by its weight; sterling is light in weight compared to plate and other elements. German silver purses were made in a variety of meshes, (never as fine a gauge as those of Whiting Davis) soldered and interwoven, with embossed wide or very thin frames, bottom fringes of chain and ball, flattened ovals and other shapes which were attractive, if heavy. Some were lined with white kidskin,

PLATE 40. Three German silver purses.

COLOR--VISION--BAG
TRADE MARK
PROCESS PATENT PENDING
New method of blending and shading of colors
ENAMEL guaranteed

Dampness or Salt Water will not effect the gloss or smoothness of this bag.
Please tell your friends about it.
Beware of Imitations.
None genuine unless stamped "MANDALIAN"
ORIGINATORS

This small card (shown exact size) describes Mandalian purse and was tucked inside.

197

PLATE 41. Five sterling purses including a coin holder and compact combination.

FIGURE 1

FIGURE 2

FIGURE 3

others with fabrics. They were always inserted into a rigid frame or attached to the frame by a series of rings which were inserted into perforations in the frame. They were almost always rectangular in shape ranging from 4–7 inches in width and 6 inches in depth depending on the fringes. They find little acceptance among collectors today though they were very popular with those who could not afford the more costly meshes nearly a century ago. If the mesh is damaged it is not easy to find someone willing to repair it as it is a time consuming process which may not warrant the expense unless sentiment is involved. German silver frames were sometimes used on the reticule type of purse with attractive results; in fact, when used as framing material, German silver is both effective and substantial.

German silver has the same appearance as sterling, was made in nice if simpler patterns than sterling, had elegant frames which were embossed as were the sterling ones, was much more durable, and commanded but a fraction of the cost of sterling. How can one tell the difference if a purse is not marked in any way? Sterling is much lighter weight, it will have a softer feeling—which is not easily described— it will have a finer mesh as a rule, it will have a whiter tone, it will have more carefully rendered embossing and usually more elaborate pattern and only sterling would be repousse work or hand chased as German silver would not warrant the expense of such labor. The purses on *Plate 40* are plated silver, even the small purse at *Figure 2,* which is a combination of mesh and beads. *Figure 1* has a very pretty frame but note the shallow design has worn, as it was stamped rather than hand engraved. The pouch at *Figure 3* is all plated silver but was badly tarnished and when cleaned the brass dominated the silver color giving it a splotchy appearance, and it tends to tarnish much faster than sterling. Sterling, being softer, will not stand the abuse that German silver and plate will, so many ladies owned both materials and saved the sterling for "good".

Gold is more likely to be unstamped than sterling for some reason, so examine the inside of the frame with care, as some of the marks may be worn, obliterated, in a place which is difficult to locate, or just plain confusing. It's worth the effort, however. As previously suggested, patent dates, makers' marks, sterling and gold symbols, serial numbers, country of origin, unusual materials such as gun metal and German silver, which portions of the article are made of a given material; all this information can sometimes be found inside the frame.

Aside from the dates, personalized inscriptions, manufacturing data, and materials, the metal purses which were most popular were engraved. Possibly this is because other types of purses were of the handicraft

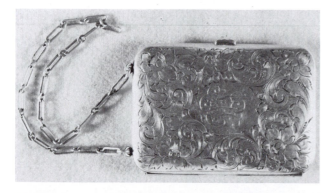

FIGURE 1

sort and the manufactured item was a novelty, rather than the reverse. The engraving (see *Plate 41, Figs. 1-2*) might cover the front of the article only or the entire piece. The engraving on a quality piece was fine enough to give depth to the pattern and added greatly to the beauty. These ornate purses (pursettes or coin purses) are in great demand today and since they are serviceable, light weight, unique, charming, and often genuine works of the engraver's art, they command a hefty price. The interior was gold washed on some, the mirror beveled, and other fittings such as the coin counter—if made of leather—was of the highest quality.

FIGURE 5

FIGURE 6

FIGURE 1

PLATE 42. Sterling holders and purses. *Fig. 2:* American actress Frances Starr. *Fig. 4:* American actress Grace Elliston. *Fig. 5:* American actress Bertha Gannard.

FIGURE 2   **FIGURE 4**   **FIGURE 7**

The designs used included: florals, a combination of florals and monograms, leaves, branches and buds, imitation basketry, geometrics, simple vertical lines, Art Nouveau heads, birds, small timepieces, animals, scenes, cupids, and water babies. Exquisite repousse work (the design is pushed out from the underside for deep relief) was done on the most expensive purses by such firms as Tiffany, Unger, Gorham and Kirk in America, and a host of superb English silver and goldsmiths whose quality of workmanship equalled and/or surpassed American. Ladies whose hobbies or pasttimes included golf, tennis, sailing, canoeing, croquet, bowling on the green, gardening, and the like received gifts commissioned specifically for them by relatives and friends. Needless to say these are avidly sought. For the less sophisticated and retiring women the designs were romantic and feminine in the extreme.

Gradually, as all classes of women began to use cosmetics, to one degree or another, and they lost the stigma from which they had suffered, purses were fitted with indented or special areas to house powder, rouge, lipstick, a comb, perfume flask, and other beauty aids. Combination purses encompassed all manner of things. There were pencil holders, (sterling of course, with tiny rings which could be hung about the neck) slots for nickels, dimes, and quarters, a small snap flap section for folding money, a mirror, an ivory writing surface, a receptacle beneath the mirror for incidentals, (pills, tickets, pins, etc.) and later, much later, cigarettes. Of course, not every purse contained all these appointments, some had but two areas and were really coin carriers, vanity cases, or held next-to-nothing. They allowed a nervous or apprehensive young woman to have something to hold which was sufficiently elegant to complement formal or evening attire.

RECENTLY THERE WAS a craze for wearing rings on every finger instead of the usual one or two on the two fingers we have come to accept as "ring fingers". This practice was actually a revival of a 16th century fad as portraits of royalty show numerous rings worn even on the thumb and index finger. The wearing of gold chains of assorted lengths, weights, designs, and widths is just beginning to wane. One season clothing was "layered" and fashion has decreed equally strange notions to be chic year after year. Such was the practice of carrying numerous purses, pursettes, vanities and the like. There seems no other plausible explanation for these virtually useless, albeit lovely, items. During the disco days the hands were so much in motion that similar small purses were hung about the neck, along with matching cigarette cases, and cylinder bags.

By the mid 1920's the vanity purse and the small

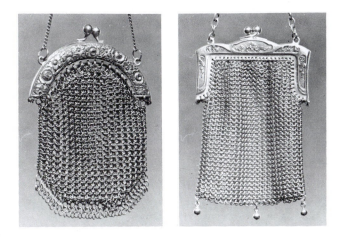

PLATE 42-A. Two excellent examples of plated silver purses.

enameled mesh purse were the fashion leaders. For their golden anniversary in 1926 the Whiting and Davis paper called the *Wadco News* announced that they would feature a special purse much like *Figure 5, Plate 36.* The women employees thanked the management for the enameled mesh bags they had received as Christmas gifts, and announced the use of a new enameled mesh machine which would make "...effects equal to those of the jacquard loom of the textile industry. By combinations of sterling silver wire, red, green and roman gold wire, surprisingly novel and beautiful fleur-de-lis, check, mosaic, bird-in-cage, in fact, any patterns in ring mesh, can be produced." In 1922 a four inch mesh bag called the "Princess Mary" with a nice lace effect, fold over flap and chain link handle sold for $7.50. The 1926 purses mentioned above were slated to retail for approximately $10.00.

Plate 37 will offer a visual comparison of the various meshes. Note how different they are. *Figure 1* may be sterling, and *Figure 2* is definitely sterling, the others are plate or base metals. *Figure 3* was made in 1901 and features the ball fringe so often found on metal purses, in fact German silver and plated purses have more elaborate fringes than sterling, [*see Figure 4, Plate 39*] possibly because the sterling being finer tends to tangle and tear more easily. German silver purses are larger than sterling, here again the cost factor would come into play. Certainly there are exceptions to every case, but this is an attempt to offer general guidelines and is not intended to be definitive and absolute in any sense.

It is difficult to determine whether a metal purse was lined or unlined as few will still have the linings today and all traces of former linings are not as easily seen in metal purses as in other types. When lined, the favorite material seems to have been white buck-

PLATE 42-B. A handsome young woman in fashionable dress with a German silver purse.

WHEN 19TH AND early 20th century American women adopted a style they did so with gusto, no half hearted likes or dislikes with them. Hats were gigantic, dresses lavish, skirts billowy and trailing, gloves, jewels, furs, shoes, hatpins; all were large, lavish and lovely. So around 1905 a style of purse swept the fashionable woman off her feet and rather than carrying merely one, she gathered as many as her fist could accommodate and rested assured she was a fashion plate. *Plate 42* shows three promising actresses of the day, each carrying two, three, and four of these charming little purses.

They are not miniatures in the true sense of the word, and apparently were held in conjunction with larger sized handbags as an affectation. They were made of sterling, plated silver, German silver, gold, gold wash, vermeil, enamels, meshes of all sorts, fabrics, tooled and gilded leathers, celluloid, ivory, and any other suitable substance. They were both lined and unlined. Sizes varied widely from as small as 2 inches square to three or four inches, generally being oblong shaped. Though the sizes varied, the carrying chains were all approximately 5½ inches long. It was fashionable to carry various sized purses ranging from the tiniest to a standard size purse of about six to eight inches, but as people tended to be much smaller a century ago than today, the purses were correspondingly smaller, except for the shopping bag which was used in lieu of the paper sacks currently utilized. A lady provided her own container for those purchases made on her daily trips to the market.

Those observed have all had some personalized aspects such as initials, names, dates, cities, affectionate phrases, dedications such as, ''To Betty with love from Ed'' or, ''To Sara from Mamma and Papa.'' It was a sentimental era and both recipient and bestower's names were visible along with the occasion commemorated. Everything was thus inscribed, dishes, glassware, jewelry, silverware, utensils, serving pieces, ad infinitum. These dates are now proof positive of the age of the individual item as well as establishing a broad time span for a category of articles. It is comforting to the historian as well as the neophyte to find patent dates thereby allaying fears and doubts as to authenticity. It is unlikely that either purses or combs are presently being reproduced with deliberately falsified dates, as they would not be profitable enough to warrant the expense required in relation to the profits, nor would their imitation be very successful.

skin or doeskin as it was sturdier than fabric which became unserviceable after prolonged contact with the metal rings.

Chain link handles were used on base metal purses and the sterling and gold ones as well, the only difference being in the quality of the workmanship, the soldering, the sturdiness of the chain, and the design of the links.

German silver and plated purses sold for approximately $5.00 and were offered as premiums to housewives who sold various products to their friends and neighbors.

Sterling purses were more apt to have a gothic shape, that is, come to a point toward the clasp frame and terminate in a collected fringe of chain forming a tassle at the bottom.

Sterling purses cost from $30.00 upward, depending of course on the amount of ornamentation, whether genuine stones were used in the frame, the gram weight of the purse, its ornateness and other factors. Currently sterling purses tend to follow the precious metal trends and were commanding amazing prices when silver reached artificially inflated peaks created by speculators a few years ago.

CHAPTER 3
THE BEADED PURSE

I n an age when there was no television, no soap opera, no afternoon bridge club, bars were the province of men only, few women engaged in sports, women seldom worked outside the home, and there was little to purchase in the local dry goods store, middle and upper class women worked endlessly on ''fancy work''. Among the items most prized was the beaded purse. Catalogues for the construction of these handbags were as numerous then as patterns for knit and crochet items are today, and their careful study reveals how patient and talented the makers must have been.

Always costly, beautifully executed bags were so difficult to make that a skillful bag knitter could com-

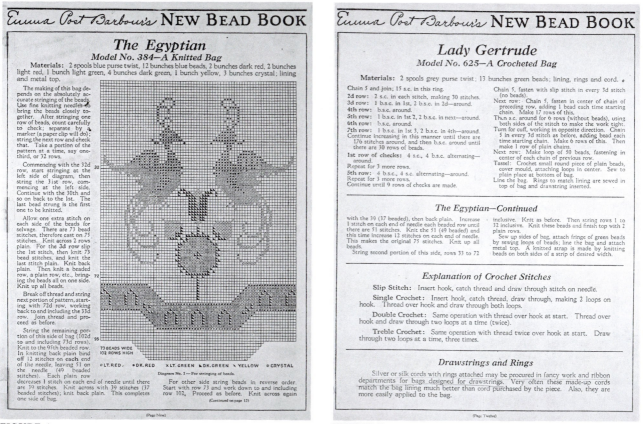

FIGURE 1   FIGURE 2

PLATE 43. Appearing in 1924, two years after King Tut's tomb was found, this beaded purse pattern was quite popular. The directions are very clear and thorough. Time to get started!

mand as much as $5.00 a bag in 1800, a truly princely sum in that time. Bags were knit or crocheted to match wedding gowns and incorporated elaborate scenes, floral sprays, landscapes, historic places or events, animal and bird life and even funereal designs. Ultimately the patterns were limited only by the imagination and skill of the beadworker and ran the gamut from landscapes to solidly beaded one color purses in elaborate frames, through huge bouquets of brilliantly hued roses, morning glories, corn flowers, poppies, and sprinkled rose buds.

A genuine prize for the purse collector would be one of these pouch type bags done in very fine beads in an old pattern in which the drawstrings were run through what appears to be "made over" material; that is material which extends from the beaded portion, often in a most unlikely color and fabric. Some of these purses date from the 18th century and unless the salesperson is knowledgeable aspersions may be cast on the purses' age which are undeserved. The lining extends above the beadwork and a facing is stitched to accommodate the cording which is knotted to prevent its slipping back into the facing. A moment's reflection will indicate that some means of carrying the purse must be supplied as the beadwork is far too delicate for this purpose.

Early purses, whether beaded or not, were of the drawstring type which could easily be completed by the beadworker in the home. As purse shapes changed, patterns and construction became increasingly complicated, completed purses were sent to factories where the metal frame and handles were attached commercially by professionals. Rigid frames were also purchased at the local "dry goods store" and the body of the purse beaded to fit the frame.

Writing in *The Designer* about 1902, Alice Gibson points out the difficulties of making bead bags and indicates how expensive such purses were, "Just now, when bead bags and chains—in fact, anything made of beads—are so fashionable, it is gratifying to learn that all the elaborate bags and purses shown in the high-class shops are not knitted, as is usually believed, but sewed, and, what is more, sewed in such a simple manner that it will no longer be necessary for us to gasp at the exorbitant prices charged for them....who ever supposed that even a novice at fancy work could make a bag with shaded pink roses, green leaves and borders, all on the same six inches, and still remain sane?"

Prices charged for designs in these stores were considered dear, ranging from seventy-five cents to a dollar-and-a-half, and prospective purchasers were encouraged by Mrs. Gibson to make their own using graph paper in a manner similar to "The Egyptian" shown on *Plate 43.*

As crochet work became fashionable in the early

FIGURE 1

FIGURE 2

PLATE 44. *Fig. 1:* Black velvet proves a perfect material for this reticule fitted with chain drawstring. The beads are small cut steel on basket, scattered beads and edging, as well as the narrow swag. This pattern was used extensively in embroideries during the first half of this century. *Fig. 2:* Although not particularly impressive at first glance, this purse of aluminum beads is quite unusual. Aluminum was used to overcome the problem of rust which plagued the steel bead. These beads are smooth, round edged and shiny—far shinier than cut steel beads. To break the monotony, diamonds are delineated by black glass beads and rhinestones. The purse is light in weight, dressy in appearance and more commodious than silver purses of the same size. As shown it is missing its fringe and needs a tab replacement, but these are being restored.

FIGURE 1

in one (bead 2, 3, 4, 5), s c 10 *. Repeat. 11th round—* Three s c in one
(bead 2, 3, 4, 5), s c 5, omit 2, s c 5 *.
Repeat. 12th round—* Three s c in one
(bead 2, 3, 4, 5, 6), s c 12 *. Repeat.
13th round—* Three s c in one (bead 2,
3, 4, 5, 6), s c 14 *. Repeat. 14th round
—Three s c in one (bead 2, 3, 4, 5, 6),
s c 7, omit 2, s c 7 *. Repeat. 15th
round—* Three s c in one (bead 2,

FIG. 32. FLUTED COIN PURSE OF
BLUE AND STEEL

Figure 32. Coin Purse.
Materials.—One spool dark blue
purse twist; 1 bunch steel beads
No. 8; coin purse top; crochet-
needle No. 10.
String beads on spool Every
stitch is beaded to the end of
the 4th round, after that beads
will be mentioned. Chain 4
(bead in each ch), and join.
1st round—One s c in 1st st,
2 s c in each of the others.
2d round—Two s c in each
stitch. *3d round*—* Two s c
in 1st st, 1 s c in 2d *. Repeat. *4th round*—* Two s c in
1st st, 1 s c in 2d and 3d *.
Repeat. *5th round*—* Three s c
in 1st (bead in 2d of 3), 1
s c in 2d (without bead) *.
Repeat. *6th round*—* Three s c
in one (bead 2d and 3d), 1 s c
in 2d, 3d, and 4th *. Repeat. *7th
round*—* Three s c in one
(bead 2d, 3d, and 4th), 5 s c *.
Repeat. *8th round*—* Three s c
in one (bead 2, 3, 4, 5), s c 3,
omit 1, s c 3 *. Repeat. *9th
round*—* Three s c in one
(bead 2, 3, 4, 5), s c 8 *. Repeat. *10th round*—* Three s c

No. 1531. OLD KNITTED BAG OF BLACK
CUT BEADS AND GOLD

3, 4, 5, 6), s c 16 *. Repeat.
16th round—Three s c in one
(bead 2, 3, 4, 5, 6), s c 8, omit
2, s c 8 *. Repeat. 17th round
—* Three s c in one (bead 2, 3, 4,
5, 6), s c 18 *. Repeat. 18th
round—* Three s c in one (bead
2, 3, 4, 5, 6), s c 9, omit 2, s c
9 *. Repeat. The next 4 rounds
are without beads. 19th round
—* Three s c in one, s c 9, omit
2, s c 9 *. Repeat. 20th round
—* Three s c in one, s c 9,
omit 2, s c 9 *. Repeat. 21st
round—* Three s c in one, s c
9, omit 2, s c 9 *. Repeat. 22d
round—* Three s c in one,

FIG. 34. COIN PURSE OF RED
AND STEEL

Omit every second stitch. 24th
round—Omit 1 stitch at each
point. 25th round—Omit 1 stitch
at each point. 26th round—
Single crochet around. 27th
round—* Single crochet 9, omit
1 *. Repeat. 28th round—Single
crochet around. 29th round—Single crochet 8, omit 1. Repeat.
30th round—Single crochet. 31st
round—Single crochet 7, omit
1. Repeat. 32d round—Single
crochet. 33d round—Single crochet 6, omit 1. Repeat. 34th
round—Single crochet. 35th
round—Single crochet. 36th
round—Single crochet 6, widen.
Repeat. 37th round—Single
crochet 7, widen. Repeat. In
the 23d, 24th, and 25th rounds
there are two figures of beads in
each section, in the 27th, 28th,
and 29th rounds there are 7
such figures, one over each
fourth one below and 2 others
half way between in the 29th
round.

Figure 34. Coin Purse.
Materials.—One spool red

FIGURE 2

PLATE 45-A. Pattern
books were very popular.
Reproduced here in its
entirety are the instruc-
tions for a purse called
''The Miser—Model
No. 509.''

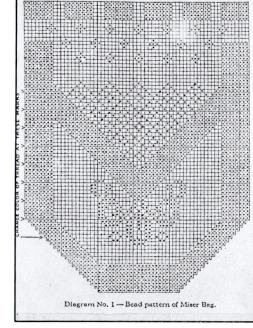

The Miser
Model No. 509—A Crocheted Bag
Materials: 10 bunches garnet beads; 2 spools blue, 1 spool yellow and 1 spool lavender
purse twist. Beads must be strung on the various colors of twist.

Chain 15; s.c. in each stitch; 3 s.c. in last stitch.
Turn; s.c. in each stitch back on other side of chain.

2d row: 17 s.c., 3 s.c. in last stitch of each end.
3d row: 19 s.c., 3 s.c. in last stitch of each end. Continue for 2 more rows, increasing 1 stitch at each end.
6th row: 1 s.c., 23 b.s.c., 1 s.c., 3 s.c. in last stitch,
repeat for other side.
7th row: 1 s.c., 25 b.s.c., 1 s.c., 3 s.c. in last stitch,
repeat for other side.
Continue for 6 more rows, increasing 2 beads each
row, and increasing 1 stitch at each end. This
makes 37 beads in your 8th row of beads.
14th row: 1 s.c., 8 b.s.c., 23 s.c., 8 b.s.c., 1 s.c.,
3 s.c. in last stitch. Repeat other side for each
row.
15th row: 1 s.c., 8 b.s.c., 25 s.c., 8 b.s.c., 1 s.c.,
3 s.c. in last stitch.
Continue for 3 more rows, increasing 2 s.c. inside
design, each row, making 31 s.c. on inside of design.
19th row: 1 s.c., 8 b.s.c., 15 s.c., 3 b.s.c., 15 s.c.,
8 b.s.c., 1 s.c., 3 s.c. in last stitch.
20th row: 1 s.c., 8 b.s.c., 10 s.c., 2 b.s.c., 3 s.c.,
5 b.s.c., 3 s.c., 2 b.s.c., 10 s.c., 8 b.s.c., 1 s.c.,
s.c., in last stitch.
21st row: Change color: 1 s.c., 8 b.s.c., 10 s.c.,
1 b.s.c., 2 s.c., 1 b.s.c., 1 s.c., 2 b.s.c., 3 s.c., 2 b.s.c.,
1 s.c., 1 b.s.c., 2 s.c., 1 b.s.c., 10 s.c., 8 b.s.c., 1 s.c.,
3 s.c. in last stitch.
22d row: 1 s.c., 8 b.s.c., 12 s.c., 2 b.s.c., 2 s.c.,
2 b.s.c., 3 s.c., 2 b.s.c., 2 s.c., 2 b.s.c., 12 s.c., 8
b.s.c., 1 s.c., 3 s.c. in last stitch.
23d row: 1 s.c., 8 b.s.c., 17 s.c., 2 b.s.c., 1 s.c.,
1 b.s.c., 1 s.c., 2 b.s.c., 17 s.c., 8 b.s.c., 1 s.c., 3 s.c.
in last stitch.

(Continued on page five)

Diagram No. 1 — Bead pattern of Miser Bag.

CHANGE COLOR OF THREAD AT THESE MARKS

The Miser—Continued

24th row: 1 s.c., 8 b.s.c., 12 s.c., 4 b.s.c., 2 s.c., 2 b.s.c., 1 s.c., 1 b.s.c., 2 s.c., 1 b.s.c., 2 s.c., 2 s.c., 4 b.s.c., 12 s.c., 8 b.s.c., 1 s.c., 3 s.c. in last stitch.

25th row: 1 s.c., 8 b.s.c., 12 s.c., 6 b.s.c., 1 s.c., 2 b.s.c., 1 s.c., 1 b.s.c., 2 s.c., 1 b.s.c., 2 s.c., 6 b.s.c., 12 s.c., 8 b.s.c., 1 s.c., 3 s.c. in last stitch.

26th row: Change color; 1 s.c., 8 b.s.c., 12 s.c., 3 b.s.c., 3 s.c., 2 b.s.c., 1 s.c., 5 b.s.c., 1 s.c., 2 b.s.c., 3 s.c., 3 b.s.c., 12 s.c., 8 b.s.c., 1 s.c., 3 s.c. in last stitch.

27th row: 1 s.c., 2 s.c. in next 2, 1 s.c., 8 b.s.c., 12 s.c., 2 b.s.c., 2 s.c., 2 b.s.c., 1 s.c., 2 b.s.c., 1 s.c., 3 b.s.c., 1 s.c., 2 b.s.c., 1 s.c., 2 b.s.c., 2 s.c., 2 b.s.c., 12 s.c., 8 b.s.c., 6 s.c. Repeat from beads for other side.

28th row: 8 b.s.c., 12 s.c., 2 b.s.c., 3 s.c., 2 b.s.c., 1 s.c., 2 b.s.c., 1 s.c., 1 b.s.c., 1 s.c., 1 b.s.c., 1 s.c., 2 b.s.c., 3 s.c., 2 b.s.c., 12 s.c., 8 b.s.c., 6 s.c.

29th row: 8 b.s.c., 12 s.c., 3 b.s.c., 2 s.c., 2 b.s.c., 2 s.c., 1 b.s.c., 2 s.c., 2 b.s.c., 2 s.c., 2 s.c., 3 b.s.c., 12 s.c., 8 b.s.c., 6 s.c.

30th row: 8 b.s.c., 12 s.c., 6 b.s.c., 4 s.c., 1 b.s.c., 1 s.c., 1 b.s.c., 4 s.c., 6 b.s.c., 12 s.c., 8 b.s.c., 6 s.c.

31st row: Change color: 8 b.s.c., 13 s.c., 4 b.s.c., 5 s.c., 3 b.s.c., 5 s.c., 4 b.s.c., 13 s.c., 8 b.s.c., 6 s.c.

32d row: 8 b.s.c., 11 s.c., 2 b.s.c., 1 s.c., 1 b.s.c., 6 s.c., 5 b.s.c., 6 s.c., 1 b.s.c., 1 s.c., 2 b.s.c., 11 s.c., 8 b.s.c., 6 s.c.

33d row: 8 b.s.c., 10 s.c., 2 b.s.c., 2 s.c., 1 b.s.c., 5 s.c., 7 b.s.c., 5 s.c., 1 b.s.c., 2 s.c., 2 b.s.c., 10 s.c., 8 b.s.c., 6 s.c.

34th row: 8 b.s.c., 10 s.c., 2 b.s.c., 2 s.c., 2 b.s.c., 3 s.c., 9 b.s.c., 3 s.c., 2 b.s.c., 2 s.c., 2 b.s.c., 10 s.c., 8 b.s.c., 6 s.c.

35th row: 8 b.s.c., 10 s.c., 2 b.s.c., 2 s.c., 2 b.s.c., 2 s.c., 11 b.s.c., 2 s.c., 2 b.s.c., 2 s.c., 2 b.s.c., 10 s.c., 8 b.s.c., 6 s.c.

36th row: Change color: 8 b.s.c., 11 s.c., 3 b.s.c., 3 s.c., 13 b.s.c., 3 s.c., 3 b.s.c., 11 s.c., 8 b.s.c., 6 s.c.

37th row: 8 b.s.c., 16 s.c., 15 b.s.c., 16 s.c., 8 b.s.c., 6 s.c.

38th row: 8 b.s.c., 15 s.c., 17 b.s.c., 15 s.c., 8 b.s.c., 6 s.c.

39th row: 8 b.s.c., 14 s.c., 19 b.s.c., 14 s.c., 8 b.s.c., 6 s.c.

40th row: 8 b.s.c., 13 s.c., 10 b.s.c., 1 s.c., 10 b.s.c., 13 s.c., 8 b.s.c., 6 s.c.

41st row: Change color: 8 b.s.c., 12 s.c., 10 b.s.c., 3 s.c., 10 b.s.c., 12 s.c., 8 b.s.c., 6 s.c.

42d row: 8 b.s.c., 1 s.c., 10 b.s.c., 2 s.c., 1 b.s.c., 2 s.c., 10 b.s.c., 1 s.c., 8 b.s.c., 6 s.c.

43d row: 8 b.s.c., 10 s.c., 10 b.s.c., 2 s.c., 1 b.s.c., 1 s.c., 1 b.s.c., 2 s.c., 10 b.s.c., 10 s.c., 8 b.s.c., 6 s.c.

44th row: 8 b.s.c., 9 s.c., 10 b.s.c., 1 s.c., 1 b.s.c., 2 s.c., 1 b.s.c., 2 s.c., 1 b.s.c., 1 s.c., 10 b.s.c., 9 s.c., 8 b.s.c., 6 s.c.

45th row: 8 b.s.c., 8 s.c., 10 b.s.c., 3 s.c., 1 b.s.c., 3 s.c., 1 b.s.c., 3 s.c., 10 b.s.c., 8 s.c., 8 b.s.c., 6 s.c.

46th row: Change color: 8 b.s.c., 7 s.c., 10 b.s.c., 2 s.c., 1 b.s.c., 2 s.c., 1 b.s.c., 1 s.c., 1 b.s.c., 2 s.c., 1 b.s.c., 2 s.c., 10 b.s.c., 7 s.c., 8 b.s.c., 6 s.c.

47th row: 8 b.s.c., 6 s.c., 10 b.s.c., 2 s.c., 1 b.s.c., 1 s.c., 1 b.s.c., 2 s.c., 1 b.s.c., 2 s.c., 1 b.s.c., 1 s.c., 1 b.s.c., 2 s.c., 10 b.s.c., 6 s.c., 8 b.s.c., 6 s.c.

48th row: 8 b.s.c., 5 s.c., 10 b.s.c., 1 s.c., 1 b.s.c., 2 s.c., 1 b.s.c., 2 s.c., 1 b.s.c., 1 s.c., 1 b.s.c., 2 s.c., 1 b.s.c., 1 s.c., 10 b.s.c., 5 s.c., 8 b.s.c., 6 s.c.

49th row: 8 b.s.c., 4 s.c., 10 b.s.c., 3 s.c., 1 b.s.c., 3 s.c., 1 b.s.c., 3 s.c., 1 b.s.c., 3 s.c., 10 b.s.c., 4 s.c., 8 b.s.c., 6 s.c.

50th row: 8 b.s.c., 3 s.c., 10 b.s.c., 2 s.c., 1 b.s.c., 2 s.c., 1 b.s.c., 1 s.c., 1 b.s.c., 2 s.c., 1 b.s.c., 2 s.c., 1 b.s.c., 1 s.c., 1 b.s.c., 2 s.c., 1 b.s.c., 2 s.c., 10 b.s.c., 3 s.c., 8 b.s.c., 6 s.c.

51st row: Change color: 8 b.s.c., 2 s.c., 10 b.s.c., 2 s.c., 1 b.s.c., 1 s.c., 1 b.s.c., 2 s.c., 1 b.s.c., 2 s.c., 1 b.s.c., 1 s.c., 1 b.s.c., 2 s.c., 1 b.s.c., 2 s.c., 1 b.s.c., 1 s.c., 1 b.s.c., 2 s.c., 10 b.s.c., 2 s.c., 8 b.s.c., 6 s.c.

52d row: 8 b.s.c., 1 s.c., 10 b.s.c., 1 s.c., 1 b.s.c., 2 s.c., 1 b.s.c., 2 s.c., 1 b.s.c., 1 s.c., 1 b.s.c., 1 s.c., 1 b.s.c., 2 s.c., 1 b.s.c., 2 s.c., 1 b.s.c., 2 s.c., 1 b.s.c., 1 s.c., 10 b.s.c., 1 s.c., 8 b.s.c., 6 s.c.

53d row: 18 b.s.c., 3 s.c., 1 b.s.c., 3 s.c., 1 b.s.c., 3 s.c., 1 b.s.c., 1 s.c., 1 b.s.c., 1 s.c., 1 b.s.c., 3 s.c., 1 b.s.c., 3 s.c., 1 b.s.c., 3 s.c., 18 b.s.c., 6 s.c.

(Continued on page eight)

The Miser—Continued

54th row: 17 b.s.c., 2 s.c., 1 b.s.c., 2 s.c., 1 b.s.c., 1 s.c., 1 b.s.c., 2 s.c., 1 b.s.c., 2 s.c., 1 b.s.c., 1 s.c., 1 b.s.c., 2 s.c., 1 b.s.c., 2 s.c., 1 s.c., 1 b.s.c., 2 s.c., 1 b.s.c., 2 s.c., 17 b.s.c., 6 s.c.

55th row: 16 b.s.c., 2 s.c., 1 b.s.c., 1 s.c., 1 b.s.c., 2 s.c., 1 b.s.c., 2 s.c., 1 b.s.c., 1 s.c., 1 b.s.c., 2 s.c., 1 b.s.c., 2 s.c., 1 b.s.c., 1 s.c., 1 b.s.c., 2 s.c., 1 b.s.c., 2 s.c., 1 b.s.c., 1 s.c., 1 b.s.c., 2 s.c., 16 b.s.c., 6 s.c.

56th row: Change color: 15 b.s.c., 1 s.c., 1 b.s.c., 2 s.c., 1 b.s.c., 2 s.c., 1 b.s.c., 1 s.c., 1 b.s.c., 2 s.c., 1 b.s.c., 2 s.c., 1 b.s.c., 1 s.c., 1 b.s.c., 2 s.c., 1 b.s.c., 2 s.c., 1 b.s.c., 1 s.c., 1 b.s.c., 2 s.c., 1 b.s.c., 1 s.c., 15 b.s.c., 6 s.c.

57th row: 14 b.s.c., 3 s.c., 1 b.s.c., 3 s.c., 1 b.s.c., 3 s.c., 1 b.s.c., 3 s.c., 1 b.s.c., 3 s.c., 1 b.s.c., 3 s.c., 1 b.s.c., 3 s.c., 1 b.s.c., 3 s.c., 14 b.s.c., 6 s.c.

58th row: 13 b.s.c., 2 s.c., 1 b.s.c., 2 s.c., 1 b.s.c., 1 s.c., 1 b.s.c., 2 s.c., 1 b.s.c., 2 s.c., 1 b.s.c., 1 s.c., 1 b.s.c., 2 s.c., 1 b.s.c., 2 s.c., 1 b.s.c., 1 s.c., 1 b.s.c., 2 s.c., 1 b.s.c., 2 s.c., 1 b.s.c., 1 s.c., 1 b.s.c., 2 s.c., 13 b.s.c., 6 s.c.

59th row: 12 b.s.c., 2 s.c., 1 b.s.c., 1 s.c., 1 b.s.c., 2 s.c., 1 b.s.c., 2 s.c., 1 b.s.c., 1 s.c., 1 b.s.c., 2 s.c., 1 b.s.c., 2 s.c., 1 b.s.c., 1 s.c., 1 b.s.c., 2 s.c., 1 b.s.c., 2 s.c., 1 b.s.c., 1 s.c., 1 b.s.c., 2 s.c., 12 b.s.c., 6 s.c.

60th row: 11 b.s.c., 1 s.c., 1 b.s.c., 2 s.c., 1 b.s.c., 2 s.c., 1 b.s.c., 1 s.c., 1 b.s.c., 2 s.c., 1 b.s.c., 2 s.c., 1 b.s.c., 1 s.c., 1 b.s.c., 2 s.c., 1 b.s.c., 2 s.c., 1 b.s.c., 1 s.c., 1 b.s.c., 2 s.c., 1 b.s.c., 2 s.c., 1 b.s.c., 1 s.c., 11 b.s.c., 6 s.c.

61st row: Change color: 10 b.s.c., 3 s.c., 1 b.s.c., 3 s.c., 1 b.s.c., 3 s.c., 1 b.s.c., 3 s.c., 1 b.s.c., 3 s.c., 1 b.s.c., 3 s.c., 1 b.s.c., 3 s.c., 1 b.s.c., 3 s.c., 1 b.s.c., 3 s.c., 10 b.s.c., 6 s.c.

62d row: 9 b.s.c., 5 s.c., 1 b.s.c., 1 s.c., 1 b.s.c., 5 s.c., 1 b.s.c., 1 s.c., 1 b.s.c., 5 s.c., 1 b.s.c., 1 s.c., 1 b.s.c., 5 s.c., 1 b.s.c., 1 s.c., 1 b.s.c., 5 s.c., 9 b.s.c., 6 s.c.

63d row: 8 b.s.c., 7 s.c., 1 b.s.c., 7 s.c., 1 b.s.c., 7 s.c., 1 b.s.c., 7 s.c., 1 b.s.c., 7 s.c., 1 b.s.c., 7 s.c., 8 b.s.c., 6 s.c.

64th row: 8 b.s.c., s.c. across, 8 b.s.c. Repeat 4 more rows.

69th row: 8 b.s.c., 7 s.c., 1 b.s.c., 7 s.c., 1 b.s.c., 7 s.c., 1 b.s.c., 7 s.c., 1 b.s.c., 7 s.c., 1 b.s.c., 7 s.c., 8 b.s.c., 6 s.c.

70th row: 8 b.s.c., 6 s.c., 3 b.s.c., 5 s.c., 3 b.s.c., 5 s.c., 3 b.s.c., 5 s.c., 3 b.s.c., 5 s.c., 3 b.s.c., 6 s.c., 8 b.s.c., 6 s.c.

71st row: 8 b.s.c., 7 s.c., 1 b.s.c., 7 s.c., 1 b.s.c., 7 s.c., 1 b.s.c., 7 s.c., 1 b.s.c., 7 s.c., 8 b.s.c., 6 s.c.

72d row: 8 b.s.c., s.c. across, 8 b.s.c., 6 s.c.

73d row: 8 b.s.c., 3 s.c., 1 b.s.c., 7 s.c., 1 b.s.c., 7 s.c., 1 b.s.c., 7 s.c., 1 b.s.c., 7 s.c., 1 b.s.c., 3 s.c., 8 b.s.c., 6 s.c.

74th row: 8 b.s.c., 2 s.c., 3 b.s.c., 5 s.c., 3 b.s.c., 5 s.c., 3 b.s.c., 5 s.c., 3 b.s.c., 5 s.c., 3 b.s.c., 2 s.c., 8 b.s.c., 6 s.c.

75th row: 11 s.c., 1 b.s.c., 7 s.c., 1 b.s.c., 7 s.c., 1 b.s.c., 7 s.c., 1 b.s.c., 7 s.c., 1 b.s.c., 7 s.c., 1 b.s.c., 17 s.c.

76th row: s.c. all around.

77th row: 7 s.c., 1 b.s.c., 7 s.c., 1 b.s.c., 7 s.c., 1 b.s.c., 7 s.c., 1 b.s.c., 7 s.c., 1 b.s.c., 7 s.c., 1 b.s.c., 13 s.c.

78th row: 6 s.c., 3 b.s.c., 5 s.c., 3 b.s.c., 5 s.c., 3 b.s.c., 5 s.c., 3 b.s.c., 5 s.c., 3 b.s.c., 5 s.c., 3 b.s.c., 12 s.c.

79th row: 7 s.c., 1 b.s.c., 7 s.c., 1 b.s.c., 7 s.c., 1 b.s.c., 7 s.c., 1 b.s.c., 7 s.c., 1 b.s.c., 7 s.c., 1 b.s.c., 13 s.c.

80th row: s.c. all around.

81st row: 8 b.s.c., 3 s.c., 8 b.s.c., 3 s.c., 8 b.s.c., 3 s.c., 8 b.s.c., 3 s.c., 8 b.s.c., 3 s.c., 8 b.s.c., 6 s.c.

Repeat for 4 rows.

1 d.c., 1 chain in every 2d stitch. Turn, leaving opening of bag. Continue for 58 rows, and repeat other half of bag. Fringe at bottom.

FIGURE 1

FIGURE 2

PLATE 45. Two examples of partially worked patterns. *Fig. 1:* Flour sack beading. Commonly used at the turn of the century for fine beading only. Done in one piece and joined at the sides. *Fig. 2:* A small beaded purse of the late 1800's. The two pieces were made separately as shown and then joined *(Both purses courtesy "The Venerable Bead," Berkeley, California).*

part of the 19th century crocheted beaded purses can be dated fairly accurately. Knit beaded bags predated crochet by a full century, though incredibly fine beaded embroideries on early bags date from the mid 1700's and brilliantly hued minute glass beads were

being made in Venice, Italy, as early as the 13th century. Although it may be impossible to determine the exact date of a given purse, the size of the beads will give an approximate age; the smaller the beads the older the purse is a reliable rule of thumb. *Plate 11, Fig. 1* and *Plate 14, Figures 3* and *4* show purses with beads so fine 1,000 to the square inch can be counted. Different sizes of beads were used to create effects and absolute uniformity was non-essential in blown glass.

From Its Inception in July, 1830, till its demise in 1879, *Lady Godey Books* contained patterns and directions for making purses of all sorts, including beaded purses (the directions for the misers' purse from *Lady Godey 1857* are given on *Plate 45A*). Other women's publications such as *Delineator, Harpers, Grahams, Petersons, McCalls* and numerous others regularly published patterns, as well as the manufacturers of knitting and crocheting equipment and materials. One of the best of these was a magazine called *The Modern Priscilla* which in 1911 published a booklet which they advertised as follows: "*The Modern Priscilla* is a profusely illustrated monthly magazine, brimful of lovely designs and interesting new ideas for needleworkers. It gives you the newest and prettiest designs for embroidery, crochet, tatting, knitting, basketry, beadwork and china painting. It is an ever growing encyclopedia of feminine handicrafts. More than a half million other women are already enjoying *Modern Priscilla.*"

Such magazines were offered for 25¢ each, while others sold for as little as 10–15¢. Some were the output of publishing companies while others were promoted by bead manufacturers and importers such as National Trading Company and Saint Louis Fancy Work Company. Women who had supervised or completed the designs themselves acted as editors. Each booklet offered new and old designs in beadwork and some of the patterns date amazingly from 1750 and earlier. They are a marvelous reference source today, if they can be located.

The beaded bag was shown along with some suggestions concerning its construction and a few simple purses were presented with complete directions to whet the desire of the novice without revealing too much and thus obviating the need to purchase the magazine. The quantity of beads was given, the colors, sizes, frames, needles or crochet hook sizes, thread weight, color, appropriate linings etc. The illustrations were unfortunately in black and white as color layouts were just becoming feasible but were too expensive for the average advertiser to use. It would have been a great boon to us today had they done so.

As the larger patterns are extremely complicated and probably would result in total frustration for the modern bag collector who might like to attempt a

FIGURE 1

No. 1505A. Blue Velvet Bag with Band of Leaves in Beaded Canvas. See No. 1505B.

FIGURE 3

FIGURE 4

PLATE 46. Five patterns from books c. 1911.

FIGURE 5

beaded bag of her own construction, a simple yet attractive pattern from one of these booklets is here included for your examination. It is possible for a skilled needleworker to complete the misers' purse and/or the Egyptian bag shown on *Plate 43* and it should be quite satisfying, realizing each is a fine antique pattern.

In 1924 the beadworker was encouraged by the National Trading Company that "Beadwork is always worth while; though fashion may change there is always a return to the beaded. The artistic work of

FIGURE 1

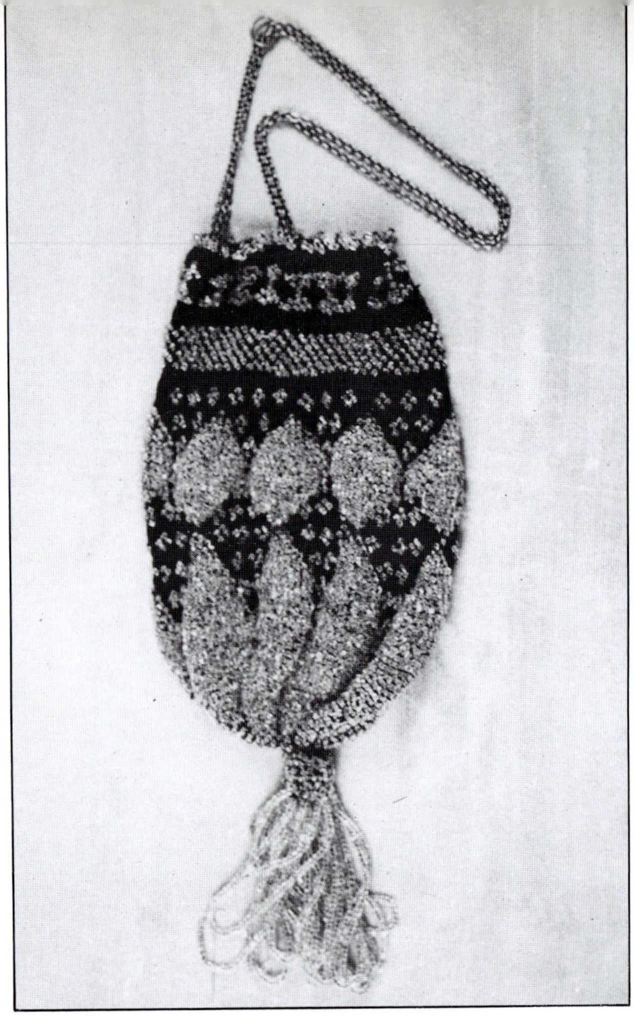

FIGURE 4

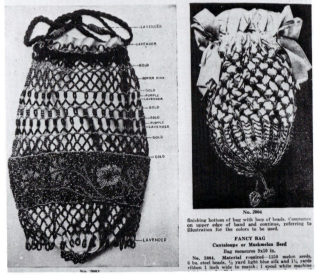

No. 2004

finishing bottom of bag with loop of beads. Commence on upper edge of band and continue, referring to illustration for the colors to be used.

FANCY BAG

Cantaloupe or Muskmelon Seed
Bag measures 9x10 in.

No. 2004. Material required—1350 melon seeds, 6 bu. steel beads, ½ yard light blue silk and 1½ yards ribbon 1 inch wide to match; 1 spool white machine

FIGURE 2

PLATE 46-A. Five more patterns c. 1911.

FIGURE 3

208

your hands today will give you much satisfaction while the vogue is strong and a work of art always lives, becoming enhanced by age in both value and sentiment.'' Reassured that the pastime was really an art gave value to the tedious job and veterans of the First World War in military hospitals ''whiled away the weary hours in making articles for which they received compensation with a very pleasant pastime.''

The ardent purse collector has proven the beautifully beaded bags have ''enhanced in value'', though few people would consider the current prices paid for these purses is in any way commensurate with

the skill and time required to produce them.

Purse collectors and those who have merely found among various estate items a purse done by some distant relative years ago, alike, are most anxious to affix a date to a given article, and nothing is harder to do with certainty. A study of known patterns of great age does reveal, however, some guidelines which aid in determining approximate dates, though a purse could have been made in the '20's from a pattern of the late 18th century and similarly one could have been done in the 1800's which is mistaken for a more recent vintage. Early patterns include some of the following

FIGURE 1

FIGURE 2

PLATE 47. Two purses exhibiting the lyre and rose pattern (courtesy Clinton Historical Society, Clinton, Massachusetts).

FIGURE 1

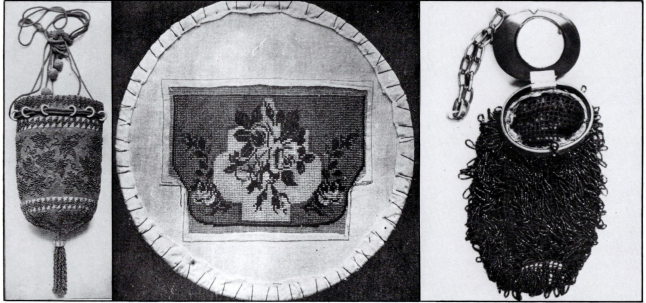

FIGURE 2   **FIGURE 3**   **FIGURE 4**

PLATE 48. *Fig. 1:* Early sautoir done by Josi Bishop in 1833. Made on a loom, it is only 12 beads wide (5/16″) and must be handled with extreme care. Its tiny beads are predominantly beige and white, but there is a sprinkling of other colors. The motto reads "Learning is wealth to the poor and honor to the rich. Love virtue. Josi Bishop 1833." Both sautoir and motto have suffered some damage in the past 150 years. *Fig. 2:* These drawstring rings are on the outside of this reticule, a practice not generally followed. *Fig. 3:* Beading done on canvas. This was recommended for amateurs as it promised the greatest degree of success. *Fig. 4:* A typical all-over pattern c. 1911 called "The Dewdrop." It has a celluloid frame and permanent inset mirror.

elements, if not all, as some patterns were so intricate that Mary White writing in *How To Do Beadwork* (1904) states, "How fortunate is the woman who owns an old-fashioned knitted bead bag! Long forgotten it may have lain in chest or treasure box, but it is now in high favour, mounted in silver or gold. Only the faint fragrance of rose leaves reminds one of its age. Quaint and sometimes beautiful are the designs of these old bags and the colouring is soft and lovely. Fine silk was used at that time and the beads were tiny, while the needles were like slender wire… One wonders how the women of that generation kept their eyesight, stringing and knitting such fine beads by candle or lamplight. The beads were strung according to the pattern and direful were the results if one bead was misplaced: the pattern, of course, would be all awry. The texture of these bags, silky and shimmering, is a joy, but not even for the pleasure of giving or owning such a beautiful thing would the woman of to-day spend so much time and pains."

IN THE EARLY 17th century professional pattern makers designed for European courts but by the 19th century when every conceivable article, and a few very implausible ones to boot, were beaded, ladies' magazines were copiously filled with patterns to satisfy all

skills and tastes. Little would be accomplished by listing all of the patterns in detail, but from close examination of countless purses the following motifs executed in *fine* beads can safely be considered as old, meaning from 200–300 years old, though most purses themselves will date from the mid 1800's to 1920. Flowers included poppies, tulips, roses, forget-me-nots, corn flowers, morning glories, water lillies, sun flowers, and chrysanthemums; in bouquets, sprays, garlands, swags, baskets, and scattered across fields beaded in solid colors. Birds included peacocks, parrots, lovebirds, and swans among the more easily distinguishable birds. Leaves were often borders of berries and acorns, ivy, grape, oak, fig, acanthus, and maple leaves. Landscapes were surely the most involved showing ships-at-sea, castles and moats, shepherds and small flocks of sheep, school houses, buildings of all sorts, state houses and important government buildings, in particular, court scenes, (usually French) cemetery views, all interspersed with animals, butterflies, and imaginative insects.

Non-naturalistic embellishments included the fleur-de-lis, musical instruments such as the lyre and harp, coats of arms, mottoes, initials in floral wreaths, religious symbols, Greek keys, dates, (what better authentication?) geometrics, Oriental rug motifs, and saw tooth terminals.

And the fringes, which were virtually mandatory! They were twisted, entwined, looped, clustered, bunched, of contrasting colors, of variegated patterns, tasseled, swagged, vandyked, chained, braided, shirred, and flounced in every imaginable way in which a bag might be bordered.

It is doubtful if these designs sprung from the minds of their creators full blown, but rather were based at least in part on prints, paintings, Biblical figures, Berlin works, historical events, tapestries, inspired and combined from other pattern books, and from personal memory catering to current sentiment.

Both the multiplicity of colors and the variations in descriptive terminology make it impractical to list all of the 122 colors and hues used in making purses, but it is interesting to note some of the combinations used in making one medium fine beaded purse in a solid pattern of sunflowers and morning glories. The design calls for 100 × 116 rows and uses the following terms, only a few of which are really exotic: pale yellow, light yellow, (opaque and clear glass), orange, amber, brown, gray blue, dark grey blue, milk white, pink, red, (white lined), dark red (glass), light and medium green, dark green (glass), black, light cold green (opaque), medium cold green, and opal. Exactly what is meant by cold green is open to interpretation. This pattern required 109 bunches of beads with 1,000 beads to the bunch, so the beader strung and applied 109,000 beads! Judging from the colors supplied with

patterns for early purses popular colors used in these bags were: opal, favored for background and large areas, along with varying shades of rose, deep and light shades of blue, green, lavender, dark red, turquoise, blue, and crystal. Yellow, orange, brown, gold and black were used sparingly and for accents only, as a rule. Various pleasing effects were achieved by interspersing opaque, lined and glass beads, but the same size beads were used in order that the surface be smooth, unless the intent was to create a raised beadwork effect in which the beads appear padded or shirred.

Beads Used In the United States were and still are imported from abroad; originally they came from Venice, Italy, Germany, then France and Czechoslovakia. Today beads also come from Japan and other parts of the world, but those suitable for purse embroideries are best obtained from Venice. Bead sources will be given at the end of the book should the reader desire to purchase them. Through the 19th and early years of the 20th century, beads were numbered according to size rather differently than today. Currently the larger the designated number the smaller the bead size in millimeters. For instance the tiniest beads which would be found in beaded purses would be classified as 5/0 and it would be fine seed beads ½ millimeter in diameter, 23 of which would measure 1 inch. It would be virtually impossible to purchase or obtain any beads this small today, unless an old purse which was beyond repair was used to supply the proper size, color and shape. Beads currently range in sizes from 18–½ millimeters and come in an infinite variety of shapes including: pearls, oat beads, rondells, crystal faceted, saucers, round rocailles, lined cut beads, cut lustres, seeds, ceylons and others.

Antique beaded purses employed the following types of beads: transparent, a bead which can be seen through; opaque, the reverse of transparent as light does not penetrate the bead; lined, a bead which had been coated with a dye or paint; iridescent, transparent beads with a coating which causes them to glisten in certain angles and lights; ceylon, those having a pearly exterior; bugle, an elongated glass shaped bead frequently black on color; half bugle, which is the same as bugle but as the name implies about one half the length; cut steel, made of steel rods which vary greatly in thickness, jet black bugle beads, called jet erroneously as the term applies to the color only; gold plated, base metal which is covered with an outer shell of genuine gold; French gilt, gold colored beads from France as opposed to those plated with the mineral gold; round steel, the same as the steel bugle but with rounded shape rather than tubular, (not as common as the bugle type); aluminum,

FIGURE 1

rather rare, large compared to the beads designated as fine beads but they were both a curiosity and a practical answer to the steel beads which unfortunately rusted under unfavorable conditions.

Beads for embroidery purposes were classified as very fine, fine, medium and large. The fine were for net, loom, knit and crochet; medium for canvas; and the large were suitable for fringing.

Embroidery beads were strung and sold in bunches, the finer beads being the most expensive. The finest beads averaged about 600 beads to the bunch, larger size seed beads were 1000 to a bunch, gold plated, French gilt and steel in different sizes about 1200 per bunch and round steel about 1500 to the bunch. This information was essential as the hand blown beads varying in color from lot to lot had to be purchased at one time. The importance of obtaining beads of uniform size, in so far as possible, was to maintain an even surface and it was necessary to determine well in advance the approximate number of bunches of beads required to complete a project.

Popular methods of making beaded purses in the early 19th century were: knitting, crocheting, beading on canvas, bead embroidery on fabric, Indian bead weaving or loomed weaving. By the 20th century knitting and embroidery on fabric had lost favor to the other methods; most designs were considered too complicated and were replaced by relatively simple patterns in solid colored beads. Knitted bags (which were the most durable), show the silk threads heavily on the wrong side and slightly on the right side, whereas loomed bags show almost no threads on either side, and are more evenly surfaced.

In knitted bags the beads were first strung on a spool of thread, following the pattern precisely. The thread used was usually silk, which Alice Morse Earle tells us was obtained from silkworms—which some women raised in small numbers—wound, twisted, and made into their own strong silk fibers. While I do not recall ever having seen any silk worms I do remember with some malicious glee the thick foliage of the mulberry tree which fell like the ribs of an umbrella to the ground and which was a perfect hiding place for small children. Some optimistic woman had hoped

FIGURE 3

FIGURE 4

FIGURE 2

PLATE 50. *Fig. 1:* Mourning picture, 1803 *(Metropolitan Museum of Art, gift of Mrs. L.H. Robertson). Fig. 2:* Reticule of beads on canvas, c. 1800–20, United States *(Metropolitan Museum of Art, gift of Mrs. Glen Ethel May Wright). Fig. 3:* An American reticule with architectural ruins as the motif, c. 1835–45 *(The Brooklyn Museum, gift of Mrs. Omri F. Hibbard). Fig. 4:* Beaded bag with shepherdess motif made by Sonia Benyon Goodrich, 1836 *(The Brooklyn Museum, gift of Miss Jennie Brownscombe in memory of Miss Goodrich).*

to feed her silk worms, imported from China, on these leaves, for such was the craze nearly a century ago in as unlikely a place as rural Massachusetts.

PATTERN BOOKS WARNED the knitter of several pitfalls such as the absolute necessity of stringing the beads from the bottom right hand row to the top, always starting from the right hand side so the beads were strung just the opposite of the order in which they were to be knit. In large purses the stringing had to be done in sections of 20 rows as the job would prove too unwieldy otherwise. Early pouch crochet or knit purses frequently commenced with a star bottom in which a chain of stitches was increased and then decreased to create points resembling a star. This proved particularly handsome when the star was beaded of one color outlined with black and the star points are

213

FIGURE 3

FIGURE 4

FIGURE 2

PLATE 50. *Fig. 1:* Mourning picture, 1803 *(Metropolitan Museum of Art, gift of Mrs. L.H. Robertson). Fig. 2:* Reticule of beads on canvas, c. 1800–20, United States *(Metropolitan Museum of Art, gift of Mrs. Glen Ethel May Wright). Fig. 3:* An American reticule with architectural ruins as the motif, c. 1835–45 *(The Brooklyn Museum, gift of Mrs. Omri F. Hibbard). Fig. 4:* Beaded bag with shepherdess motif made by Sonia Benyon Goodrich, 1836 *(The Brooklyn Museum, gift of Miss Jennie Brownscombe in memory of Miss Goodrich).*

to feed her silk worms, imported from China, on these leaves, for such was the craze nearly a century ago in as unlikely a place as rural Massachusetts.

PATTERN BOOKS WARNED the knitter of several pitfalls such as the absolute necessity of stringing the beads from the bottom right hand row to the top, always starting from the right hand side so the beads were strung just the opposite of the order in which they were to be knit. In large purses the stringing had to be done in sections of 20 rows as the job would prove too unwieldy otherwise. Early pouch crochet or knit purses frequently commenced with a star bottom in which a chain of stitches was increased and then decreased to create points resembling a star. This proved particularly handsome when the star was beaded of one color outlined with black and the star points are

variegated. Stars were equally effective when used in purses knit of one color and beaded in one other sharply contrasting color such as black and crystal, blue and steel cut and other combinations. Small coin purses were invariably made in variations of this pattern. These star bottom purses date from 1846 which was also the year when steel and gold beads were first used.

French steel cut bags were first introduced to the American market in 1910. They bear the same indelible patterns and colors which make them immediately distinguishable from all other purses; the shimmering bugle and steel beads in gold, bronze, silver, black and greys. They are found in other colors from time-to-time but these five colors are commonly combined; the body of the purse done in one color and the other four used in the decorative scheme. The weight of these beads placed such a strain on the lining and the areas sewn to the narrow embossed metal frame that they are seldom found in good condition. The beading separates at the sides and top and though they are exquisitely executed in elegantly understated patterns, they tend to need repair, be repetitious and lack the appeal of other beaded bags. If uncertain as to the country of origin, examine the inside frame for the imprint ''Made in France'' and ''Hand Made in

PLATE 51. *Figs. 1 & 2:* Each side of a beaded handbag made by Ellen Coxe in 1838 is shown *(The Brooklyn Museum, gift of Mr. Omri Hibbard).*

FIGURE 1

214

France'' on the fabric mirror holder. One of these fine quality French steel beaded bags in a beautiful floral design with fancy silver, gold, and red flowers, was priced at $28.00 in 1929.

Flat crocheted beaded purses about 3 inches in diameter called Tam O'Shanter purses were extremely popular around 1900, and are relatively easy to find today. They were used for safeguarding rings (which had been removed when shedding the gloves every lady wore as a matter of course) in addition to coins, tickets, and other small items.

Home Needle Magazine, among many domestic magazines of its genre, gave directions in April, 1901, for making one of these 8 pointed star patterns which appears to have been a basic Tam O'Shanter. It is so simple that the directions are as follows for those who may have a cover available to them or have a damaged or worn purse to replace: ''Make a chain of four and join. Into this circle make 8 stitches in single crochet, 2 stitches into each of those forming the circle. Into each of these 8 stitches work 2, 1 with and one without beads, having at the completion of the round 16 stitches, 8 with beads and 8 plain. Continue working in this manner, adding 1 bead in the stitch, widening the previous round with a single plain stitch between each section, marking the divisions of

FIGURE 2

the star. When there are 9 beads so worked, the widest part of the star having beads is reached. The following rounds are worked by omitting the last bead in each section, substituting therefor a plain stitch, and continuing to widen as before the same place as formerly, that is at the stitch just before the bead, so this line may be preserved unbroken, until there remains a single bead at each section which will mark the tip of the star. There then will be a perfectly flat circular mat which should be 3 inches in diameter. If at the conclusion of the star the mat is less than 3 inches increase it to the desired size by the addition of several rows of plain crochet. The work is now at its widest and largest point and is continued by working rows of plain single crochet and narrowing at each point which was previously widened. Continue to narrow in this manner for about 8 rounds when this part will be found to double over upon the mat like portion and will present the appearance of a miniature Tam O'Shanter cap from which its name is taken. When this circle is narrowed to the size of the top selected, work 2 rows in double crochet which should stand up like a band, to which the top is to be attached. The top will cost 50¢ and the mounting an additional 20¢. One bunch of #9 beads will be sufficient to make the purse and they should be strung upon silk before the work is commenced. Use crochet needle #1 and ½ ounce spool of Corticelli Purse Twist."

A similarly shaped purse with a half rounded clasp top, twisted fringed bottom and beaded length of silk passed through a ring, was obviously intended to be a chatelaine purse, as was another measuring about twice the size. The designer, a certain Mary Shuster, declared a 5 inch frame with chatelaine top will cost $3.75 but a "less expensive one can be bought of the same dimensions." This is an interesting sidelight as such information is seldom revealed and it does indicate the costliness of these bags at that time.

SELDOM EVER DOES the collector have the opportunity to accurately date a purse and authenticate its maker and owner, unless of course the purse is a family heirloom. In this respect two purses in this text are most interesting. They are the Sara Day Wilder purse and the Elisabeth Ayers purse [*Plate 49*].

The Sara Day purse was purchased from a lady who said her grandmother had been an antique dealer some years ago and she had kept some articles when she retired from her business at an advanced age. Her granddaughter brought me the purse accompanied by a fragile silhouette of Sara Day, some genealogical material, and some framed fragments from a wedding dress which supposedly was worn by Sara Day. It was difficult to decipher the penmanship and it was not possible to determine with any accuracy who traced the little genealogical chart but the purse is without

question one of the oldest completely beaded domestic purses I am acquainted with outside a museum.

A mere 5¼ × 4¾ today, it is missing the silken fabric top which would have extended its length and provided the drawstring and carrying cords. It is not in mint condition by any means, as it was knit of the finest silk thread and completely beaded in 15 different colors, including the unusual shade of cornflower blue found only in very old beaded objects. The beads are of varying sizes but the majority are so small they are best observed through a magnifying glass. At one time the purse was silk lined as it was too delicate to have ever been used unlined.

The real appeal of the purse lies in its motif, however, as it is a funereal purse, the design of which was poular between 1800 and 1830. At the base are 4 rows of deep cobalt beads, topped by 9 rows of variegated green beaded lawns, in the midst of which are a pair of trees with large opaque glass bead trunks. Though space did not allow a willow tree, traditional symbol of sorrowful sentimentality, the intent may have been present. Between the trees is a tombstone topped by a funeral urn bearing the large initial *S*. The colors of the entire pattern are vivid to the point of gaiety; aside from the tombstone there is not the slightest hint of morbidity about the purse design. Why then the gravestone? The answer lies in the preoccupation in the 18th and 19th centuries with death and mourning. For women in particular it was a relatively short, mean, hard life; women lived but 32 years on the average; men but 40.

Alice Morse Earle in her invaluable *Costume in America* tells a humorous story in this connection which bears repeating, "A handsome pattern for knitting a bead bag was a treasure beyond price; its written rules were given only to nearest and dearest friends. Simple designs could be counted out from existing bags. Many a tale of domestic jealousy and social envy centered around these bags. In one New England town Matilda Emerson reigned a queen of the bag makers; her patterns were beyond compare; one of a Dutch scene with a windmill was the envy of all who beheld it. She was a rival with Ann Green for the affections of the minister, a solemn widower, whose sister kept house for him and his three motherless children. Matilda gave the parson's sister the written rules for a wonderful bead bag, (the design having originated in Boston), a bag which displayed when finished a funereal willow tree and urn and grass-grown grave, in shaded grays and purple and white on a black ground; a properly solemn bag. But when the parson's sister assayed to knit this trapping of woe, it proved a sad jumble of unmeaning lines, for Ann Green had taken secretly the rules from the knitter's work box, and had changed the pencilled rules in every line. When the hodgepodge appeared where the orderly

FIGURE 1

FIGURE 2

FIGURE 3

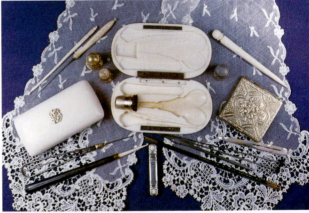

FIGURE 5

FIGURE 4

PLATE 49. *Fig. 1:* Silhouette of Sara Day Wilder, early 19th Century, *Fig. 2:* Right, purse of extra-fine beads, by Sara Day Wilder. Left, similar design with fringe. *Fig. 3:* Purse making tools. Case is dated 1840, has mother-of-pearl ribbon threader, tiny graduated set of crochet hooks, ivory hooks, celluloid knitting needles, and four extremely fine needles one-quarter size of "O" needle. *Fig. 4:* Reticule by Elizabeth Ayers, 19th Century *(courtesy "The Venerable Bead")*. *Fig. 5:* Ivory sewing kit c. 1840 with solid gold thimbles and silver needle case.

FIGURE 1

FIGURE 3

FIGURE 4

FIGURE 2

FIGURE 6

FIGURE 5

PLATE 52. Indian purses and bags. *Figs. 1 & 4:* Fine beads on leather *(courtesy "A Stitch In Time," Richmond, California). Figs. 2 & 3:* Leaf motif in large beads *(Collection of Bronwen Heuer). Figs. 5 & 6:* Indian purses, Tuscarora and possibly Canadian.

218

symbols of gloom should have been seen, the sister believed that Matilda had purposely written them wrong in order to preserve her prestige as a bag knitter and she so prejudiced her brother that he coldly turned from Matilda and married, not Ann, but a widow from another town.''

The Sara Day purse design differs only in that the ground color is opalescent, the roses are variegated red pink, and the total effect is so cheerful the tombstone appears incongruous in this setting.

THE ELISABETH AYER purse was found in a shop in Maine and contained an abbreviated account of the maker which subsequently was substantiated, much to the delight of the purchaser, through the Bureau of Vital Statistics in Massachusetts. Miss Ayer was a maiden lady living in Haverill, Massachusetts, between 1826–1861 and she died at the age of 35 of a lung disorder. The bag is interesting for a number of reasons. First the name, (spelled Elisabeth rather than the traditional Elizabeth) is nicely done in black beads, the y extending in typical early 19th century fashion, and the given name separated from the last name by a small design. Secondly, the light grey silk fabric top was found in very good condition as well as the grey cord handles. It is unlikely this is the original silk, though grey was the ''approved'' color for reticule tops, for some reason or other. Third, the pattern is separated from the name and top by a saw tooth design in red beads which is classic with these early purses. The beads themselves are fine to medium fine, the pattern a colorful one of a crystal ground terminated in a crystal twisted fringe.

As these purses were purchased in 1980 from antique dealers across the nation from one another, it shows that fine old purses which can be documented are still available to the collector and add greatly to the value and appeal of a collection.

Sophia B. Goodrich and Ellen Coxe have also left us a record of their bead accomplishments done in 1836 and 1838[*Plates 50 and 51*]. Note how similar the patterns are and though the beads are greatly magnified, how small and fine. The Cox purse is different in that it has a sterling frame when most reticules of the time were drawstrings. The very complex architectural ruins and landscape purses are neither dated nor signed but are equally fine. Each offers ample proof that the narrow top to which the bead work was attached was made of silk, or velvet, presently quite frayed. Later beadworkers were to confine their efforts merely to initials, in lieu of names.

THE AMERICAN INDIANS, particularly the Crow, Fox, Sioux, Ojibwa, Cree, Tuscarora, Arapaho, Plains, Woodlands, Plateau, Menominee, Blackfoot, and Pennacock were skilled beadworkers. They made purses and other articles both for their own use and for trade with the colonists and for sale at trading posts from 1860 onward.

THE USE OF glass beads from Europe commenced as early as 1675 and articles so decorated were of enormous value to the Indians. They used such techniques as weaving, netting, spotstitching and lazy stitching. Since all of these methods were also used by all beadworkers, a simplified explanation of each is of value to the collector.

SPOT STITCH BEADING

This is an effective method where an overall design is not required as the beads are threaded in the desired pattern such as a flower, leaf, or geometric laid on the material and sewn into place between sections of the pattern, such as every 3rd or 4th bead. Some designs were ''filled in'' with parallel rows of beads once the outer edges were established.

An invaluable source of information concerning Indian beading is found in *North American Indian Arts* (A Golden Guide, Western Publishing Company, Inc., Racine, Wisconsin, 1970).

BEAD WEAVING

Bead weaving was done both with and without benefit of a loom. When a small loom was used, about 30 warp threads were attached to the loom and the beads which had been accurately threaded on a beading needle, applied. In single weft weaving, one weft strand is passed through the beads above the warps. When double weft weaving, one weft strand is passed through the beads above the warps and the other below them. Cross warp weaving uses a wood heddle which separates the warp for the insertion of the beaded weft and the beads pushed tightly together. Woven patterns were generally elongated. It should be noted there is no foundation material—aside from the warp—in a sense the beading creates the material. The warp threads are always visible between the beads so the silk or warp material should not be a sharply contrasting color.

NETTING

Netted beading is done in various ways to produce netting in which the beads are substituted for knots or loops. It is an ancient type of finger weaving, though needles or weaving frames may be used. In simplified terms, a strand is fastened to a needle or wrapping it around a bobbin and passing it back over itself to make a series of loops. The loops were also twisted or knotted to produce nets.'' The intricate fringes on beaded bags, both domestic and European, used the netted bead-work techniques to great advantage. (See *Plate 56A* for excellent examples of knotted bead fringe.)

FIGURE 1

FIGURE 2

FIGURE 3

FIGURE 4

FIGURE 5

FIGURE 6

PLATE 53. *Fig. 1:* Old reticule *(Collection of Evelyn Wittsell)*. *Fig. 2:* Art Deco period purse *(Collection of Bronwen Heuer)*. *Fig. 3:* Fine bead with orange carnation design. *Fig. 4:* Butterfly motif *(Collection of Penelope More)*. *Fig. 5:* Bead handle and frame *(ibid Fig. 4)*. *Fig. 6:* Very old reticule *(courtesy "The Venerable Bead," Berkeley, California)*.

Indian beaded purses, which are obtained from time to time, are easily distinguished from other types of beading as they are colorful, the beads employed large, and a great portion of the naturalistic pattern was done in crystal tube and round beads. The purses were often made expressly for tourists and were not intended to be worn as the handles consisted of just two strands of twisted beads! The Tuscarora Indians sold their beadwork to the tourists visiting Niagara Falls as early as 1840 and many of these purses, made

of fine challis wool dyed a brilliant red, blue, and black were crowded with heavy crystal beads, padded in patterns which resemble the examples on *Plate 52*.

Lazy Stitch Beading

This method would appear to be the simplest beading technique of them all as shown in a beading guide of 1911. The material to be beaded was marked off by a series of dots spaced ⅓ of an inch apart over the entire surface. A needle was brought up from the underside of the material on the dot, beads were looped and then fastened securely to the underside on the same dot. The entire surface of the bag was thus covered with looped beads in a simple yet effective fashion which even an unskilled worker could readily handle. Another method was to string a desired number of beads, attach to the fabric at intervals of 8–10 beads—depending on the size of the bead and considering their weight—either horizontally or vertically, cover the entire surface of the fabric and fasten at the ends of the rows. The above is called a "Dew drop" design.

Originally the styles offered were the same as those which the Indians themselves favored; the straight-sided, elongated, practical bags which were gathered by drawstrings near the top and were done on fine supple animal skins. They were decorated with quills, shells, and colorful beads in simple yet handsome geometric patterns worked in subdued, harmonizing colors rather than the gaudy, overdone bags which they ultimately sold to the tourists. Early bags were flap style with rounded bottoms fastened by a hook and eye; later flat chatelaine type bags were more to the tourists' liking. Fringing often was done in the same size bead as used in the body of the purse. The small colorful purse with large straight cut end beads is probably of Canadian origin as the leaf appears to be a veined maple and the beaded handle is strung on stout cord. The beading is nicely executed and some of the beads are quite fine.

Shoulder bags, consisting of a band which passed behind the neck and over the shoulders leaving the bag resting on the chest were worn by Chippewa men, while yet another version passed over one shoulder and the bag was worn at the side. The designs were angular, the purses nearly square, the symmetrical patterns of naturalistic leaves, florals, arrows, stars, fruits and the like, were done in concentric shaded rows of brilliant colors, boldly executed.

Beadwork, following quillwork, began with the Indians from the eastern part of the United States as early as 1675 when the Europeans traded glass beads with them, in exchange for furs, scouting and other services. Floral motifs became popular in the mid and late 1800's possibly inspired by European embroideries.

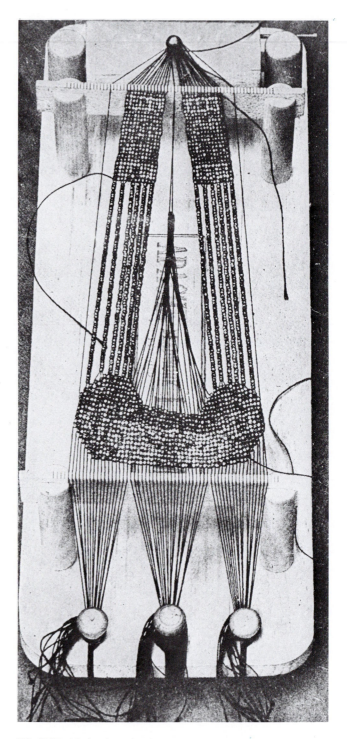

PLATE 52-A. Apache bead work loom.

A type of bag known as the "four tab" bag made by the Nez Perce and Athabascan tribes of western Canada were made of cloth, usually trade cloth in the shape of an inverted hand with four tabs, each tab was beaded and feathered.

FIGURE 1

FIGURE 5

FIGURE 4

FIGURE 6

FIGURE 2

FIGURE 3

PLATE 53-A. *Fig. 1:* Floral *(author's collection).* **Fig. 2:** *(Collection of Sharon Peterson).* **Fig. 3:** Old envelope-type *(courtesy "The Venerable Bead," Berkeley, California).* **Fig. 4:** Fine bead reticule *(Collection of Penelope More).* **Fig. 5:** *(author's collection).* **Fig. 6:** Fine bead reticule *(ibid Fig. 4).*

FIGURE 1

FIGURE 2

FIGURE 3

FIGURE 4

FIGURE 6

FIGURE 5

PLATE 54. *Figs. 1, 2, & 3: (Collection of Penelope More).*
Fig. 4: (Collection of Bronwen Heuer). **Figs. 5 & 6:** *(author's collection).*

FIGURE 1

FIGURE 2

FIGURE 3

FIGURE 5

FIGURE 6

PLATE 54-A. *Fig. 1: (courtesy "A Stitch In Time," Richmond, California). Fig. 2: (author's collection). Fig. 3: (Collection of Michaela Bennet). Fig. 4: (Collection of Penelope More). Fig. 5: (Collection of Bronwen Heuer). Fig. 6: (Collection of Sharon Peterson).*

FIGURE 4

FIGURE 1

FIGURE 2

FIGURE 3

FIGURE 4

PLATE 55. *Fig. 1:* Crystal and white envelope with tapestry insert. 6 1/2″ by 6″ from Germany *(author's collection).* *Fig. 2:* Reticule with oak leaf motif *(courtesy "The Venerable Bead," Berkeley, California).* *Fig. 3:* Beaded pattern and matching frame *(Collection of Bronwen Heuer).* *Fig. 4:* Floral of fine beads, dated 1917 *(Collection of Michaela Bennett).* *Figs. 5 & 6:* Sentimental reticules *(ibid Fig. 2).*

FIGURE 5

FIGURE 6

PLATE 55-A.
Fig. 1: 19th Century France with Russian motto reading "In remembrance of" *(Costume Institute of The Metropolitan Museum of Art, gift of Mrs. Louis Coblentz).* *Fig. 2:* Abstract pattern *(Collection of Penelope More).* *Fig. 3:* Unusual French steel cut Collection of Mrs. Pat Costello). *Fig. 4:* 19th Century French pastoral *(ibid Fig. 1).* *Fig. 5:* Egyptian motif with both sides shown *(courtesy "A Stitch In Time," Richmond, California).* *Fig. 6:* Netted figural *(author's collection).*

FIGURE 1

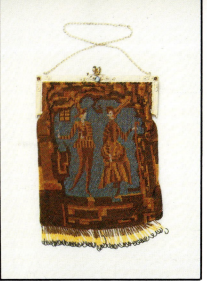

FIGURE 6

FIGURE 4

FIGURE 2

FIGURE 3

FIGURE 5

PLATE 55-A.
Fig. 1: 19th Century France with Russian motto reading "In remembrance of" *(Costume Institute of The Metropolitan Museum of Art, gift of Mrs. Louis Coblentz).* *Fig. 2:* Abstract pattern *(Collection of Penelope More).* *Fig. 3:* Unusual French steel cut Collection of Mrs. Pat Costello). *Fig. 4:* 19th Century French pastoral *(ibid Fig. 1).* *Fig. 5:* Egyptian motif with both sides shown *(courtesy "A Stitch In Time," Richmond, California).* *Fig. 6:* Netted figural *(author's collection).*

FIGURE 1

FIGURE 6

FIGURE 4

FIGURE 2

FIGURE 3

FIGURE 5

226

FIGURE 1

FIGURE 3

FIGURE 4

FIGURE 2

FIGURE 5

FIGURE 6

PLATE 56. *Fig. 1:* Tulip bottom reticule *(author's collection).* *Fig. 2:* Fine bead scenic *(ibid Fig. 1).* *Fig. 3:* Sterling frame and handle *(Collection of Michaela Bennett).* *Fig. 4:* Memorial purse, c. 1830 *(courtesy "The Venerable Bead,").* *Fig. 5:* Message reticule reading "My name is found here" *(ibid Fig. 4).* *Fig. 6:* Floral with Greek key border *(ibid Fig. 4).*

227

FIGURE 1

FIGURE 2

FIGURE 3

FIGURE 4

FIGURE 5

FIGURE 6

PLATE 56-A. *Fig. 1:* Fine monochrome with silver frame *(Collection of Penelope More). **Fig. 2:*** Geometric, with ornate fringe *(Collection of Michaela Bennett). **Fig. 3:*** Elegant plated frame and flared skirt *(author's collection). **Fig. 4:*** French-cut steel *(Collection of Mrs. Michael Conte). **Fig. 5:*** French cut steel with unique fringe and color scheme *(ibid Fig. 3). **Fig. 6:*** French-cut steel in delicate shades *(ibid Fig. 1).*

FIGURE 1

FIGURE 2

FIGURE 3

PLATE 57. *Fig. 1:* Paisley, over-the-wrist one piece bag *(Collection of Penelope More).* *Fig. 2:* Triangular gold bead. *Fig. 3:* Egyptian head *(Collection of Sharon Peterson).* *Fig. 4:* Gold thread over satin *(ibid Fig. 3).* *Fig. 5:* Elaborate scenic in plain frame. European *(author's collection).* *Fig. 6:* Embroidered and beaded handle and frame *(courtesy "Coleman's Curiosity Shop").*

FIGURE 5

FIGURE 4

FIGURE 6

229

Just as the Chinese had their phoenix bird, so the Indians had a thunder bird which they believed descended from heaven and that from him man sprang. The thunderbird is nearly impossible to recognize as a bird, but the symbol was prevalent with many tribes.

The Iroquois embossed their velour pouches by crowding the pony beads and raising the design with padding, a typical example is shown on *Plate 52, Fig. 2. Figure 4* on the same plate has the earmarks of Apache work, as does *Figure 1* (not old) but the same geometric designs were, with modifications, used across the continent. Either the entire bag, the exterior or just the interior was made of buckskin, meaning smoked deer, buffalo, antelope or elk hides tanned in this manner. White was a color used on choice pieces.

PLATE 57-A. *Fig. 1:* Crystal beads on black background *(Collection of Mildred Strouss).* **Fig. 2:** Art Nouveau *(author's collection).* **Fig. 3:** Geometric with Peking glass handles *(Collection of Bronwen Heuer).* **Fig. 4:** Colored French beads *(author's collection).* **Fig. 5:** A European scenic with medium beads *(author's collection).* **Fig. 6:** Heavily beaded, curved frame *(Collection of Mrs. Gene Gittlesohn).*

FIGURE 1

FIGURE 2

FIGURE 3

FIGURE 4

FIGURE 5

FIGURE 6

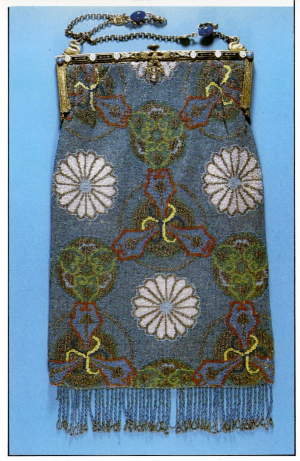

FIGURE 4

Sinew was used by some tribes for applying the bead work and fine needles by others.

Quillwork, a technique which originated with the American Indian and practiced only by them, consisted of sewing the dyed quills of the porcupine onto garments and accessories. Beads were so much easier to use that they supplanted the quills eventually. These items today command thousands of dollars and ideally belong in museums where they can be properly cared for and admired by future generations.

MANY PURSES CONTAIN a bead or two which appear to be obvious errors, in fact so obvious that one

PLATE 58. Solid bugle beads (*Collection of Sharon Peterson*). *Fig. 2:* Tambour, gold thread and pearls (*courtesy "A Stitch In Time," Richmond, California*). *Fig. 3:* Oriental seed pearls and crystal (*Collection of Judith Osborne*). *Fig. 4:* A lively pattern (*author's collection*). *Fig. 5:* Paisley fine beaded purse (*Collection of the late Doris Gladding Hass, San Jose, California*).

FIGURE 1

FIGURE 3

FIGURE 5

FIGURE 2

wonders why the maker allowed an otherwise beautifully executed work of art to be marred by a white bead, for instance, in a field of maroon or a black bead in a rose petal. There are several explanations from which the reader may make a choice, although all are plausible and it is possible various explanations apply in differing situations. The most romantic and historic is the fear of the artisan to compete with the Almighty in creating a perfect piece of handiwork. The Lord alone, they reason, is capable of producing a flawless work of art so the artisan shows his humility by deliberately making an error so evident that no offense is shown to the diety. This practice is followed by many cultures even today and is a touching symbol in an egotistical world.

The second explanation is more mundane and realizing the complexity of some of the patterns and the tedious nature of the work, one easily ascribed to;

the error once made in misreading the pattern while stringing the beads would be virtually impossible to rectify when discovered and the beadweaver simply hoped the mistake would not be too noticeable.

Lastly, as many of the purses have passed from one owner to another, a bead may have been replaced at a later date by an inexpert needleworker with whatever beads were at hand, rather than the correct shade or size, to prevent further damage to the design.

Keeping the ''humility bead'' practice in mind may allow one to reconsider an otherwise perfect beaded purse when a glaring error proves offensive.

Plates 53–59 endeavor to present as wide a selection of beaded examples as possible. They cover a time span of at least one hundred and fifty years, from approximately 1800 to the mid 1930's.

FIGURE 1   FIGURE 2   FIGURE 3   FIGURE 5

FIGURE 4   FIGURE 6

PLATE 58-A. *Fig. 1:* Solid carnival beads *(Collection of Mrs. Gene Gittlesohn).* *Fig. 2:* Fine medallion center floral *(Courtesy ''Ladyfingers,'' Carmel, California).* *Fig. 3:* Blue sequin purse, c. 1930. *Fig. 4:* Coralene beads on black satin. *Fig. 5:* Unusual red beads with celluloid frame *(author's collection).* *Fig. 6:* Josef of Paris. Tambour and seed pearls *(courtesy ''A Stitch In Time,'' Richmond, California).*

FIGURE 1

FIGURE 2

FIGURE 3

FIGURE 4

PLATE 59. Four outstanding examples of beading. Each is by virtue of pattern, beading, and condition, worth in excess of $400.00, and would be very hard to find today. The patterns are so complicated they are not likely to have been made later than 1910 and possibly much earlier as some may have been reframed. *Fig. 1:* Huge domestic beadwork *(author's collection). Fig. 2:* Steel beaded from Austria *(ibid Fig. 1). Fig. 3:* Extra fine beads *(Collection of Penelope More). Fig. 4:* Extra fine beads *(Collection of Michaela Bennett).*

CHAPTER 4
THE CHATELAINE PURSE

No purse is more romantic yet practical than the chatelaine. Though the term is unfamiliar to many people, when acquainted with the purse they recall a grandmother or other elderly person who at one time wore one of these unusual purses.

The term chatelaine comes from the French and means keeper of the fort or castle, the keeper of the keys, mistress of the chateau or the castellan who was the wife of the keeper. It is the combination of the French words laine (wool) and chateau (house or mansion), so it is easy to see how the keeper of the keys to the linen closet or armoire where the valuables were kept locked, was once known as the chatelaine. Eventually the meaning was transferred from the person to the object and the chatelaine became an ornamental hook, clasp, or pin worn at the waist of the mistress of the house or castellan, containing a series of chains

from which objects such as a pomander, keys, watch, purse, trinkets, sewing implements, or other small objects were hung for ready use.

The purse chatelaine had only one hook, one end of which was attached to a ½″ ring which in turn connected a pair of chains to the purse frame. It is nearly impossible to assign exact dates to the use of the chatelaine as skirt widths waxed and waned tremendously, but as early as the 12th century the chatelaine hook was worn over the girdle, then over a narrow belt and by the late 19th century was hooked over the waistband of the long slender skirts then much in vogue. In 1900 the Gibson Girl came into her own wearing a white shirtwaist, high stiff collar with bow tie, a skirt so nipped in at the waist, the feminine figure resembled an hour glass, and a chatelaine purse hung at her left side.

The chatelaine was worn on a four inch chain

PLATE 60. Four old chatelaines from the author's collection. *Fig. 2:* Beaded jet with tennis motif frame. *Fig. 3:* Very old. Sterling frame and hook, bargello work.

FIGURE 1

FIGURE 2

FIGURE 3

FIGURE 4

PLATE 61. Chatelaine decorated with melon seeds.

aluminum or other metals. The choicest examples were sterling, though one rare example is of aluminum which was such a novel mineral when first introduced in 1824 that it took precedence over precious metals. It is not as attractive as sterling or plate, however, as it has a dull finish resembling pewter. It had the advantage of being comparatively light weight, resisted oxidation, and was very durable. The fasteners ranged from simple twist, plunger or stud mechanisms, spring or snap closings of various complexities, to ball and socket and bar latches. Fringes and tassels were of the cut steel variety and were simple loopings or strands, though not all chatelaines were so trimmed.

A RARITY AMONG purses today is the finger ring purse which may be mistaken for the chatelaine purse as both have loops, but the finger ring purse has a much larger ring, approximately 1 inch in diameter, and contains a large bead which prevents the attached chain from slipping beyond it and acts as a jewel on the finger. The finger ring purse shown [*Plate 66, Fig. 1*] is a handsome sterling example resembling a miniature carpet bag with exquisite repousse work. It is hallmarked Birmingham, 1906, and inscribed to Anna Fristedt.

Such purses were naturally made of light weight materials such as sterling silver, gold mesh, soft leathers such as doeskin or suedes, and knit or crochet of very fine beads. Finger purses were rather small ranging in size from two to four inches in width to four and a half inches in depth. They were expressly designed for their jewel-like effect and were ill suited for other than the smallest objects and a bit of change. Worn dangling from a finger they were not intended as chatelaines as they are far too elegant and fragile. There is little doubt that they would have aroused attention and they were as beautiful as it was possible for the silversmith or other artisan to create.

ALTHOUGH THE CHATELAINE bag was usually round, approximately five inches in diameter, it was also constructed in oblong, square, pear, and oval shapes, among others. Rectangular purses ranged from 6–8 inches on the average including the frame and fringe. Most popular was the rounded shape of solidly beaded knit, the design whorl commencing in the center, swirled in petals or sections, or merely beaded from side to side with no discernable pattern. The universal bead was cut steel, very fine, beveled flush on two sides, of random sizes or flattened to catch the light. Earlier versions of the chatelaine from the 19th century were beaded in colored glass beads, both fine and extra fine sizes, the patterns being quite traditional florals, commonly backed with velvet, plush or other high piled material which prevented the inevitable damage to the beads which would occur if the beaded

and the hook added another 1–3 inches to the overall dimensions. Not all hooks were of the same depth; some were as long as 2¼″, others as shallow as 1″, but the connecting ring was nearly always ½″ in diameter. One hook contained a patented narrow bar with serrated edges controlled by a plunger spring which when depressed gripped the skirt material firmly and prevented movement or loss of the purse. The front of these chatelaines was always heavily embossed in decorative motifs which ranged from mythical figures, leaves, crowns, fleur-de-lis, rosettes, grapes, birds and animals, fish, coats of arms, cat tails, Neptune, king of the seas, shells, cherubs, waterlilies, women's heads with flowing hair, nothing fanciful escaped the imagination of the designers of purse frames and chatelaines. The designs were done in high relief rather than intaglio and constitute the most striking element of the chatelaine for today's collector.

Even the links of the chains were sometimes ornamented with raised designs, though they were more likely to be simple interlocking ovals, twists, disks, cables and double rings.

Unfortunately some chains were made of steel which oxidized and rusted when not heavily silver plated, but for the most part they were made of brass plated with silver or nickel, gun metal, sterling, and

FIGURE 3

FIGURE 2

PLATE 62. Four beaded chatelaines.
Fig. 1: Sterling silver frame and hook, fine beading, c. 1870, origin unknown *(The Costume Institute, Metropolitan Museum of Art, gift of Mr. Samuel B. Hawley).* **Fig. 2:** Velvet with steel beads and silk, c. 1870–85, France *(Museum of Fine Arts, Boston, Elizabeth Day McCormick Fund).* **Fig. 3:** Ornate frame and closing, fine beads, c. 1870–85, France *(ibid Fig. 2).* **Fig. 4:** Made by Aunt Susan Wetherbee Cushman, date unknown, United States *(Costume Institute, Metropolitan Museum of Art, gift of Mrs. Frederick M. Ives).*

FIGURE 1

FIGURE 4

236

FIGURE 5

PLATE 63. *Fig. 1:* Brown pigskin with embossed silver mount and hook *(Costume Institute of The Metropolitan Museum of Art, gift of Mrs. Leopold Arnaud)*. *Fig. 2:* Cut plush velvet with embroidery, 1870 *(author's collection)*. *Fig. 3:* Sterling purse with maker's mark, c. 1900, Russia *(Collection of Emily Rothstein)*. *Fig. 4:* Steel beads, aluminum frame *(author's collection)*. *Fig. 5:* Ornate metal frame, suede back *(ibid Fig. 4)*.

FIGURE 1

FIGURE 2

FIGURE 4

FIGURE 3

237

tion. The first purse measures 3 ¼ × 4 ¼ inches including the narrow sterling frame chased at the ends with a stylized fish and terminated at the bottom with a pretty sterling bead-like tassel. There is a tiny ring in the center of the frame but no other chains or attachments which would indicate how this purse was carried. The small ring might be intended for a larger chatelaine ring connector. The body is of tiny carnival colored beads with an indistinct crystal bead monogram in the center which appears to be an F.S. Confusion arises over the sterling hallmark IK G which might be that of John Kidder, London mark, 1780. Although the purse is entirely hand made and sewn of the coarsest of materials the antiquity of the mark is suspect.

The third purse is also pouch shaped and made of silk bargello stitch in tones of gold, blues, and white trimmed with silver thread and tassels. The lining is of handwoven linen, with a finer linen tape both in natural linen color, obviously *very* old. The sterling frame is marked in an octagon punch, triple trefoil, a crowned H and W H for William Hull, Chester mark of 1780–90. Too many marks are as troubling as too few!

Plate 60, Fig. 4 is unfortunately in extremely poor condition but as it is unique it was included. The side worn nearest the body is of well preserved, smooth, cocoa colored leather. When new, the fabric front (backed by tanned leather) was solidly beaded with carnival beads and large flat backed green and red glass beads which were sewn over the raised pattern. The glass beads were drilled and side attached by coarse black thread. The beads themselves are not uncommon but used in this fashion on a chatelaine they are rare indeed.

PLATE 64. Chatelaine cuts from *Lady Godey,* 1858-1875.

FIGURE 1   FIGURE 2

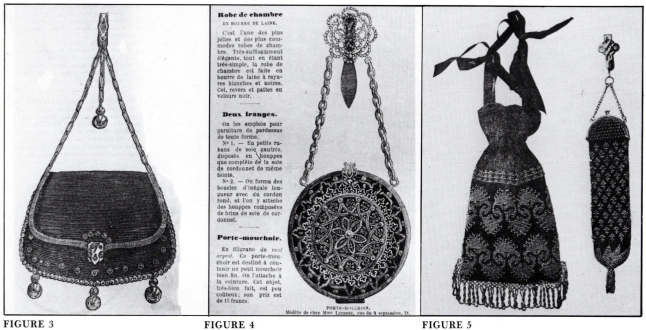

FIGURE 3   FIGURE 4   FIGURE 5

FIGURE 1

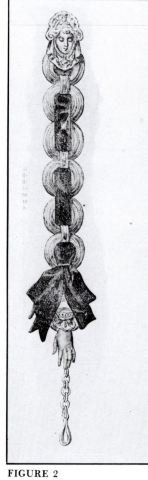

FIGURE 2

PLATE 65. Chatelaines from *Lady Godey* (1858), *La Mode Illustré* (1875) and *Priscilla Beadwork* (1911).

FIGURE 3

FIGURE 4

Parisian chatelaine, wrought in gold, to hold a woman's purse on her belt. *The Workshop.*

FIGURE 5

239

FIGURE 1

FIGURE 2

FIGURE 3

FIGURE 5

PLATE 66. All sterling chatelaines from the author's collection except *Fig. 1*, a finger purse dated 1906, engraved script ''Anna Fristedt'' courtesy of Maury Rosen.

FIGURE 4

The semi circular frame is centered by a large crown surmounted by a plunger resembling the traditional cross used on crowns. Within the wreath scrolls on either side of the crown, a young girl gazes ahead. The detail on one side is still sharp enough to clearly discern a jewelled ornament encircling her head. The spring equipped brass hook, signed ''Perfection'' is decorated with a typical Art Nouveau water lily and clover. Dimensions are 8″ × 4¾″.

Chatelaines in the closing years of the 19th century were attached to the gracefully curved purse frame by rings soldered at the top of the frame equidistant from the fastening device. The gold Parisian chatelaine [*Plate 65, Fig. 5*] which holds a woman's purse to her belt is quite different, in that it contains an oval opening below the ornate bow ribbon and suspended lotus blossoms which could have been intended to hold a miniature painting on vellum or ivory. The side sections might have terminated in hooks, as elaborate chatelaines of the 18th century contained upwards of five hooks; though the caption for this drawing did not indicate either circa or additional accessories for this handsome, costly piece of precious jewelry.

Nineteenth century fashion books referred to the chatelaine and aumoniere interchangeably; however, the aumoniere was simpler than the chatelaine and required only loops, straps, or chains which passed through the essential belt or girdle, whereas the chatelaine entails a hook which slid over the pocket or skirt top in addition to other devices which encircled the waist. Some of these chain belts fell low on the hips rather than fitting closely about the waist. The purse was attached to the chain and hung some distance down the thigh. Both terms had been in common use for centuries.

Figure 2 on *Plate 60* is an unusual sort of purse as few chatelaines were beaded in any sort of beads but cut steel, yet this one has a body and fringe of the finest jet beads knit with brown silk. Was this deliberate or did the knitter not have the black silk and merely proceeded with the darkest color on hand? As with other chatelaines the beaded outer layer is nowhere attached to the soft leather lining aside from the frame. The square shape is definitely not traditional. The unmarked frame of highly embossed plate showing daisies and buds emerging from a spiral cornucopia shaped vase meet at the top in a stylized French bow and crossed oddly shaped tennis racquets with an applied tennis ball adhering to the strings.

ONE OF THE earliest references to the chatelaine was made in a letter written in 1821 from a correspondent in Paris to an American friend, ''When the corner of the white handkerchief of fine lawn had only a little embroidery, then one of these corners served as a

purse to the French ladies; and after tying a knot they fastened their ring of keys to it. Now these handkerchiefs are so beautifully embroidered, that they require more management in the display of them; and those fashionable dames who will not take the trouble of carrying a little basket or ridicule, have a silver purse they fashion to their belt.''

In 1863 the British magazine *Queen* noted, ''For some time past chatelaine bags have been very popular in England. They have been worn at the side suspended from the waistband. These have generally been made of leather and studded with steel, and for travelling have been found very convenient. For home wear they are made of gimp or embroidered velvet.'' Though the phrase ''for some time past'' is vague indeed, ancient engravings indicate the chatelaine had been worn for centuries, though intermittently, according to the dictates of skirt widths, as previously noted. It is significant that leather is mentioned for this was the material most used for chatelaines over the centuries, though all-leather examples are found only in museums today.

It was a relatively simple matter to add a chatelaine hook to some purses converting them to wear on the belt or skirt, others were chatelaines from the outset. *Plate 62, Fig. 4* shows a beautifully beaded purse with a double chain which seems overly long and the hook is somehow dissimilar to it. It has a plunger clasp but neither it nor *Figure 2,* discussed in the next paragraph, are fitted with that large ring found on nearly every other example. They are not devaluated in any way, merely curiosities, as their owners may have altered the chains to suit the prevailing fashion.

Most extraordinary were the French chatelaines C. 1870–85 which were so nearly identical they were virtually indistinguishable from one another in size, color, material, workmanship, pictorial detail, fringe and each had a side fold-over flap opening which in itself was distinctive. They must have been worked by the same person using the same basic factors on each. The only way they differed was that the one shown [*Plate 62, Fig. 2*] was fitted with a chatelaine hook and chain, the other has a cord handle. Note the large tubular bead used on the fringe to the one above it. The same bead is used on the body as part of the decoration. The leaves and flower appear to be stump worked or raised embroidery with couched cording. It is also fortunate the Museum of Fine Arts in Boston is in possession of both purses.

A curious purse appeared in the *Delineator,* August, 1904. A replica of a reticule from 1850, it consisted of a combination of melon or cantaloupe seeds and steel cut beads in a design which formed a fragile cage about a satin pouch completed with a ribbon carrier. The directions indicate the pattern would have been relatively simple for the accomplished bag maker

FIGURE 1

PLATE 67. *Fig. 1:* An 1880 photo showing a woman wearing a chatelaine purse.

of the day, but they must have been delicate as none have been discovered in present day collections. The chatelaine shown is of crocheted silk and the bag is mounted on a silver frame. [*Plate 61, Fig. 1*] Variations of designs are suggested by combining different colored beads with the seeds.

241

CHAPTER 5
THE MINIATURE PURSE

Almost every collection includes a few miniature purses, some so small they are mistakenly thought to be dolls' accessories. Actually they were called sovereign purses in England, and "Gold Dollar Purses" in the United States. Made in sterling mesh, leather with an expandable top, sometimes called a gate top, velvets with steel snap fasteners, solid brass, steel beads with gilt metal mountings, exquisitely carved ivory with brass handles, mother-of-pearl, circular shaped beaded with sterling or more commonly plated stamped designs. They have comical or sentimental motifs, silver enameled, flat pouches worked in bright colored tiny bead patterns, handleless oval shaped tortoise shell with applied piqué work in gold; the variations were endless.

Since they are so small they can often be purchased for far less than a purse of more conventional dimensions. They are seldom large enough for more than a coin or two for that was their original purpose. The chatelaine rosary case made by Whiting Chain Company between 1911–1929 (which has the finest chain mesh imaginable) enameled in two pastel colors and decorated with a cross and secular figure in low relief, might originally have been worn by a Roman Catholic nun. Descriptive literature from this firm indicates they manufactured several styles of this case in various simple patterns, and a mystery was thus solved for a collector who had wondered about her tiny purse for some years.

The smallest purse found is a mere one inch square and accomodates a dime or similar small coin. [*Plate 41, Fig. 3a*] It is made of sterling mesh and has a diminutive chain handle which fits over a finger, provided the finger is slender. A scale model of the larger sized bag, it could well have been a salesman's sample to show his firm's latest styles to wholesale customers. As small versions of the product were space saving and less ponderous for the representatives of manufactured goods to carry, items ranging from cut glass to furniture are occasionally found today and command premium prices.

Around the turn of the century a most significant purse became popular. It appeals to collectors today for good reasons; it was beautiful, useful, and relatively inexpensive. The general contours were oblong shaped measuring approximately 3 × 5 inches; though some were smaller, few were larger. They were made of sterling silver, embossed—some on both sides—and floridly monogrammed in Old English script, occasionally dated as in example [Plate 41, Fig. 3c]. They had fairly standard ten inch flat oval link chain, and push release snap closings.

Their interesting aspect was the fitted interiors for they varied from mere coin holders. Most common were nickel, dime and quarter flat disks which depressed with the aid of a spring, to elaborately designed mirror, cigarette holder, wee sterling pencil and ivory writing pad, powder and rouge compartments, card holding receptacle, and glove leather currency holder creations. They were worn over the wrist and were just the right size; any larger and they would have been cumbersome, smaller they would have been useless. No handsommer purse was ever manufactured and just about every silversmith made them in an infinite variety. Like the German silver purses, they were featured in advertisements found in women's magazines as incentives to salesmanship (or in this case salesladyship), among the prizes given for inducing one's acquaintances to subscribe to the magazine, through glowing wholesale jewelers' ads, and through more legitimate channels. A number of these lovely smallish purses were shown and discussed in Chapter II.

Among the miniature beaded purses are found the elegant gold, silver, and pearl French loomed purses measuring 4 × 3½ inches, mere junior sizes of the more familiar full sized versions, silk crocheted monocolored beaded pouchettes swagged with bead fringes and handles no larger than needed to accommodate a comb, mad money, a handkerchief or other trivia.

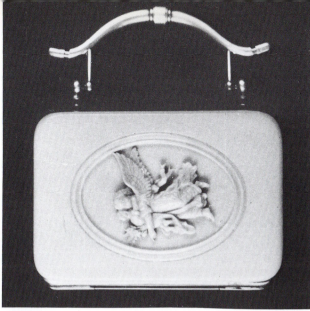

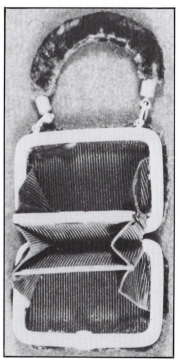

PLATE 70. Miniature or child's purses. *Fig. 1:* Deeply carved ivory with brass handle and angel motif, silk lined *(author's collection).* **Fig. 2:** Tam O'Shanter purse with stolen kiss motif *(Collection of Gerri Levine).* **Fig. 3:** Deeply carved ivory with leather handle in floral motif *(Museum of Fine Arts, Boston, gift of Mrs. Yves Henry Buhler).* **Fig. 4:** Trunk shaped miniature with embossed brass frame.

ANOTHER PURSE WHICH resembles a child's bag is in the shape of a trunk with substantial brass fittings and curved handle, [*Plate 70, Fig. 4*] covered with what appears to be fur or sheared lamb's wool. The interior of the purse has a brass frame beautifully chased with flowers and leaves and the center section is joined by a hinged cap which forms a coin and currency receptacle. The lining is deep purple waled-cord, accordion pleated to hold calling cards no larger than 3¾ × 2¾ inches. A supremely feminine purse, the fine fittings indicate it was more than a childs' toy.

The four choice little purses [*Plate 69*](which Lady Godey of 1859 called "gold dollar purses") measuring a little less than 1½ inches by 1¾ inches *would* hold a gold dollar of that day, but nothing else. There is no explanation of these purses nor directions for making them so they remain a mystery. Were they gold dollar gift holders, coin purses for reticules, were they beaded or petit point, were they conversation purses to be admired when held in the hand, were they exercises for the young to sharpen their needle skills; who knows?

The colored illustrations indicate the patterns so clearly that directions were not needed; skilled workers of that day were accustomed to inadequate directions in sewing, cooking, canning, in fact every phase of the homemaker's life was like a trackless path, and experience counted for all.

Many, though by no means all, of the tiny purses are a sort of combination calling card and change

FIGURE 1   FIGURE 10   FIGURE 3

FIGURE 7

PLATE 68. Miniature purses. ***Fig. 1:*** Red plus, mid-19th century *(author's collection)*. ***Fig. 2:*** Sterling silver with dime for comparison *(ibid Fig. 1)*. ***Fig. 3:*** Collection of Tam O'Shanters *(courtesy "The Venerable Bead," Berkeley, California)*. ***Fig. 4:*** Small Indian pouch *(ibid Fig. 3)*. ***Fig. 5:*** Enameled purse, c. 1920 *(Collection of Michaela Bennett)*. ***Fig. 6:*** Beaded crochet purse *(Collection of Bronwen Heuer)*. ***Fig. 7:*** Four old purses including two ring purses *(ibid Fig. 3)*. ***Fig. 8:*** Rosary case plus two beaded purses, one with a scenic *(Collection of Sharon Peterson)*. ***Fig. 9:*** Four old purses including one chatelaine *(ibid Fig. 3)*. ***Fig. 10:*** Beaded envelope purse with strap handle *(ibid Fig. 1)*.

FIGURE 5   FIGURE 6

FIGURE 9

FIGURE 4

FIGURE 2

PLATE 69. *Lady Godey* gold dollar purse, 1858.

FIGURE 8

purse. Their interiors consisted of a number of open sections, usually covered in bright colored silk, and containing a brass hinged cover which bound the section for small coins and folding currency together. *Plate 68, Fig. 7* shows four diminutive purses, two of which are finger ring purses, and a solidly beaded purse with two steel rods which allow the narrow neck to open slightly for the insertion of a coin or two and possibly a small container of smelling salts; nothing more. This beaded purse dating from around 1800 was made on a mould, a process in which the bead network is not sewn down to any fabric and the mould allowed the purse to take its exact shape; then the beaded mesh was placed over a more substantial fabric for strength. Needless to say this type of beaded purse is the most fragile and demands utmost care in handling.

CHAPTER 6
RARE AND UNUSUAL PURSES

Not all purses were intended for utility alone; some are amazingly beautiful, amusing, startling, outsized, deliberately hidden from view, weird combinations of purse and muff, momentarily faddish, of materials no longer permitted to be manufactured or imported, or have a limited appeal. They are all fun, however, and deserve attention if only through enhancing a collection as oddities.

One of the most eye catching materials periodically in vogue is the sequin. It is difficult to conceive this shining, flat, metallic disk being used as trimmings for clothing and accessories in 1767 when Diderot compiled his famous *Recueil de Planches sur les Sciences et les Arts.* Originating in Venice, Italy, in the 13th century, they were made of gold and silver, later they were variously colored, sized, and shaped, and the disk was drilled in various places. Originally attached by hand, they still are, so each disk overlaps the other in rows to conform to the shape of the object being decorated. Applying these paillettes, as they are known in beading circles, is a costly and time consuming process and sequin purses are intended only for evening wear today. The example [*Plate 58A, Fig. 3*] has a simple shape and the blue beading and frame indicate it is from the 1930's.

Most elegant among the beautiful evening purses are the gold thread bags from France. When gold threads are used the patterns are raised, and relatively simple bead or rhinestone sets accentuate the designs and exquisite workmanship. The purse on *Plate 57, Fig. 4* has a gracefully curved frame surmounted with medium sized pearls, a rhinestone set twist closing, matching patterns on each side, "Made in France" stamped in gold on the white faille lining, and a beveled mirror in matching case. A sure sign of quality in any object be it a purse, furniture, toilet set or hanging mirrors, is beveling, (the slanted indentation on the edge of the mirror which is hand done). Beveling has always been expensive and when found on a purse mirror—provided the mirror is original to the purse—it denotes a superior product. The attention

to detail is seen in the prong set rhinestones and the tiny gold beads applied at the pouch seams. Another distinguishing feature is the small brass tab, ranging in size from ½-¾ inches long, in the shape of an oak leaf, wreath, standing basket of flowers, circlet, or abstract geometric shape, among others, to match the Art Deco designs used during the period. On purses using this type of closing, these tabs attached to a ring near the plunger. They were held when depressing the plunger to separate the sides of the frame and though they are frequently missing now, the ring will still be there indicating their former presence. Invariably found on quality French purses, they are also found on high quality domestic purses as well.

Women made their own personalized purses of silks and satins which they embroidered on both exterior and interior. In the case of a purse made by B.M. Gould, every stitch is done by hand including the satin stitched name and puckered mirror holder, done in green thread on peach colored satin. The simplicity of the exterior is noteworthy as it is done in diamond shapes gathered so the diamonds appear to be raised; again, all the stitches are hand done.

Few handbags are as elaborate as the Josef of Paris hand beaded and tamboured purse shown [*Plate 58A, Fig. 6*]. The lustrous flat sided pearls are top sewn (about every third or fourth bead is attached to the wide silk tapestry base) in a whorled pattern. The front center is delicately tamboured in pastel buds and full blown flowers. The frame is set with baguette and rose cut rhinestones completed by a short gilt chain. The lining is immaculate white satin, neatly fitted with mirror, lipstick, and compact compartments. The flawless workmanship is superior to that done in the Orient in the 1930's.

A handsome purse in black satin has knotted fringe at the base, dainty embroidered floral circlets and monogramed K.F. Both this and the "Gould" purse are nearly a foot square and are elegant in dimension and simplicity. The frames were purchased at local establishments in advance of making the purse

PLATE 71. Satin, with monogram "KF".

and sewn onto the frames at home, as opposed to the beaded purse which was often sent to the factory for assembling when completed, as this finishing touch required a considerable degree of skill.

AMONG THE UNUSUAL purses which are more odd than beautiful is a small comical one which comes straight from the Roaring Twenties [*Plate 80A, Fig. 3*]. The frame is of inexpensive steel with an impressed figure in an oval and some crude swags, a body of soft pigskin, and attached to the frame is an unusual single twist which allows a garter and hook attachment, the other end of which was joined to milady's girdle hose support. The purse was thus kept out of sight and the flapper's "mad money" was secure from her escort's knowledge, or anyone else's for that matter. Ugly as this purse is, there is something amusing and touching about it. Vanda Foster mentions an English version called "Keptonu" which athletic ladies kept thus hidden while playing tennis or skating.

The fierce little mink with shining eyes and vicious, bared teeth was sacrificed to make this strange purse during the days when stoles, stone martin skins and fur capes insured that a lady was fashionably dressed. The drawstrings are mink tipped and the body is of beige satin damask, badly frayed and disintegrating with age. The overall measurements are

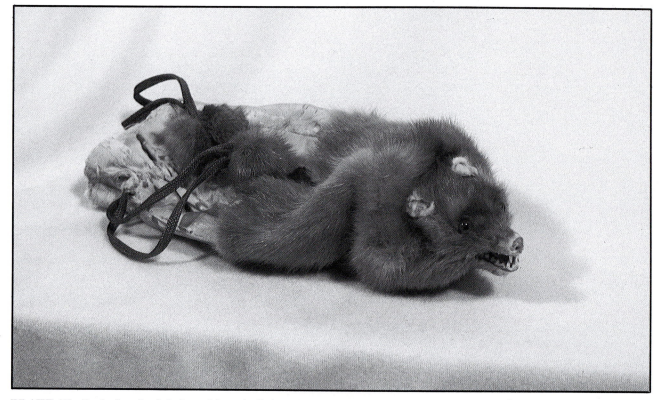

PLATE 72. Reticule of mink fur with satin lining (*author's collection*).

247

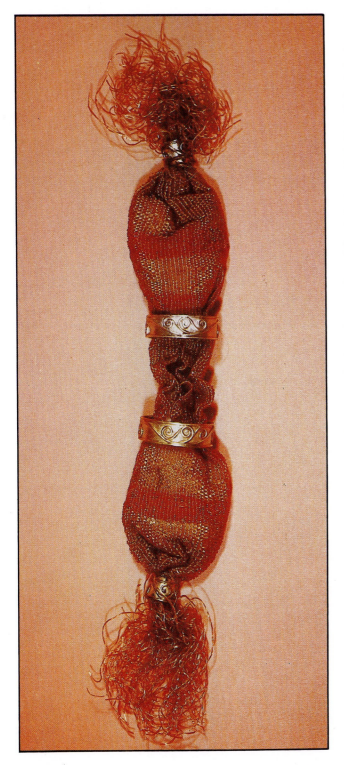

PLATE 73. Most unique purse in the world—"The Silk Purse From a Sow's Ear" *(courtesy Authur D. Little Inc., Cambridge, Massachusetts).*

12 inches in length by six inches wide [*Plate 72*].

Perhaps the most unusual purse ever made was the result of a dare. Arthur D. Little was the founder of a firm of consulting engineers and experts 1,300 strong who are capable of solving problems for governments, corporations, individuals, and municipalities. In short, anyone who has a technological, sociological, or agricultural dilemma anywhere in the world may find a solution by consulting this Cambridge, Massachusetts, firm. Dr. Little literally accepted the challenge of making a "silk purse out of a sow's ear" in 1921, by chemically reducing a batch of sow's ears to gelatin and tissues from which a fiber, dyed red, was spun and loomed into two miser's purses. The one shown may be seen at the Cambridge headquarters and the other is on display at the Smithsonian Institution in Washington, D.C. [*Plate 73*].

Quoting from a tongue-in-cheek paper by the firm, "We admit frankly that it is not very strong or very good silk, and that there is no present industrial value in making it from glue.... We have no intention of producing sow's ear silk for the market. We made this silk purse from a sow's ear because we wanted to, because it might serve as an example to clients who come to us with their ambitions or their troubles, and also as a contribution to philosophy.

"The most discouraging thing to hear, if you are interested in real progress and in the forward march of events, or more particularly if you have set your heart on doing something that you believe should be done, is some old saw that is repeated merely because the words that tell it have been learned parrot-wise....

"Things that everybody thinks he knows only because he has learned the words that say it, are poisons to progress. The only way to get ahead is to dig in, to study, to find out, to reason out theories, to test them—and then to hold fast to that which is good...." Amen!

MUFFS HAVE BEEN in and out of fashion since 1620 when they were sported by fashionable women and men, in fact the most absurdly gigantic fur specimens were carried by the French courtiers and for purposes which had very little to do with warming the hands and much to do with exhibitionism. In the United States from the 1800's till the commencement of the First World War muffs were immensely popular. On March 8, 1881, a certain Alice Pass patented a combination muff [*Plate 76*] and satchel which she described as "an invention to increase the conveniences of muffs by adding a satchel thereto. The invention consists in making a satchel muff with a gathered satchel opening upon the top and with hand apertures below arranged at right angles with the satchel opening; and also in the combination with the exterior side of the muff, of a pocket, as will be fully described."

Why anyone would go to the extreme of patenting a device as simple as this is hard to understand and one wonders how many were manufactured a hundred years ago.

To prevent accidental loss of the muff, the wearer inserted the hands and wrist into the loops before slipping the hands into the muff portion. All the cords and tasseling were popular bits of decoration. When the cords were loosened, objects dropped into a space in front of the muff. This muff was made in velvet, brocades, or possibly fur, and would have been a very feminine accessory.

Some years ago the lush, magenta colored, silk plush velvet [*Plate 82, Fig. 6*] was acquired with a vintage wardrobe and it is interesting to note its similarities to the Pass muff. Every stitch is hand done, from the smocking in the middle, to the black satin lining. It does not have a wrist loop but can be drawn up one arm to the elbow, as the bound hand openings expand to five inches. The interesting aspect of the muff is the purse (which someone apparently added years later) very much like the Pass muff, made in the heaviest of black grosgrain material. The probable age is the 1890's, as this type of velvet has not been available for at least seventy-five years.

FREQUENTLY COLLECTORS ARE confused by the similarity of the terms Art Nouveau and Art Deco, but the likeness does not extend beyond the terms. The Art Nouveau movement spread rapidly through Europe and became universal, though it was short lived (approximately 1885–1915) and when the Art Deco period found favor (1920–1935), the reaction against the foregoing movement was decisive and completely contradictory in nature.

The year 1900 ushered in a new century and a new style which relied little upon classical forms or

PLATE 74. Reticules from *La Mode Illustré,* 1875.

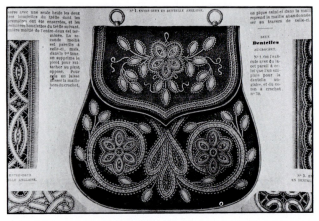

FIGURE 1

FIGURE 2

FIGURE 3

FIGURE 4

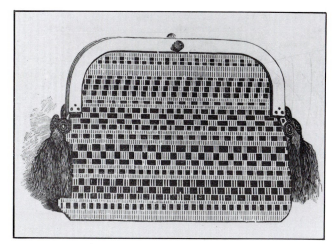

PLATE 75. The Protection Purse from *Lady Godey,* 1878.

PLATE 77. The Applique Reticule from *Lady Godey,* 1878.

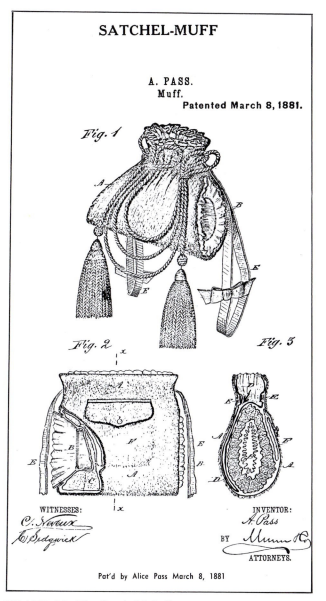

PLATE 76. The Satchel Muff, patented March 8, 1881.

outmoded symbols. Art Nouveau as the name suggests, (new art or style) was primarily concerned with nature rendered in curving lines, strange animals, birds and fish such as goldfish, sea horses, octopus, lizards, snakes, dragonflies, peacocks, owls, swans; and among the leaves and flowers the waterlily, lotus blossom, seaweed, chrysanthemum, sycamore, cat-tails, and lily-of-the-valley. The human female figure was lean, elongated, and swathed in flowing gauze materials, the hair always full blown encircling the entire figure or face and acting as a background for the whole piece.

Art Nouveau craftsmen merged the decorative and applied arts, giving each equal status. Indeed many of them were versatile artists who designed, painted, wrote poetry, and other forms of literature, sculpted, and were able musicians and architects. They executed their creations in wood, leather, glass, textiles, furnishings and jewelry.

A true collector's prize is a tooled leather purse of the Art Nouveau period. Used until they wore out, these genuine leather purses were never inexpensive as they were hand cut, tooled, laced, finished, and were individual creations. That shown [*Plate 80, Fig. 4*] has a tanned leather exterior and suede interior, with similarly covered mirror. The raised tool-

PLATE 77-A. Ads from the December, 1902 *Ladies Home Journal.*

ing, frequently found on the front side only, has the typically coiling vines, leaves and tendrils which these artists found so appealing. The frame, also hand forged, is copper with a coat of nickel plate. It has a plunger fastener with an oblong floral tab which securely locks the purse when turned. The shape is ovoid, squared off at the bottom and finished with flat lacing. There is a strong resemblance to the tooled bags of Louise Germain and Mlle de Felice who worked in France about 1910. [*Plate 81*] This purse, though not offered for sale, when displayed at a recent show attracted more attention and its sale was solicited more often than any purse ever handled.

The 1927 Sears Roebuck Catalogue listed as their most expensive purse an imported Spanish steerhide pouch bag, a purse very much like the afore mentioned purse, selling for $7.95. The description could easily fit as well, "Our finest Spanish steerhide. Very high grade pouch bag, 7 × 8 inches of extra quality imported steerhide in a rich tope brown shade. Hand tooled effect. Gun metal patented 'Turn-loc' safety frame. Suede leather lining. Expertly hand laced with leather all the way around bag and handle. Practical,

roomy size. Steerhide change purse and beveled mirror in separate pockets. Leather gussets. Made to give long wear."

Somehow this purse seemed older than the Sears model and sure that the tooling was hand done, the frame was rubbed with fine steel wool revealing a patent date of October 5, 1915 and another for May 15, 1917, and a manufacturer named JEM Company (Jemco?) as well. This illustrates the necessity of cleaning the frames and areas where identification is most likely to be hidden under coats of dirt, polish, or foreign matter. In a surprising number of cases some marks will be revealed. It would appear that the more expensive, older purse had been copied or the rights had been sold to Sears and Roebuck at some time, as the unique locking system appears to be virtually identical.

Such new ideas as multiple frames, back straps—so the purse could be carried in two ways—mirrors in the pull tab, exterior handkerchief pockets, snake effect trims, frameless Paris style bags, were offered from as little as 45¢ to $7.95.

Plate 80 contains three purses [*Figures 1, 3, and*

PLATE 78. *Fig. 1:* Petit point purse, enameled and jeweled *(author's collection).* *Fig. 2:* Needle and petit point *(Collection of Sharon Peterson).* *Fig. 3:* Austrian petit point. Sterling silver frame. *Fig. 4:* Magnificent petit point on ornate plated frame *(courtesy of Mary Hamilton).* *Fig. 5:* Hand-woven Austrian tapestry *(Collection of Joan Feast).*

FIGURE 1

FIGURE 3

FIGURE 4

FIGURE 5

FIGURE 2

252

PLATE 78-A. *Figs. 1 & 2:* Crewel and petit point work *(Collection of Mildred Strouss).* *Fig. 3:* Hand-woven tapestry *(courtesy "The Venerable Bead," Berkeley, California).* *Fig. 4:* Fine petit point *(Collection of Michaela Bennett).*

FIGURE 1

FIGURE 2

FIGURE 3

FIGURE 4

Pusilo Collection

PLATE 79. Purses of exceptional quality. *Fig. 1:* Enameled, 14K gold finger purse with compact in top *(author's collection)*. *Fig. 2:* Tortoise with gold piqué. Leather lined *(courtesy Barbara Holmes, Aptos, California)*. *Fig. 3:* Plique-a-jour frame on plush, with metallic embroidery *(Pusilo Collection)*. *Fig. 4:* Cartier purse in grey suede and gold trim with monogram "AMC", early 20th Century, France *(Costume Institute of The Metropolitan Museum of Art, gift of the estate of Agnes Miles Carpenter)*.

5] which are properly classified as miniatures but were assigned to the leather section as each is made of that material.

Particularly interesting is the purse found at *Figures 1 and 2*. It is made of a very fine, soft leather into which the pattern has been impressed, for no carver could make such an intricate pattern. It is only 5 by 2½ inches, and has six separate compartments, one of which is metal framed and secured by a bar. The copper snap fastener is patent dated Feb. 26 and Mar. 12, '78, and shows a lighthouse in the foreground of turbulent seas. Inside is a faded label which reads, "J.W. Cowing, Dealer in Dry Goods and Clothing...

groceries, hats, caps, boots, shoes, books, stationery... Drugs and Jewelry...Jackson, Minn." The purse was priced at $1.50. The design is a wild and jumbled mixture of such incongruous things as, ivy leaves, windmills and turreted castles complete with moats, wild boars pursued by hunting dogs, steps leading to two cottages by a waterwheel, a log bridge across a small pond, and a man on horseback hurrying off into the distance. The front has a female figure strumming a lute, while a large ship under full sail appears ready to drown them. Clearly the imagination of the die maker knew no bounds and was not repressed by reality. The purse has the musty, strange odor that

PLATE 79-A. All from the collection of Dr. Joan Feast. *Fig. 1:* Genuine coral beads on silver and gold tissue with salmon moire lining. *Fig. 2:* Cultured pearls on beige satin with silver thread embroidery and Cornelian clasp. *Fig. 3:* Tambour work. Probably done in China, c. 1920. *Fig. 4:* Modern Chinese petit point purse showing Panda. *Fig. 5:* Tapestry purse with cameo and marcasites.

FIGURE 4

FIGURE 2

FIGURE 3

FIGURE 1

FIGURE 5

FIGURE 2

FIGURE 3

FIGURE 1

PLATE 80. *Figs. 1 & 2:* Unusual coin purse dated 1876, shown open and closed *(author's collection). **Fig. 3:*** Child's purse of leather with brass handle and stamped scenic, European, date unknown *(ibid Fig. 1). **Fig. 4:*** Art Nouveau, tooled leather with twist lock top, "Jemco" c. 1900 ***Fig. 5:*** Made of pigskin with patent date of 1897. ***Fig. 6:*** Leather pouch with "accordion" closure.

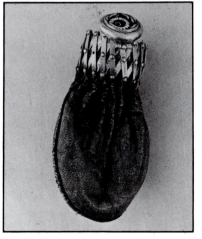

FIGURE 4

FIGURE 6

FIGURE 5

256

old things often have.

Figure 3 is much like the miniatures found on *Plate 70*. The brass handle is sturdy and shapely, bearing the single word "Patent"; evidently the clasp which opens when depressed, was patented, but there is no date. It is lined with pale green satin and has numerous compartments or divisions. The impressed figures on the front are clothed in peasant dress quite foreign to American styles.

Figure 5 is almost an exact duplicate of the others, was patented in 1877, and was made in New York. *Figure 6* is an extremely tiny gate-top pouch 2 inches long, fitted with a small ring and brass cap, probably of the same or earlier vintage.

A highly specialized purse is the sporran, a large pouch of skin with the hair on worn in front of the kilt by Scotch Highlanders in full dress and used as a purse, which evolved from the 15th and 16th century game bags. Resembling an outsized pear in shape, the 6¼ inch by 4¼ inch example shown on *Plate 80A* is capped by a semi-circular piece of silver topped by a pommel. One side is decorated with a thistle and fine inscribings such as were found on early American sterling combs. That this particular purse is ceremonial in nature—as are all kilt purses today—is evident from the almost unbendable leather so closely joined that the small flap opening which contains whatever can be forced into the pocket, is a mere ¾ of an inch wide! They can hardly be of any practical value. The fur side of this sporran is worn and may have been overlaid with decorative tasselling. It was obtained at auction (but had been priced at ten times the knocked down price) by some antique dealer who wished to dispose of it.

Plate 83 shows four very interesting purses. Though purchased in the United States at auction, the extremely fine petit point envelope purse [*Figure 1*] measuring 8½ × 5 inches was made in Germany. The purse has been unfolded so both sides may be viewed at a glance; the word "KINO," appearing along the right side remains a mystery. It may be the name of the needleworker, the name of the building on which it appears, a city; no one knows. The illustration is a strange combination of a gothic cathedral complete with red tile roof, framing ultra modern skyscrapers. The hurrying figures in the foreground add perspective and depth. The turreted entrance and walled city on the opposite side seem of another age.

The owner of this humorous gilt-metal cat purse [*Figure 2*] says she has been approached by total strangers wondering about it. It has about the same dimensions as a small animal with bright Persian turquoise eyes, jeweled collar, molded whiskers, gilt ears, and unlike a real puss, opens through the middle. A true novelty, it is carried in the hand as a rule, despite the long chain.

A touch of elegance can be claimed for the Elizabeth Arden plush green velvet clutch purse [*Figure 3*] with clear celluloid ends and high quality rhinestone frame and tabs. The cream colored satin lining is of the type which (before the day of nylon and other synthetics with their acknowledged benefits), was the most sumptuous fabric imaginable, called slipper satin. Well heeled and glamorous ladies wore slipper satin undergarments of such beauty no synthetics yet created can defy them. Only the mirror, lipstick case and compact remain intact in the fitted interior, however, there are sections allotted for another case, a container just slightly larger than the lipstick and a comb. The comb seciton held three pale yellow celluloid teeth, mute evidence of a former occupant. Each container is fitted with a small emerald green baguette closing or slide, the golden metal is crosshatched and the mirrors are both beveled. The former owner apparently did not know how to open the lipstick container (not as silly as it sounds with these old holders) and the geranium colored lipstick is as lush as when it was inserted nearly 50 years ago!

The armadillo purse [*Figure 4*] is a curiosity though not actually a rare purse; it is included for those who are unacquainted with them. An inoffensive nocturnal creature which seldom emerges from its burrow in the ground, its body is encased in an armor of small bony plates and when attacked it can roll into an armored ball. The poor creatures have been used for all sorts of utensils and bags. They can be purchased in South American countries and Mexico and make tough, long lasting purses of a novel shape. This one includes the paws and long carrying handles.

Although the following silver-plated purse is a chatelaine and is properly grouped in Chapter IV [*Plate 66, Fig. 2*] its construction is unique enough to list it here. Mesh chatelaines are usually of the flat topped interlocking type and more often than not made of sterling, (or it is possible the sterling examples have survived because they are choicer than those made of plate). It is the body, however, which differentiates it from other purses as it has stamped flower-like flat pieces with solid centers and the four petals are openwork joined by rings to every other flower piece.

Today it is rare to find the hook attached to the chatelaine and still rarer to find the hook is a simple fleur-de-lis with the same crosshatching as on the body and the small tabs which decorate the rings closing the bottom edge. The widely spaced ring mesh is impractical, however, and the purse must have been lined at one time.

One of the most elegant purses of all times is the enameled purse [*Plate 79, Fig. 1*]. Although the style was used by many firms, this purse, made by a manufacturer whose trademark was a padlock with the

initials R&G Co., is distinctively of 14K white gold, filigreed on its octagon sides and exquisitely enameled on the top. Even the yellow enameled dome through which the finger ring passes, is gold. Strangely, the mesh is enameled in blue, brown, and white diamonds which contrast sharply with the lavender and pink floral top. Fitted with a mirror and a powder receptacle, it measures a mere 3½ inches deep and 2½ wide and would accommodate only the smallest of articles. Its original cost would probably have been close to $175.00 in the mid 1920's and cost the present owner twice that amount.

A strange and somewhat gaudy purse-compact combination, called the "ELSA", was made by Whiting-Davis about 1925 [*Plate 82, Fig. 3*]. The mesh is enameled in both brilliant and pastel colors interspersed with touches of gold, the overall effect is approaching the Art Deco as the vandyked ends carry out the elongated design. The compact, consisting of tiny cake rouge, powder and comb receptacles with oval mirror, is attached to the exterior of the mesh and is enameled and embossed to show a pair of dancers in French court costumes. The combination of colors and motifs is atypical of this firm and exemplifies the extremes of the Flapper Era.

ORIENTAL PURSES ARE something of a novelty and the two here presented are no exception [*Plate 83A*]. The small brown tobacco pouch with the attached netsuke is Japanese, while the red embroidered silk purse is from The Camel's Bell Gift Shop, Peking, China. Although it appears to be just an elegantly embroidered sack-like container the frame is most unusual. Constructed of a delicate scrolled wire set with small jade pieces, the braided silk carrying cords are all that hold the frame together, quite unlike Western purses which are held shut by clasps, twists, plungers and other locking or gripping mechanisms. The dimensions, 7 inches by 10 inches are generous and the English label indicates it was intended for export or sale to tourists at least a half century ago. The embroidery of traditional design is hand done and the gold thread is of good quality. It is lined with beige colored China silk, still in fine condition.

The tobacco pouch is believed to be from the late 19th century and was of course the property of some Japanese gentleman. The delicate fabric has typical stork, plum blossom, and water lily patterns in brown and gold, lined with blue and gold silk in a reverse pattern. It is the netsuke, attached by a series of brass chains which is of interest to Westerners. The netsuke, (pronounced nets-key, ne = root and tsuke = fasten) is closely associated with smoking. It is a small object carved in wood, ivory, etc. or wrought in metal, the back usually pierced and strung with carrying cords. The tobacco pouch was used by upper class mer-

FIGURE 3

258

FIGURE 1

FIGURE 2

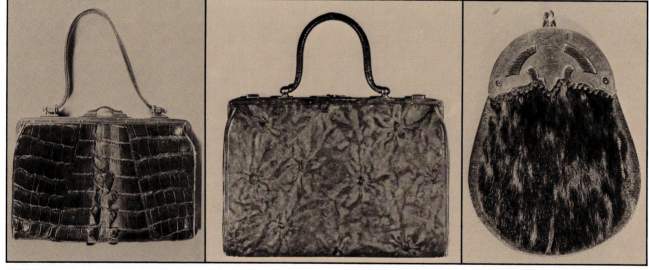

FIGURE 4   FIGURE 5   FIGURE 6

PLATE 80-A. All from author's collection. *Figs. 1 & 2:* Front and back views of large tooled leather handbag, c. 1940. *Fig. 3:* Flapper's purse of soft leather with girdle attachment. *Fig. 4:* Genuine crocodile handbag with solid brass fittings, c. 1920. *Fig. 5:* Stamped leather handbag with copper fittings, c. 1900. *Fig. 6:* Sporran from Scotland.

chants, and fashionable men below the rank of samurai. Before Japanese men adopted Western style clothing they wore loose fitting kimonos belted with a wide sash. The top of the netsuke rested over the sash, the chains hung behind it and the pouch was then readily accessible (see *Fig. 3*). This netsuke is made of ivory and low grade silver center dragon. Some netsuke are very valuable and they are typically Japanese. The other type of container or purse was

the inro. It was also carried at the girdle and was used for carrying medicine, the family seal, jewels etc. Lacquered and inlaid, held together by cotton cords and an ojime bead, with a netsuke terminal, they were also used before the Japanese adopted Western styles. Each makes an interesting addition to a purse collection.

Among the choicest purses one could encounter is shown in *Plate 79A, Figure 1*. This elegantly understated gold and silver thread purse is embroi-

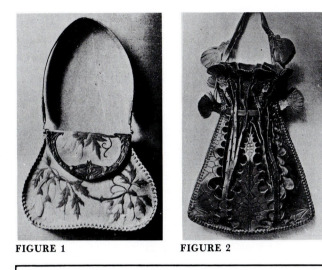

FIGURE 1   FIGURE 2

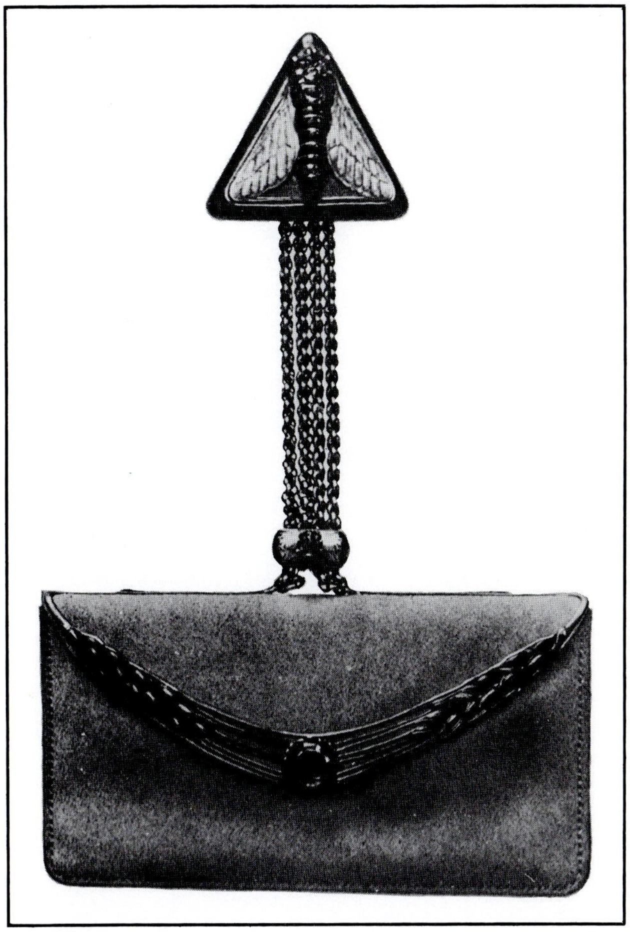

FIGURE 3

PLATE 81. Tooled Art Nouveau purses, c. 1900, France. *Fig. 1:* The leaf motif is repeated on the frame. By Mlle. de Felice. *Fig. 2:* Unusual reticule type with leaf tabs. By Louise Germain. *Fig. 3:* Leather chatelaine on metal chain. An unusual shape. By Lucien Gaillard.

dered with genuine coral beads and set with three rows of larger corals, much like the coral tiaras in the previous section. It is lined with salmon colored moire silk and fitted with a short chain handle. The body is solidly embroidered with silver thread, centered with French knots. Each of the flower petals is outlined in gold thread and accented with pink embroidery thread. Each of the coral beads is sewn onto the material and outlined in gold thread. The front and back of the purse are identical. The approximate age of this French 5 × 6 inch purse, made for a specialty shop in San Francisco, is 1920. So much handwork would be prohibitively expensive in recent times.

Figure 2 was also made in France for Milnor Company and is also hand embroidered on fine, beige, heavy satin material. Each of the flowers is set with a good quality pearl of smallish size, framed with gold thread, couched as embroideries from China were early in the century. It is entirely possible such was the case as the work is extraordinarily fine. The tab pull is a matching flower, the plunger is cornelian; the lining is of peach colored satin and ocntains an attached divided change purse, and beveled satin covered mirror. It is 6 inches square.

Figure 3 has no identifying marks other than the words "Trinity Plate" but the overall tambour work suggests strongly it was made in China. The entire surface of the purse is covered with fine tambouring in colors which are not too subtle. The frame is set with green Peking glass and marcasites, while the lining is stamped in gold with the previous owner's name. The mirror is the height of refinement; the pear shaped, beveled glass is bezel set and the back is shirred into a pocket for some small object or currency. It is 6½ inches by 7 inches.

BETWEEN 1940–1960 THERE was a craze in the United States for deeply tooled, top-grained cow hide leather purses, some of which were so elegant it would be shortsighted to neglect them, though they are not actually antique purses. A skilled leather worker asserts such depth of design as seen in the handbag [*Plate 80A, Figs. 1, 2*] is not available today. This handbag, like others from the same time period, was hand

PLATE 82. (right), *Fig. 1:* Chinese silk with tassels *(courtesy "A Stitch In Time," Richmond, California)*. *Fig. 2:* Fabric reticules with mirrored bottoms. *Figs. 3 & 4:* The multicolored mesh "Elsa" by Whiting Davis, c. 1925 *(Collection of Sharon Peterson)*. *Fig. 5:* Contemporary gate-top mesh with attached holder. German. *Fig. 6:* Satin embroidered reticule *(Collection of Bronwen Heuer)*. *Fig. 7:* Velvet muff and purse combination *(author's collection)*.

FIGURE 1

FIGURE 2

FIGURE 3

FIGURE 4

FIGURE 5

FIGURE 7

FIGURE 6

tooled, the design most likely an original creation and the leather the finest obtainable.

The talented leather artisan created the purse for a lady friend or relative whose name is found on the lining along with his own. Unless the recipient was herself an outdoorswoman, it is obvious the leather worker, named Herb, used sports motifs which he enjoyed, giving little thought to the ultimate wearer. The front flap is decorated with flying birds departing from a realistic marshland. The back side shows a magnificent buck and doe in a stippled forest scene of birches and pines. Apart from the fine tooling, it is the careful attention to minute details which classify this handbag a true work of art. Such detailing can be observed in the fine braided handle, the matching guard loops and the double braided edges. A lining of dark leather hides the inevitable soil which ruins the interiors of most purses. Mock lacing—made by skillfully cutting the leather—matches the outer edge lacing and even the snap fastenings are tooled flower petals which merge into the pattern of grasses and stems. The purse is an ample 13 inches long and 8½ inches deep.

SIXTY OR SEVENTY years ago little thought was given to the extinction of some creatures and the alligator, crocodile, lizard and even such exotic skins as ostrich were used to make rather small purses, the dimensions of which were dictated at least in part by the size of available skins. Today, protected by endangered species laws which prohibit their importation, very few handbags of this nature enter the country. Antique leather and reptile handbags are being snatched up at garage sales, estate sales, rescued from attic trunks and old clothes bags and are being lovingly restored.

FIGURE 3 (closed)

FIGURE 1

FIGURE 2

Those few new articles which are currently retailed sell for phenomenally high prices, a crocodile bag fetching as much as $3,500! The above price is for an extraordinary imported purse handcrafted to last a lifetime (Stefan Mann Co., Carmel, CA). Little wonder the antique versions are being restored regardless of cost.

The alligator is native to the southern parts of the United States, while its cousin the crocodile is native to the African, Asian, South American and Australian continents. Though it is commonly thought the skins found in purses of the 1920's were from domestic North American reptiles, especially the alligator, crocodiles were just as often used for handbags and other goods. For nearly a half century the alligator has been protected as a vanishing species, but recently (1977) has become such a nuisance in swampy areas of Florida and other southern states that limited hunting has been resumed. It is difficult to tell the difference between the alligator and crocodile when viewing only the finished product, however, there are two essential differences: 1. the crocodile has a tiny oil gland which appears as a pin point on each scale of the underbelly; 2. the natural skin color of the mature crocodile is olive with black markings, while the alligator is shiny black with dull yellow markings.

The 8½ × 6½ inch example shown at [*Plate 80A, Fig. 2*] is approximately 70 years old. It is worn along the twill leather-covered edges and the handle, but the body of the handbag is shiny, dark and pliable. It was made in three sections; the center section is taken from the side of the reptile which runs into the tail. It consists of a double row of fin like pieces which are here used for decorative effect. The outer sections

FIGURE 3 (open)

PLATE 83. *Fig. 1:* Exceedingly fine hand-woven tapestry, thought to be German *(Collection of Bonnie Stone).* *Fig. 2:* Gold cat with turquoise eyes *(ibid Fig. 1).* *Fig. 3:* Elizabeth Arden purse, c. 1930, shown open and closed. *Fig. 4:* Armadillo pouch with shoulder strap *(ibid Fig. 1).*

FIGURE 4

FIGURE 3

FIGURE 1

FIGURE 2

PLATE 83-A. *Fig. 1:* Extraordinary red silk purse embroidered with gold thread, c. 1930, China. The braided silk carrying cords are all that hold the wire frame together. *Fig. 2:* A Japanese "netsuke," from which a silk tobacco pouch is suspended by brass chains. This particular netsuke is carved from ivory with a dragon of low grade silver mounted in the center. *Fig. 3* shows how the pouch was worn attached to the kimono sash.

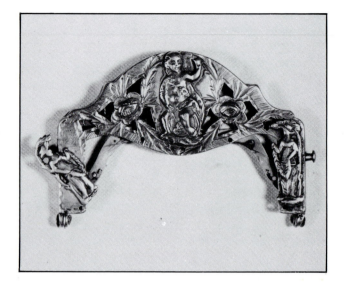
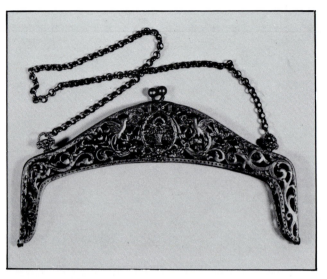

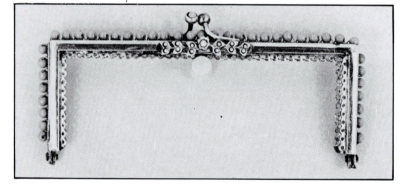

CHAPTER 7

CARE AND REPAIR OF PURSES

People who are unacquainted with the fascination of purses are amazed that they rank among the most sought after collectible articles of costume and in response to the ''why'' question the reasons are worth considering.

One of the chief appeals the purse has for collectors is size. Purses are lightweight, usually not more than a foot square, are easily transported, (although a box of solidly beaded purses is surprisingly heavy), and they occupy very little space when displayed. In an age when more and more of us are living in apartments and small homes, space becomes a considerable factor to the collector and many of the more cumbersome articles of antique furniture, large art works, and glass, silver, and porcelains which require special cabinets and caution in handling become a liability rather than an asset. Collections of miniature purses are very suitable to the collector who has a minimum of space.

Many are drawn to the infinite variety of patterns, designs, shapes, fabrics, and colors which are found in the purse. Among the thousands of vintage purses there is seldom an exact duplicate since most were hand made and have an individual character. Even though the same basic pattern be employed, the addition of names and monograms, dates, trimmings, variations in color schemes, linings, frame ornamentation or the lack of it, fringes, clasps, and the materials themselves, all make for diversity and distinction in what might first be thought a monotonous subject.

High on the list of attractions for the collector is the sheer beauty of purses aside from any intrinsic value they may have. The most popular bag is the multi-colored and patterned beaded purse, as a case in point.

Many collections originated from a single family heirloom which had setimental significance. The fact that great Aunt Josie spent endless hours creating a purse outweighs any artistic merits it might lack. A work of caution might be valuable in connection with trying to ascertain the age of an article by comparison with the approximate age of its owner. The mere fact that a purse was owned or created by a distant relative of advanced years does not in itself guarantee the article is correspondingly old. It might have been a gift to the lady in the closing years of her life, or never have been hers at all—as household items have a way of being intermixed or of doubtful origin—and over the years memories become confused as to ''who made what and when''. One is on firmer ground when the article is dated or bears a name firmly establishing ownership; as previously stated this is why such purses as the Elizabeth Ayer, Ellen Coxe, Sophia Goodrich and Sara Day purses are unique. In any event, many a purse is beloved because of its touching family connections.

Even if the purse maker is unknown, an appreciation for the consummate skill involved and the fact that the article is hand made intrigues many collectors and would-be collectors. Many ladies are still expert at crocheting and knitting and could easily produce the non-beaded type of purse or satchel, but there are probably only a handful of artisans in existence who could or would be able to make the intricate beaded purses which constitute the bulk of collections today. In an increasingly mechanized and automated world there is a growing recognition of the importance of handicrafts.

As an accessory of dress the purse, though considered a minor item, is historically significant. It has been largely ignored in favor of larger pieces but it is an important cultural artifact for students of costuming for the stage, textile researchers, bead workers, museum decorative arts departments, and fashion designers; in short anyone interested in the development of the human species since recorded time.

THOUGH SOME PURSES are too fragile or costly to be used, the socially inclined lady can use her purses for evening wear, weddings, afternoon teas, the opera, costume events, or just for the fun of it as a conver-

sation piece. Caution should be exercised with beaded purses as the silk thread may be weak, the beads loose, and many linings are not sturdy enough for the jumble of things ladies are now accustomed to lug about in their purses. The most practical purses for wear today are the mesh, fabric, and leather types, though they are not as stunning as the multicolored beaded bags.

THE FOLLOWING SUGGESTIONS will help to preserve the antique purse:

1. Store purses in layers with dividers of light weight cardboard or acid free tissue paper to prevent beads, fringes, and handles from entangling.

2. Insertion of sachet inside purses will help prevent the musty odor which old fabrics often acquire.

3. Fabric purses can be steam pressed by stuffing them with turkish toweling and steaming them on the hand. Work slowly and carefully. This works very effectively on satin, velvet, silk, linen, pongee and similar fabrics.

4. Silk tassels can be steamed and then combed with care to remove knots and tangles.

5. Thorough but gentle cleaning of fabric purses will enhance their appearance and prolong their life. Brush with a soft brush to remove spots, or use moistened cloth and mild soap.

6. Gently washing beaded purses by swishing carefully in warm soapy water will remove grime and dust, remember: the beads will last forever, but the thread will not, so use care.

7. Metal frames can be brightened by rubbing with fine steel wool; use caution not to damage material or beads nearest the frame.

8. Ask your shoe repairman for dressings for leather purses. Some exotic leather purses are best professionally cleaned.

9. Never wash metal beaded purses, even those which are colored. There is no way to reverse the inevitable rusting which will result. Many an otherwise magnificent bag has thus been permanently ruined.

10. Loose threads should be tied or glued immediately to prevent further deterioration and loss of irreplaceable beads.

11. Purses made of crocheted cord which has discolored may be restored by a mild solution of bleach.

12. Old beaded purses which have frayed or torn drawstring tops can be fitted to stamped brass or other frames, which are obtainable from the Venerable Bead or other dealers in antique purses. This prevents further deterioration of the beading, adds rigidity, and a sturdy chain handle. If the lining is not intact such previous alterations are visible in some old beaded purses.

The Venerable Bead offers fine repair of valuable purses, but it should be kept in mind, the repair of beaded bags is an art and a tedious one at best, which in all likelihood does not adequately recompense the repairer, regardless of the fee, for the work is hard on the eyes, wearisome, often the beads required for repair are difficult to obtain, and all the repair is done by hand.

13. Never attempt to wash the fine doeskin linings found in German silver and some other rigid framed purses. The skin will shrink almost to the vanishing point and have to be removed. Many a fine lining has been ruined this way, unfortunately.

14. Store all types of metal mesh purses which snag easily, separately from beaded purses. Those marvelous fringes are very susceptible to entanglement and only a very skillful beader can restore them.

15. As with comb collections, storing or displaying antique purses in a clean place where the temperature is relatively constant will be most beneficial in prolonging both their attractiveness and longevity.

A word of caution: Unless you are sure of what to do, are dexterous enough to do it, have the time to be patient, have an inexpensive purse on which to practice and can obtain the proper materials: *Relegate The Repairs To An Expert.*

IF YOU ARE determined to try here are some helpful hints from one of those experts:

1. Determine if the bag is to be used or to be displayed only. Obviously, the repairs may not be the same or even possible if someone wants to carry and fill the purse. Mere decoration restoration is much more easily achieved if durability is not a factor.

2. Evaluate the area of repair and the construction technique employed. Knitted bags are the hardest to repair, whereas crocheted bags can be recrocheted in the damaged areas making sure the beads are strung before the crocheting is undertaken. Beaded petit or needlepoint repairs are not as difficult, as a long straight stitch with the beads prearranged is used. Take care that the beads are angled correctly. Transparent glue will aid in keeping the beads at the correct angle.

3. It is important to match the weight and approximate the kind of silk to that originally used, and the size of bead must also be the same.

4. Start and end the thread with a tiny knot and some back stitches, using great care not to break more of the original thread or beads when running the needle through them to anchor the thread. The silkatine threads used in bags from the 1920's are extremely fragile now and unless care is taken the area may be worsened rather than improved or repaired.

5. Study the repairs to be made and determine in advance what steps are to be followed to satisfactorily effect them.

6. Loomed purses must be repaired by an expert as whole rows may unravel if the restorer is not

familiar with this method. This is particularly applicable to French steel bead purses with intricate patterns.

7. If sufficiently thin needles are not available, try gluing the end of the thread or using monofilament nylon thread without a needle. Monofilament thread does not knot well so the ends may cause problems.

8. If weakened, replace carrying tapes or cord with new cord or old cord in better condition, particularly if they are to be hung.

9. As they are a common problem, fringes can be dealt with in any of the following ways:

    A. Remove if beyond repair or if the pattern is too complicated to duplicate skillfully.

    B. Match the beads and duplicate the loopings.

    C. Replace with shorter loops or simpler design to use the available beads.

    D. If the fringe or other section demands a small quantity of beads and the handle is beaded fabric, the beads may be pirated from the underside of the handle.

    E. If the beaded tassel at the end of a beaded purse or any purse is skimpy or has missing loops they may be purchased from the address given at the end of the book and reattached in the desired length.

10. Relining a purse can lengthen its life as the strain on the beads is relieved by having objects within the purse come in contact with the lining, not the beading. Linings are easily replaced by removing the old lining if it is still available, use it as a pattern, but remember to use *old materials* in constructing the replacement.

11. Leaving some purses in a state of "arrested decay" is suggested in the following instances:

    A. Purses which are too delicate to repair

    B. When the damage is too extensive to permit repair

    C. When the damage is too trivial to attract attention

    D. Purses of such importance that they stand on their own merit and would be historically impaired if restored.

LEATHER PURSES WHICH have laced edges are subject to leather fatigue or rot which occurs chiefly at the corners and the base where contact with rough or hard surfaces is most frequent. The only solution is to have the purse relaced by a skilled leather worker. Most large cities will have an establishment which sells leather supplies exclusively and will be able to provide the name of such a repairperson. Leather crafts instruction guides are also available through the public libraries if one has the time and inclination to personally undertake such repairs.

AS FRINGES ARE so often found in disrepair, ten simple but effective patterns for repair of beaded purse fringes are here presented. If you can thread a needle (be sure it is a fine German or British steel beading needle as others are poor quality) you can repair and beautify your purses using these fringe patterns. Remember the spacing depends on the size of the bead, the number of beads used and how dense a fringe is desired; the length is usually from 2–4 inches depending on personal preference and appropriateness to the design of the purse.

1. String 3 inches of background beads singly, then use 25 contrasting colored beads making a loop so there are 12 beads each side, finish off by running the thread back through the beads and knot. (For very fine beads)

2. String several inches of background beads, attach to the bottom of the purse in a looped U shape; on the next U, insert the needle close to the first loop and twist around the second insertion continuing across the bag.

3. Depending on the size of the bead, string about ½ inch of background color beads, ¼ inch of another color used in the design, ½ inch of a third color, and finally another ½ inch of a fourth color. End in a small loop of 8–9 tiny beads which helps prevent damage to the loop and loss of beads.

4. Using a colored crystal bead such as is found in necklaces, run three strands of beads to about 2 inches through the hold and attach to the bottom of the purse or a line of beads which is spot tacked to the purse bottom. Use a crystal several times larger than the fringe beads, and in another color.

5. Suspend a large bead or sequined ball from several short lengths of beading. This is a very nice treatment for old black velvet, jet-trimmed purses.

6. An unusual and pretty fringe is as follows: using medium beads in a dark shade, string ½ inch, attach a clear bead, another ½ inch of dark beads, thread through a large crystal bead and repeat as shown to form a wide V; attach to the bottom of the purse and continue across.

7. A simple twisted fringe may be made by stringing 65 or 70 fine cut or steel cut beads, twisting several times to the left, and attaching to the bottom of the purse so the tassels touch each other. Starting at the lower left edge, string the same number of beads and after twisting several times through the previous loop, attach to the edge very close to it; repeat until the opposite side is reached. If a side fringe is desired use fewer beads placed at greater intervals, gradually increasing in depth to the bottom. This makes a very sturdy fringe.

8. To give a lacy finish to an otherwise plain purse a vandyke with looped fringe does nicely and is not too difficult to achieve. Use 11 beads to make the vandykes—the pointed sections—and 39 beads for the fringe looping.

9. A variation of the above pattern is done in two colors or as many as can be artistically and aesthetically combined. The handsome fringe is graded into 3 points or vandykes; a larger bead is used to complete the ends of the strands. The accurate pattern in concise form follows. Note: in each strand there are 3 gold beads beyond the black bead and a larger black bead terminal, as is shown in strand 1 only. Use gold and black or whatever combination is desired to separate the beads in like manner.

Strand							
1. 14	gold,	1 black,	3 gold	14. 25	gold,	1 black,	3 gold
2. 16	,,	,,	,,	15. 21	,,	,,	,,
3. 19	,,	,,	,,	16. 17	,,	,,	,,
4. 25	,,	,,	,,	17. 11	,,	,,	,,
5. 30	,,	,,	,,	18. 17	,,	,,	,,
6. 36	,,	,,	,,	19. 21	,,	,,	,,
7. 40	,,	,,	,,	20. 25	,,	,,	,,
8. 44	,,	,,	,,	21. 30	,,	,,	,,
9. 48	,,	,,	,,	22. 36	,,	,,	,,
10. 44	,,	,,	,,	23. 40	,,	,,	,,
11. 40	,,	,,	,,	24. 44	,,	,,	,,
12. 36	,,	,,	,,	25. 48	,,	,,	,,
13. 30	,,	,,	,,				

10. Rather than using beads, many purses were completed with a tassel made of the same silk used in the knit or crochet work by folding a large gathering of silk, knotting it through the middle securely and attaching it to the center and bottom of the purse. Currently the closest material must be used in this process, as the old silk is no longer available. This is particularly appropriate to pouch shaped bags.

METAL MESH PURSES (circa 1910–1930's) often suffer a loss of the enamels which make them so attractive, as the folds of the mesh come in contact with one another, as well as hard surfaces.

If the mesh is so badly worn as to render the pattern valueless, a new pattern can be devised, or the entire surface painted with lacquers (which can be obtained at hobby shops in a wide range of colors and hues) for a very nominal sum. The existing pattern may be determined with the aid of a magnifying glass and retouched at the same value or as close to the same value as possible. The purse should be stuffed with tissue or other material to prevent the newly enameled sides from touching and each link given a daub of the lacquer and allowed to dry thoroughly by hanging the purse in the sun or in a warm area.

Although the range of colors is confined to the reds, pinks, and salmons, mauves, and similar shades, one of the most durable and easily applied substances is nail enamel; the applicator is also easy to manage and could be used for other lacquers as well. When the color is completely dry, the same overcoat used for the nails is applied, creating an amazingly durable surface. Should one become tired of the color scheme it would be possible to remove the lacquer with acetone or merely paint over the existing design and create a new one at will.

DISPLAY

1. If hung on a wall as decoration make certain the weight is evenly distributed, better still, place heavily beaded purses in display cabinets with glass shelving.

2. If you have a hat rack of the old folding type with ten glass tipped knobs, it makes an attractive and sturdy holder for some of your favorite purses.

3. Very fragile purses which cannot stand handling or possible accidents can be effectively placed in frames or shadow boxes for safekeeping.

4. If hung, use push pins with glass heads or metal picture hangers.

5. Arrange purses in groupings as you would prints or paintings rather than in straight lines. Use one kind of purse in one area or mix according to size and design. Open shelving may be used in some circumstances.

6. Arrange a purse in a shadow box by using an ornamental heavy gilt frame, cover and insert a piece of plywood with padding and velvet, add some decorative items such as a picture of a long departed relative, some dried flowers, ribbons and bows, colorful old postcards, hatpins, combs, odds and ends of jewelry, laces; in short, any delicate or unusual item from the past which would harmonize with the purse.

7. Purchase or construct a folding screen (3 or 4 panels) to contain sturdy peg board. Insert such objects as golf tees, sold in packages of 100 for less than a dollar at some discount houses; hooks, metal hangers or holders of the types used in home workshops, etc. Such a screen will hold a great quantity of purses most effectively.

8. Since combs occupy a minimum of space they are easily layered in bureau drawers. Especially useful are those many drawer types which are found in children's rooms, for the bureau is narrow and the drawers rather shallow.

9. For those special purses or those frequently used, a convenient and safe holder is the old fashioned hall tree with brass arms fixed at various heights. Additional supports can be added for an extensive collection having appropriate handles.

10. An open or closed steamer trunk which can accommodate a host of articles makes a fine receptacle. Additional shelving can be added. If glass shelving is used many layers can be seen at once.

CHAPTER 8

COLLECTING THE ANTIQUE PURSE

It has been said that collectors fall into two categories: the truly wealthy who are so discriminating they care only for those extraordinary items which are museum quality and in fact do ultimately intend to donate their treasures to museums or establish their own museums (ie. Ford, Rockefellers, Gardners, Whitenys, Guggenheims, Walters etc.). Their collections may be a consuming passion and absorb a great deal of their energies and interests or they may be a symbol of great wealth, power, and social clout or a mixture of all the foregoing. This does not necessarily diminish the pleasure and satisfaction they must derive from collecting art, objets d'art, jewels, silver, etc., but entails less of a sacrifice and becomes more of a game, the pleasure of the pursuit being paramount to the actual acquisition.

The second group is interested in items which are indicative of a given era and they collect all things within that framework, being less interested in single choice items than in a form of kleptomania and these holdings proliferate madly regardless of their lack of artistic merit or rarity. The collector has neither the money nor the inclinations of the connoisseur, but he takes great pleasure in his antiques and surrounds himself with them.

There is a place for both these groups in collecting and each serves a valuable function by preserving the past in one way or another. As a hobby collecting will provide a hedge against lassitude for there is always more to learn about each category; speculation leads to inquiry and in the realm of combs and purses the quest is ceaseless as so little research has been done here or abroad.

For the most part purse and comb accessories will not be in excess of say $10,000 (except for very desirable tiaras or a purse of such age or so studded with jewels as to be unobtainable,) most will be less than $100, subject to many conditions in each individual case, of course. There are some generalized recommendations which are worthy of consideration whether one is an advanced or novice collector which

should be shared with one another. If they are repetitious or less than original, they are nonetheless valuable.

WHEN SELECTING PURSES for a collection keep the following in mind:

1. Select purses in prime condition unless the specimen is sufficiently choice and/or valuable to warrant its repair or inclusion in a collection such as a rare 18th century pocket or early 19th century tooled leather purse.

2. Diversify by selecting either a varied cross section of each type or concentrate on a particular type or category of purse; i.e. miniatures, precious metals, beaded scenic et cetera.

3. Learn everything you can about the category of your choice by familiarizing yourself with specimens; attend antique shows, visit shops, join clubs or organizations where collections may be viewed and shared, visit museums and with the aid of their personnel examine those collections available, read whatever texts, costume books and various materials pertaining to purses—albeit limited—that you can obtain. The more that is known about a collection the keener the appreciation one has for it and one may become in the process, a recognized authority on the subject.

4. Invest in the finest specimens you can afford; quantity is secondary to quality in collecting and more pleasure is derived from a superb article than a mediocre one. It may be a secondary consideration with the avid collector of any item, but if marketability is a future intent, the intrinsic value of each article should be determined at the time of purchase.

5. Both collectors and dealers—who are merely advanced collectors in a sense—make a practice of improving their holdings. If you tire of a particular category of purse or know it to be inferior, trade or sell and invest in superior replacements.

6. If you chance upon a purse of the caliber of the prestigious Cartier, Tiffany, Schiaparelli, Chanel,

or other designer, even though some restoration or cleaning is required, do not hesitate to acquire it if at all possible, as these purses are true gems and deserve a category of their own aside from antique considerations. The workmanship, design, materials, and techniques employed in making these one-of-a-kind purses are worthy of study (for purposes of comparison if nothing else) and will ultimately command large sums. Their current value would best be determined by a competent appraiser such as a large auction house which would be familiar with items of this caliber rather than a dealer who might have limited knowledge or only passing acquaintance with such rarities.

7. If beaded purses are your main interest, many communities have bead organizations which will be of great aid to the collector in identifying the types of beads available, how beading is done, facilitate the exchange of materials and knowledge which might otherwise be difficult or impossible to obtain. The social aspects are not to be overlooked as well.

8. Some collectors who appear to derive the most pleasure from their collections use them as fashion accents, not on rare occasions, but in the course of their daily lives. They have an enormous good time and create minor sensations with their beaded reticules, vintage needle and petit point bags, revitalized reptile skin bags, and sterling coin purses. The hottest item in the smart shops and boutiques today is the return of the reticule. They are being shown in a wide variety of fabrics, colors, and designs. If sturdy and attractive ones can be drawn from one's collection or purchased in assembling a collection, a lady would be ultra smartly attired as the reticule would have the added bonus of being antique.

Think of what a stir carrying a miser's purse would create, and even more fun, the chatelaine which attaches to the belt. Some antique dealers of late have sported just such a curiosity and could not have attracted more attention than if they had been wearing a bikini in Siberia.

9. Aside from those purses which are constructed of precious metals and studded with valuable gems (such as the solid gold purses), or very old and therefore priceless, (which one would probably never encounter save at a prestigious auction or when traveling abroad) collecting purses is not likely to cause financial hardship and since there are no hard and fast rules to consider either, the searcher should please only himself or herself when selecting purses for a collection. If the purse is to be worn consider its size, color, durability, usage, one's social life, what the purse is to contain, and like factors. If the purse is merely to be displayed these considerations are of lesser importance, and age, beauty, rarity, cost, condition, et cetera, deserve thought. It matters little if

others like your selection as long as you are pleased.

As a side note, a noted fashion designer decided to obtain one good example from each decade commencing with the 1920's and working backward in time. He was eminently successful and in a recent publication stated he had amassed a collection dating back to the mid 17th century. He has, of course, been avidly pursuing purses for over 20 years and has access by virtue of his profession and living in a metropolitan area, to a wider range of offerings than the average person. The idea is an intriguing one and offers one sort of handbag classification.

10. Little has been said about obtaining purses and/or combs. Bargains are where you find them, but flea markets, garage sales, thrift shops and so called estate sales seldom produce sleepers, though if one has the time, energy, transportation, and patience to withstand disappointment it may be worthwhile. Remember, other dealers will have had first chance to purchase before the event is open to the public, either when the booths are being arranged, or in the case of estate sales, the dealers most likely to purchase an item will have been contacted by those in charge as a matter of course. Dealers are known to specialize in given areas and lists of potential dealer customers are maintained as standard business practice. The dealer will make many purchases over a period of time whereas sales to the general public will be limited. Often an appraiser will have been called in to acquaint the seller with the current values and little will be vastly underpriced. Those who operate estate sales as a business are well aware of what an item is worth, (as incidentally are auctioneers and if you are known to them, they will frankly tell a customer what an item is likely to be knocked down for and they are usually right), and will price it accordingly. For the customer it can, and should be a lark, but keep in mind the business person is not, as the expression goes, ''in business for his health'', and he will not knowingly undervalue an item without good reason.

Another possible source is friends, but a word of caution about friends. They will invariably overprice their items as few, if any, will know the actual values and they also feel, friend or no, they are being taken advantage of. It would be wise to have an independent appraisal of the item offered for sale and both abide by the decision to avoid conflict, embarrassment, and a possible end of the friendship. For a nominal fee the item can be assigned a fair value and both seller and purchaser will be satisfied. This is not to say that friends do not have very fine items, especially the elderly who often wish to dispose of personal items when moving to smaller quarters, or unhappily when their health deteriorates and things must be sold to augment their finances or dispose of in the event there are no heirs to an estate. Without

a doubt the private transaction can be rewarding, but requires the utmost in diplomacy.

Auctions are often suggested as the best means of collecting and being an ardent auction devotee I concur. There are some great bargains to be had at auctions and aside from shows and shops, auctions are both exciting and from time-to-time stupefying, when in your eagerness to win the bid you realize you have paid so outrageous a price the item cannot be disposed of profitably in your lifetime. Unless you are "auction wise" or have an unlimited purse, do be careful. We have all seen the two inordinately stubborn bidders who wanted the same item, refused to concede to one another, and succeeded only in bidding the lot up to fifty times what it should have brought. Such competition brings much joy to the auctioneer's life. Take care how you bid. Examine the merchandise carefully at the preview, do not bid unless you have examined the lot prior to the sale, watch the experienced bidders and note when they drop out. That may signal that the lot is bid in excess of its value. Have some idea what your bid limit is and adhere to it, and avoid being carried away by the excitement of the moment. There are so many other tips to profitable auction buying that several good books have been written on the subject. Some auctions are social events and everyone goes to watch, talk, bid, or meet someone whom they cannot otherwise reach. Sometimes you will make acquaintances who will be very beneficial to your collecting or business. By sheer chance I met at an auction a lady who had a marvelous diversified collection of purses which initially served as the backbone for this book and were eventually sold. A tip of the hat to her!

Considering all the foregoing sources, the shop is most often the best place to transact business for the shopkeeper will be appreciative of a good customer, will search for the customer when doing his buying, will apprise other dealers of your needs, will deal with you on a one-to-one bases, will extend the most favorable terms, and may well be the most knowledgeable. It is a fallacy that dealers are a dumb lot and do not know their merchandise so the "smart" shopper can outwit them. Selling antiques is their *business* and even though one may occasionally be uninformed or in remote areas, less than sophisticated, the average dealer is hard working, long suffering, and sharp; he has to be as the competition is fierce, and in a battle of wits the customer who thinks himself superior is a fool. Treasures may be found in junk shops and in plush shops for reasonable prices, neither has a monopoly on goodies, but prize items will not often be overlooked and consequently priced low. Sow's ears aside for the moment, one should not expect as a matter of course to get something for nothing!

11. Regard your collections less as an investment than an aggregation of items of personal choice; your collections should not be purely speculative as one would consider stocks and bonds, neither of which has any beauty aside from the value they represent, but your lovely antique combs, purses, and other items are a pleasure in themselves. The antique market, like all other facets of commerce, will fluctuate, especially those purses, combs, and hair ornaments which are made of precious metals and gems, as styles change, improvements are made, mines are discovered, and fads are initiated and die. None of these trends should sway the collector as a quality piece will never lose value and charm. A gold purse bought a century ago is even more charming today and is easily worth ten times the purchase price for the workmanship, style, and materials were all elegantly simple; classics for all time.

CHAPTER 9
A PORTFOLIO
OF ANTIQUE PURSES

Plate 85. An evening purse belonging to the Post Cereal heiress Marjorie Merriweather Post (Davies). Six inches in diameter and with a solid covering of seed pearls, the purse has a platinum frame trimmed in rubies, sapphires, emeralds and diamonds, as is the fringe. The clasp is a carved ruby, with diamond initials set in platinum. *(Smithsonian Institute, photo by Erica and Harold Van Pelt.)*

Unless otherwise credited all purses shown in this chapter are presently in the collection of the author.

Plate 86. The face of Charlie Chaplin decorates this rare celebrity purse made by Whiting and Davis circa 1914-1918. It is a small (3 1/4 ″ by 6 1/4″) black and white enamel mesh, with a 26″ cable-twist chain.

Plate 87. This silver-plated, fine mesh purse with its inset clock (still in working order) was popular in 1910, but a curiosity today.

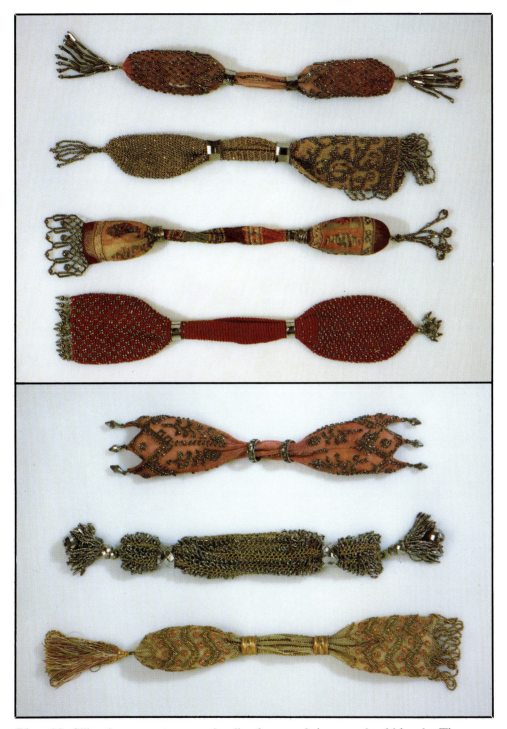

Plate 88. Silk misers purses, seven in all, of cut steel, brass and gold beads. These are from France, circa 1800-1840. Note the delicate pastel shades and heavy beading. *(Museum of Fine Arts, Boston, Elizabeth Day McCormick Collection.)*

Plate 89. The framed tapestry insert of this purse is centered on a super-fine beaded background. The delicate ribbon and rose motif is finished with a heavy twisted fringe. The quality of this tapestry and village scene suggest a European origin. It is 7″ by 11″ in size.

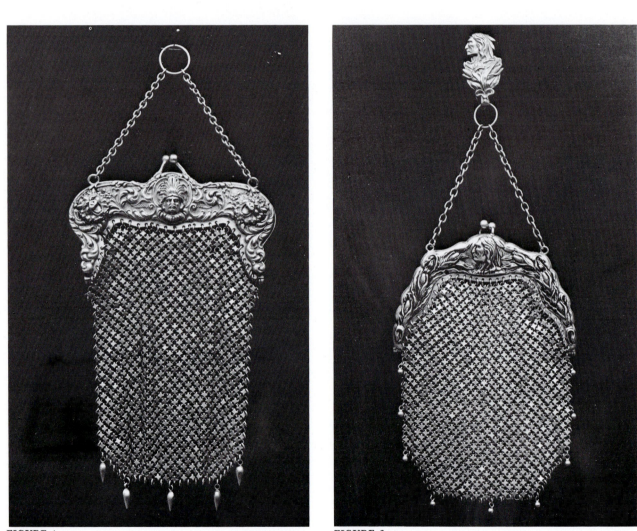

FIGURE 1

FIGURE 2

Plate 90. These Whiting and Davis flat mesh chatelaines have a value of several hundred dollars, each, thanks in part to their American Indian motif, which adds to their choiceness today. Made between 1900 and 1914, *Figure 1* is 4 1/4″ by 6 1/4″ and 159 grams sterling, *Figure 2* is 4 1/2″ by 7″ and weighs 170 grams sterling.

FIGURE 1

Plate 91. This pastel scenic tapestry is of superior quality, with an ornate brass frame set with lapiz cabachons. The reverse side features a rose within a scroll. It is 8″ by 4 1/2″. (*Courtesy of Mary Lauderdale.*)

FIGURE 2

FIGURE 1   **FIGURE 2**

PLATE 92. Early 19th Century Chinese K'ssu panels, probably taken from a wall hanging, are here attached to a purse of suede leather. The huge jade tab is symbolically carved, and the gold thread is enhanced by yellow sub-embroidery. The figures are outlined in darker threads. The rarity, coupled with workmanship employing almost microscopic stitching, makes this one of the most valuable purses shown in this portfolio. It is 9″ by 7 1/2″ in size.

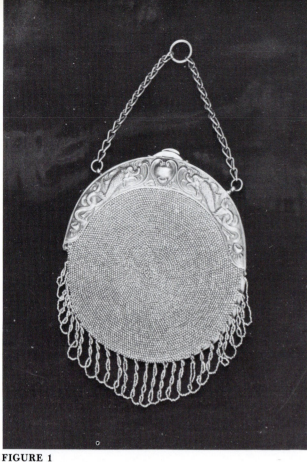

FIGURE 1

FIGURE 2

FIGURE 3

PLATE 93. Three chatelaines circa 1880-1914. *Fig. 1:* Typical solid cut steel-beaded chatelaine (minus hook), with a comical fish and entwined water lilies. The back is of suede leather and the purse measures 5 1/2″ in diameter. *Fig. 2:* Sterling mesh and frame decorated with ocean waves, cattails and crowned head of Neptune. Containing 11 1/2 ounces of sterling silver, it is a heavy chatelaine, and measures 8 1/2″ by 4 1/2″. *Fig. 3:* A velvet jet beaded body with an unusual sterling frame and hook having a matching pattern. *(Metropolitan Museum of Art, gift of Everett S. Lee.)*

283

FIGURE 2

FIGURE 3

FIGURE 4

PLATE 94. These stunning Mandalian purses illustrate the terminal decoration which secures the mesh to the base of the purse. They are 4 1/2″ by 8 1/2″. *Fig. 1:* A combination of teardrop and chain fringe. *Fig. 2:* A brilliant abstract featuring a chain fringe. *Figs. 3 & 4:* An enameled teardrop harmonizes with the pearlized body decoration.

FIGURE 1

FIGURE 2

FIGURE 3

Plate 95. Small purses are found in all cultures. These three are unique. *Figure 1:* Clear celluloid American "flappers" purse of the 1920's, decorated with subtle enamel-and rhinestone pattern. It has heavy silk tassel decoration and matching carrying cords, and measure 2 1/2″ across. *Figure 2:* Probably 19th Century Chinese, this silk purse and its silken tassels are tightly bound with silver thread. *Figure 3:* A flat purse of the U.S. Plains Indians, 6″ across, made of extra-fine beading on glazed cotton with a snap fastening and a frail bead carrying handle. Though made no later that 1900, the brilliant bead design has a contemporary feeling.

285

FIGURE 1

FIGURE 2

FIGURE 3

FIGURE 4

PLATE 96. Pearlized Mandalians and Whiting Davis "Dresden" mesh purses. Mandalian produced one of the prettiest effects in enamel mesh purses with their "Lustro Pearl." Their ads described the finish as "Essence of Pearl, a very costly solution heretofore confined to High-Grade Pearl Necklaces…now on Mandalian Mesh Bags…lustrous and silky finish positively will not chip off." *Figs. 1 and 2* are fine examples of this technique, and represent the zenith of the enameled purse. *Figs. 3 and 4* are Dresden mesh, with understated patterns which find more acceptance today than when introduced in the 1920's.

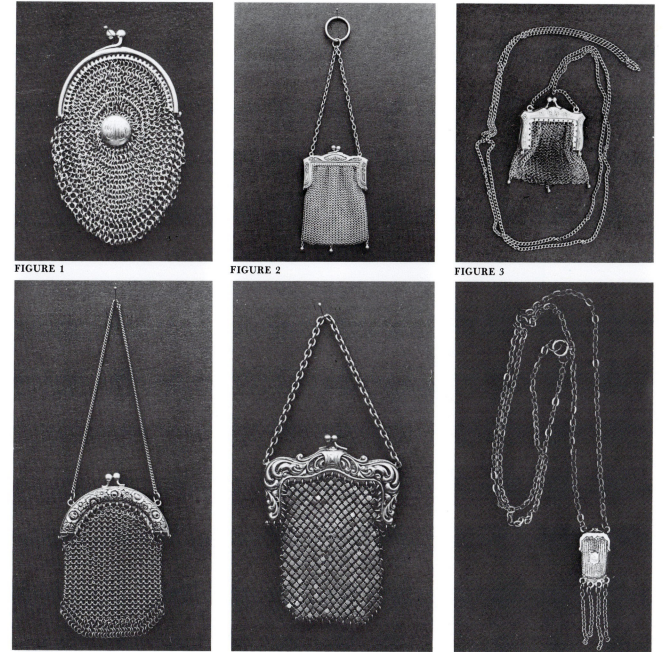

FIGURE 1

FIGURE 2

FIGURE 3

FIGURE 4

FIGURE 5

FIGURE 6

Plate 97. Six small sterling mesh purses employing various types of mesh. Sizes range from 1 1/2″ to 4″. The one with the embossed frame has a finger ring, and the long chain on another measures 30″.

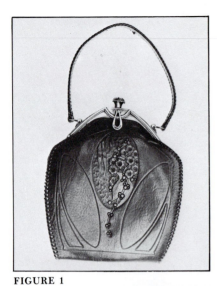

FIGURE 1

FIGURE 2

FIGURE 3

Plate 98. A sterling wrist purse (c. 1915) with enameled violets and a sapphire clasp. *Figures 3 and 4* show hand-tooled Art Nouveau purses (c. 1917-1921) with the "Turnloc" system seen in both open and closed positions.

FIGURE 4

FIGURE 5

FIGURE 6

288

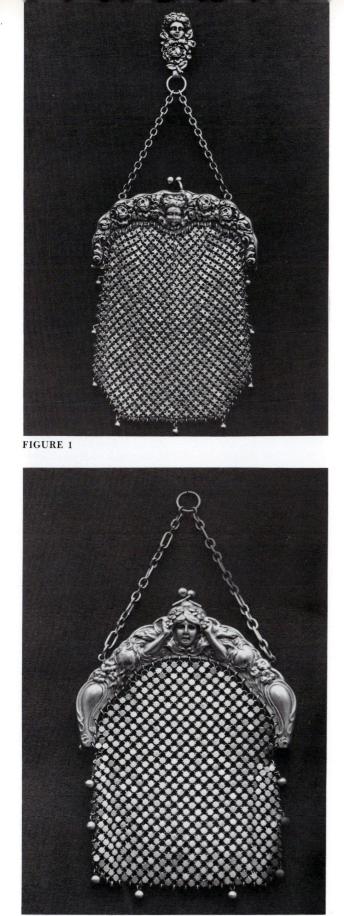

FIGURE 1

FIGURE 3

FIGURE 2

Plate 99. Both "cherub" purses are sterling silver and feature fine repousse work, with terminal decor of teardrops and balls. The purse with the Art Nouveau flower garland head is silver-plate over brass.

FIGURE 1

FIGURE 2

PLATE 100. *Fig. 1:* A showy, but finely-made sterling silver purse with repousse florals, weighing in at 11 1/2 ounces. *Fig. 2:* A gilt-colored, fine-soldered mesh, engraved with the name "Mary E. Clives" and made by the Napier Company. It has an attached compact with a mirror lid. *Fig. 3:* Soldered mesh with an attached coin holder, mirror top and sliding wrist attachment.

FIGURE 3

VALUE GUIDES, SOURCES, BIBLIOGRAPHY, INDEX

ANTIQUE COMB VALUE GUIDE

The price of combs will be greater than that charged for purses, and the truly rare comb will be very high or beyond the reach of any but the most dedicated collector or well endowed museum. There are fewer categories to consider as well. Those examples shown will be of combs and hair ornaments most likely to be available.

CELLULOID SIDE OR BACK COMBS

These are the combs most frequently seen, though they are much nicer in most cases than those currently available. They are all celluloid. *Plate 58* consists of unset examples only. *Plate 88* is of celluloid, casein, and hard rubber, some set with jet or French glass.

Plate 58

Fig. 1. $70	Fig. 6. $ 65
Fig. 2. $55	Fig. 7. $ 60
Fig. 3. $85	Fig. 8. $125
Fig. 4. $70	Fig. 9. $100
Fig. 5. $75 tiara	

Plate 59

Fig. 1. $ 95	Fig. 6. $135
Fig. 2. $145	Fig. 7. $ 95
Fig. 3. $100	Fig. 8. $ 95
Fig. 4. $125	Fig. 9. $ 70
Fig. 5. $145	Fig. 10. $110

Plate 60

Fig. 1. $ 75	Fig. 6. $ 65
Fig. 2. $165	Fig. 7. $ 80
Fig. 3. $120	Fig. 8. $ 70
Fig. 4. $ 80	Fig. 9. $150
Fig. 5. $125	

Plate 61

Fig. 1. $100	Fig. 6. $ 65
Fig. 2. $250	Fig. 7. $ 55
Fig. 3. $110	Fig. 8. $115
Fig. 4. $ 65	Fig. 9. $155
Fig. 5. $ 70	

Plate 62

Fig. 1. $110	Fig. 6. $ 65
Fig. 2. $115	Fig. 7. $ 85
Fig. 3. $165	Fig. 8. $ 95
Fig. 4. $100	Fig. 9. $110
Fig. 5. $ 85	

CARVED IVORY HIGH BACK

Plate 41
Fig. 1. $400–600
Fig. 2. $500 up
Fig. 3. $450 up

Plate 87-A
Fig. 2. $250 each up

CELLULOID LOW BACK COMBS (all set combs)

Plate 52

Fig. 1. $125	Fig. 4. $150
Fig. 2. $275	Fig. 5. $135
Fig. 3. $195	Fig. 6. $125

Plate 53

Fig. 7. $125	Fig. 10. $195
Fig. 8. $135	Fig. 11. $100
Fig. 9. $185	Fig. 12. $225

HAIR ORNAMENTS

Plate 65
Figures 2,3,5,6, about $50 each

Plate 75
From $50 to $125

HAIR PINS

Plate 28
Fig. 1. Mother-of-pearl with sterling, $85 up
Fig. 2. Gold, $55 each up, depending on the price of gold
Fig. 3. Right hand side sterling, large, $85 up

STERLING ORNAMENTAL

Plate 27
Fig. 1. $150–200 each
Fig. 2. $200–300 each

COMBS OF PRECIOUS METALS AND/OR GEM STONE ORNAMENTATION

(Sold at auction in New York, 1981–82)

Plate 91
Fig. 1. $1,500
Fig. 2. $2,500
Fig. 3. $5,000

Plate 89
Fig. 2. $800

Plate 90-A
Fig. 1. Set of three combs $750

Plate 69
Fig. 1. $3,500

This 16th century woodcut is entitled "The Combmaker." Poem reads in part: "Thou who would in order array thy locks neglected/And with comb restore thy wind-blown tresses/Hither, each one of green years, intent on love/Or woman or man, or maiden, hither come!"

TORTOISE SHELL

Plain: depends on size but not nearly as desirable as carved. Approximately ½ the price of a carved one of comparable size, age, condition, etc.

Carved:
Plate 43
Fig. 1. $175 up
Fig. 2. $600 up
Fig. 4. $95 up

Plate 64
Wedding ornament $275 up

Plate 67
Coral topped pins $300 pair

Plate 68
Ornately carved though small,
Fig. 1. $150 up

Plate 89
One of a kind comb, Fig. 3. $300 up

Plate 95
Fig. 1. One prong, two prong ornament, comb, $150 up

Plate 88
Fig. 1.–2. Small combs approximately $60 each; larger size $85 up depending on size and ornamentation. Black is not a currently popular color.

TIARAS

Tiaras are so expensive and rare it is impossible to quote any sensible prices on the diamond, coral, pearl, and those set with precious gems. Even imitation tiaras are seldom ever seen for sale in the United States, though they are found in Europe.

Pectinarius. Der Kammacher.

Quisquis inornatos disponis in ordine crines,
Pectine turbatos restituisq́ comas.
Huc viridi quæcunq́ studes in amoribus æuo,
Seu mulier, seu vir, siue puella, veni.

Hîc tibi pectinibus de millibus elige certum,
Qui placeat, fusis sitq́ medela comis.
En potes exiguis ingentia commoda nummis,
Pectinis auxilio conciliare tibi.
Manè vagos crines qui pectine comat eburno,
Auertit cerebro plurima damna suo.

APPENDIX II
ANTIQUE PURSE VALUE GUIDE

How may the value of an antique purse be ascertained? Nothing is more aggravating to antique dealers than the thoughtless person who brings items from home for the dealer to "just give some idea of the value". The same person would never consider asking for free advice from the family doctor, lawyer, accountant or other professional, but does not hesitate to keep the dealer from making other sales at shows with an endless stream of questions, (sometimes ingeniously sly, but none the less obvious to an experienced dealer) or recounting long tales about "what I have at home or gave away", (always better and cheaper than a similar item being sold).

Observing these suggestions, which really constitute nothing more than good manners, will get the collector more courteous service, and in the event the dealer cannot be solicited in a shop, bring articles for examination only after requesting permission and only when it is obvious you will not prevent the dealer from making sales, the primary reason for the dealer being at a show. Never bring a purse or comb for the purpose of evaluation under the guise of intending to sell it to a dealer unless you actually intend to sell it to *THAT* dealer.

Everyone wants to feel the items he treasures have more than sentimental value; indeed the first question asked of dealers regarding an item is not what is the quality of the piece in your opinion, or how rare is it, but how much is it worth?

How much a comb, purse, or hair ornament is worth does depend to some extent, as the wag likes to state, on how much someone is willing to pay for it, but all items no matter how insignificant have some base value, otherwise they would be worthless. It is nearly impossible to state with any absolute certainty what an individual piece will command in one section of the country as opposed to another. Who is offering the piece for sale and where, is as important as why; what condition the piece is in, its age, who made it, where it was made, its rarity, its pattern, quality of the workmanship, its design, its beauty or lack of it, its usefulness, its fragility, the conditions of sale, its weight when considering silver, carat when considering gold, and a host of other factors must be considered. As the purses found in the book are *representative* of a certain type of purse some will be used in the following price guide to enable the collector to determine the relative value of the purses they now hold and aid them in future purchases. The price given does not, nor can it in fairness to the many people who donated their purses for illustrative purposes, indicate what individual purses are worth, only what the current value of purses similar to them would be.

Antiques in general are highest on the West Coast and the Southern states; lower in the Eastern and mountain states.

The following 10 point scale was used in determining the high and low price range.
1. Uniqueness
2. Condition
3. Elaborateness of design
4. Age
5. Rarity
6. Famous or signed manufacturer
7. Size of the beads if beaded
8. Extremes in size
9. Machine or hand made
10. Precious metal or other

Beaded Purses

Fig. 5.	Plate 55	High – $ 175	Low – $125
Fig. 2.	Plate 56	High – $ 300	Low – $150
Fig. 2.	Plate 58 A	High – $ 250	Low – $150
Fig. 3.	Plate 59	High – $ 350	Low – $225
Fig. 2.	Plate 53	High – $ 125	Low – $ 75
Fig. 3.	Plate 54	High – $ 185	Low – $ 95
Fig. 5.	Plate 54	High – $ 200	Low – $100
Fig. 1.	Plate 55	High – $ 225	Low – $150
Fig. 1.	Plate 57	High – $ 250	Low – $200
Fig. 4.	Plate 57	High – $ 145	Low – $ 80
Fig. 5.	Plate 57 A	High – $ 275	Low – $175
Fig. 6.	Plate 54	High – $ 400	Low – $300
Fig. 4.	Plate 49	High – $ 175	Low – $125
Fig. 2.	Plate 49	High – $ 200	Low – $125
Fig. 4.	Plate 58 A	High – $ 85	Low – $ 55
Fig. 2.	Plate 57	High – $ 175	Low – $100
Fig. 3.	Plate 56 A	High – $ 195	Low – $125
Fig. 1.	Plate 56 A	High – $ 185	Low – $125
Fig. 5.	Plate 58	High – $ 300	Low – $225
Fig. 3.	Plate 54 A	High – $ 120	Low – $ 70

The Chatelaine Purse

Sterling

Fig. 1.	Plate 66	High – $ 250	Low – $200
Fig. 5.	Plate 66	High – $ 300	Low – $250
Fig. 2.	Plate 67	High – $ 550	Low – $300
Fig. 2.	Plate 63	High – $1,000	Priceless

Silver Plate

Fig. 3.	Plate 67	High – $ 150	Low – $ 65
Fig. 2.	Plate 66	High – $ 145	Low – $115

Aluminum

Fig. 4.	Plate 63	High – $ 140	Low – $ 65

Beads, jet

Fig. 2.	Plate 60	High – $ 135	Low – $100

18th C. Fabric

Fig. 2.	Plate 62	High – $ 600	Low – $400

Leather

Fig. 1.	Plate 63	Too rare to price	

19th C. Russian

Fig. 3.	Plate 63	High – $ 350	Low – $200

Chatelaine without hook: Reduce the price in most cases by $50 or more

Knit and Crochet Bags

Beaded heavily	$50-up—Purse such as Fig. 4. Plate 46
Beaded lightly	$40-up—Purse such as Fig. 3. Plate 44 for example
Unbeaded	$20-up—No example shown

Fabrics

Beaded with intricate pattern	Plate 26	Fig. 5 High – $ 200	Low – $ 100
Beaded with simple pattern	Plate 82	Fig. 6 High – $ 85	Low – $ 50
Unbeaded	Plate 44	Fig. 3 High – $ 75	Low – $ 35
Unbeaded plain	Plate 74	Fig. 4 High – $ 80	Low – $ 50
Embroidered	Plate 71	High – $ 85	Low – $ 40

French Steel Cut Beads

Heavily beaded gold & silver only	Plate 56 A	Fig. 4	High – $175	Low – $125
Light beading gold & silver only	Plate 68	Fig. 6	High – $ 75	Low – $ 50
Heavily beaded various colors	Plate 54 A	Fig. 4	High – $400	Low – $275
Ornate pattern various colors	See Chapter 9		High – $600	Low – $400

Indian Bags

Plate 52	Fig. 5	High – $150	Low – $ 75
Plate 52	Fig. 2	High – $135	Low – $ 65
Plate 52	Fig. 4	High – $200	Low – $100

Indian Purses (not shown)*

Dreamer bag c. 1850	Plains Indians	$3,000
Trade cloth c. 1870	Nez Perces Indians	$ 300
Hide bag with tassels c. 1900	Woodlands Indians	$ 350–500
Overall multicolored beads c. 1900	Sioux Indians	$ 400–600
Beads sewn in rows c. 1890	Crow Indians	$ 150
Sinew sewn on buffalo hide c. 1850	Plateau Indians	$ 500–700
Completely quilled hide bag c. 1860	Arapahoe Indians	$3,000–5,000

*Courtesy American Indian Artifact Company, Watsonville, California

Ivory

Usually very small purses carved on one side only.

Plate 70	Fig. 1	High – $250	Low – $175
Plate 70	Fig. 3	High – $300	Low – $200

Misers Purses

Over 18″ are probably older and worth more.

Plate 32	Fig. 2	High – $120	Low – $ 70
Plate 32	Fig. 3	High – $150	Low – $125
Plate 32	Fig. 5	High – $165	Low – $145
Plate 32	Fig. 7	High – $200	Rare color
Plate 33	Fig. 2	High – $100	Low – $ 60
Plate 33	Fig. 3	High – $150	Low – $100

German Silver Purses

Plate 39	Fig. 1	High – $ 85	Low – $ 65
Plate 39	Fig. 2	High – $135	Low – $ 75
Plate 39	Fig. 3	High – $ 75	Low – $ 35
Plate 39	Fig. 4	High – $125	Low – $ 70

Sterling Pursettes, Coin Holders, and Vanities

Plate 41	Fig. 1	High – $175	Low – $135
Plate 41	Fig. 2	High – $ 65	Low – $ 35
Plate 41	Fig. 3	High – $120	Low – $ 50
Plate 42	Fig. 3	High – $225	Low – $150
Plate 42	Fig. 6	High – $250	Low – $125

Miniatures

Very difficult to price. As a rule of thumb perhaps ½ of the price of standard size similar purse.

Name Brand Purses

Cartier may run upwards from $1,000 depending on the ornateness.

Elizabeth Arden	Plate 83	Fig. 3	$150 depending on the fittings, condition
Josef of Paris	Plate 58 A	Fig. 6	$100

Needlepoint, Petitpoint, Tapestry

Needlepoint, petitpoint and hand woven tapestry are worth at least $100 if in good condition, attractive, and nicely framed. In Europe such pieces are extremely expensive and are more highly regarded than in the United States.

Plate 78	Fig. 7	High – $200	Low – $150
Plate 78	Fig. 6	High – $250	Low – $200
Plate 78	Fig. 1	High – $150	Low – $100
Plate 78	Fig. 3	High – $250	Low – $200
Plate 78	Fig. 4	High – $250	Low – $200
Plate 78	Fig. 5	High – $275	Low – $200
Plate 78A	Fig. 4	High – $400	Low – $150

(Reticules considered under beaded bags and other classifications.)

Leather and Reptiles

Tooled leathers	Art Nouveau	Plate 80	Fig. 3	$150–225
Tooled leathers	20th century	Plate 80	Fig. 1–2	$100–145
Alligator	$ 90 up			
Crocodile	$100 up			
Ostrich	$100 up			
Lizard	$ 60 up			

Whiting-Davis and other Mesh Purses

Plate 35	Fig. 1	High – $175	Low – $100
Plate 35	Fig. 2	High – $175	Low – $110
Plate 35	Fig. 3	High – $250	Low – $150
Plate 35	Fig. 4	High – $300	Low – $225
Plate 35	Fig. 5	High – $200	Low – $155
Plate 35	Fig. 6	High – $300	Low – $225
Plate 35	Fig. 8	High – $275	Low – $175
Plate 36	Fig. 3	High – $275	Low – $200
Plate 36	Fig. 4	High – $250	Low – $200
Plate 36	Fig. 5	High – $135	Low – $ 85

The price of gold mesh handbags depends to some extent on the price of gold at any given moment. Gold has fluctuated from a high of nearly $900 and a low of $320 so it is nearly impossible to state accurately what a gold mesh purse is worth but if these prices seem high, they are in line with those which have been quoted on similar purses during the last three years.

Plate 34	Fig. 1	$1,500
Plate 34	Fig. 2	$ 185
Plate 34	Fig. 3	$3,000
Plate 34	Fig. 4	$1,200

Sterling Mesh

Plate 37	Fig. 1	$250
Plate 37	Fig. 2	$275

INSTITUTIONS OWNING PURSE AND/OR COMB COLLECTIONS

Brooklyn Museum
Eastern Parkway, Brooklyn
New York 11238
Phone: 212-638-5000
Days: Wed.-Sat. 10-5,
Sun 1-5, Closed Mon.
and Tues.
Admission: Contribution
Collections: Among the best
in the United States of
both combs and purses.

Cincinnati Art Museum
Eden Park   45326
Phone: 513-721-5204
Days: Tues.-Sat. 10-5,
Sun. 1-5
Admission: $1.00
Collections: Costumes and
textiles.

Clinton Historical Society
Mr. John J. Graves, Curator
210 Church Street, Clinton,
Massachusetts 01510
Phone: 617-368-0084
Days: Contact for
appointment.
Admission: Free
Collections: Combs
including the Harris Comb,
general line of antiques.

Cooper Hewitt Museum
2 East 91st Street, New York
City, N.Y. 10028
Phone: 212-860-6868
Days: Tues. 10-9,
Wed.-Sat. 10-5, Sun. 12-5,
Closed Monday.
Admission: Free
Collections: Both combs and
purses, some very old.

**Daughters of the American
Revolution Museum**
1776 D Street, N.W.,
Washington, D.C. 20006
Phone: 202-628-1776
Phone or write for particulars.

**M.H. deYoung Memorial
Museum**
Golden Gate Park, Great
Highway and Stanyan
Streets, San Francisco,
California, 94121
Phone: 415-558-2887
Days: Wed.-Sun. 10-5
Admission: Adults $1.50,
Free first Wed. of month
Collections: Both categories.

Essex Institute
161 Essex Street, Salem,
Massachusetts
Phone: 617-745-9500
Days: Mon.-Sat. 10-5,
Sun. 1-5
Admission: $1.50
Collections: Both categories

Fine Arts Museum, Boston
465 Huntington Avenue,
Boston, Massachusetts 02115
Phone: 617-267-9300
Days: Tues. 10-9,
Wed.-Sun. 10-5,
Great dining facility
Admission: Tues.-Sat.
$2.00, Sun. $1.25,
Free Tues. 9-5
Collections: Outstanding
collection of purses. Fewer
combs, but nice.

**Greenfield Village
Henry Ford Museum**
Village Road and Oakwood
Boulevard, Dearborn,
Michigan 48126

Phone: 313-963-0879
Days: Daily 9-6
Admission: Adults over 65
$4.00/under $4.75
Collections: Fine collection
of combs.

**Gulbenkian, Calouste
Foundation**
Avenue De Berna 45-A 1093
Losboa, Lisbon, Portugal
Days and admission fees:
Write for particulars
Collections: The most
comprehensive collection of
Rene Lalique in the world,
including some fantastic
combs.

**Leominster Historical
Society**
17 School Street,
Leominster,
Massachusetts 01453
Phone: 617-537-5424
Days: Mon., Wed., Fri. 10-3
Tours of the museum for
recognized groups may be
arranged at the mutual
convenience of the groups
Admission: Free, donation
Collections: Fine collection
of combs, possibly the best
in the United States which
can readily be seen. Contact
Mrs. Evelyn Hachey.

Mercer Museum
Pine and Ashland Streets,
Doylestown,
Pennsylvania 18901
Phone: 215-345-0210
Days: Tues.-Sun. 10-5,
Closed January through
March

Admission: Adults $2.00,
over 65 $1.50
Collections: Outstanding
permanent collections of all
sorts of things. Comb-
making tool collection the
best in the United States.
Some horn and tortoise
combs.

**Metropolitan Museum
of Art**
Fifth Avenue and 82nd
Streets, New York City,
New York 10028
Phone: 212-870-5500
Days: Closed Monday,
Wed.-Sat. 10-4:45,
Sun. 11-4:45
Admission: By contribution
Collections: Superb
collections of both combs
and purses, purse collection
more extensive. Covers
bags from 17th century.
Combs from the 18th
century, mostly domestic.
If planning to visit the
Costume Institute, write
well in advance for permission to visit. Reference
library open to qualified
researchers, write or call.
One of the world's great
museums and one of the
largest, the staff are the
most accommodating of
any museum and are a joy
to deal with.

Continued on next page

Institutions Owning Collections—continued

Millers Museum of Antique Combs
Box 316 Homer,
Alaska 99603
Phone: 907-235-8819
Days: As the museum is not as yet open to the public, advise writing or telephone.
Admission:
Collections: Outstanding collection of combs. Entire museum devoted to combs and headdress. Owners are Betty and Ralph Miller. The town is small but very scenic.

Museum of the City of New York
Fifth Avenue at 103 St.,
New York City, N.Y. 10029
Phone: 212-534-1672
Days: Weekdays 10–5, Sun. 1–5
Admission: Free
Collections: Costumed mannequins showing both purses and combs.

Old Sturbridge Village
Sturbridge,
Massachusetts 01566
Phone: 617-347-3362
Days: Daily 9:30–5:30, Closed Monday from Nov. 1–April 1 and holidays
Admission: $7.00
Collections: Purse and rare pockets and pocketbooks, in bookstore area. Extensive grounds and a great deal to see. Not the run-of-the-mill attraction.

Smithsonian Institution
On the Mall, Jefferson Drive, 9th and 12th Streets, N.W. Washington, D.C.
Phone: 202-357-2700
Days: Daily 10–5:30, extended summer hours
Admission: Free
Collections: Various collections housed in several museums. Martha Washington purse in First Ladies' Hall, National Museum of American History and Technology.

Victoria and Albert Museum
South Kensington,
London SW7 2RL
Phone: 01-589-6371
Days: Daily
Admission:
Collections: Extensive textile collections, some combs.

Walters Art Gallery
600 North Charles Street, Baltimore, Maryland 21201
Phone: 301-547-9000
Days: Tues.–Thurs. 11–4, Sun. and holidays 2–5, extended summer hours.
Admission: Free
Collections: Some extra-ordinary combs, many European from as early as the 5th and 6th centuries B.C. through the 19th century.

Wadsworth Atheneum
Main and Prospect Streets, Hartford,
Connecticut 06120
Phone: 203-278-2670
Days: Tues., Wed., and Fri. 11–3, Thurs. 11–8, Sat.–Sun. 11–5
Admission: Adults $2.00; over 65, $1.00
Collections: Many purses and combs which are being catalogued. Write or phone for information.

Winterthur
The Henry Francis DuPont Winterthur Museum, Delaware 19735
Phone: 302-656-8591
Days:
Admission: Write for information on price and reservations
Collections: Fine collections of both combs and purses.

Please note that many museums have extensive holdings which have not been catalogued for one reason or another and they are kept until this can be accomplished before a special display is made of them. They accompany costumes as accessories of dress but are seldom, if ever, exhibited as independent categories. It is wise to write well in advance of visiting an institution to state your purpose and request permission to see collections, if such can be arranged. All museums have been very helpful and their collections will be varied, rare, and in some cases, priceless, so do not expect to be able to handle the specimens nor use the facilities unaccompanied by museum personnel.

BEAD SOURCES:

Bead Store, The
417 Castro St.
San Francisco, Calif. 94114

Berger Specialty Company
413 East 8th St.
Los Angeles, Calif. 90010

Ditmar
4 West 37th St.
New York, New York 10018

Elliot, Green and Company
37 West 37th St.
New York, New York 10018

Fashion Company, The
35 Carson Avenue St.
San Francisco, Calif. 94114

Frankel, Fred
19 West 38th St.
New York, New York 10018

Gampel Supply Corp.
39 West 37th St.
New York, New York 10018

Grey Owl Indian Craft Manufacturers
150-02 Beaver Road
Jamaica, New York 11433

Har Man Importing Company
48 West 37th St.
New York, New York 10018

House of Beads
828 Lincoln Road
Miami Beach, Florida

Margola Import Corporation
48 West 37th St.
New York, New York 10018

Northern California Bead Society
1580 B Solano Ave.
Albany, California 94707

Ostro, David, Inc.
833 South Spring St.
Los Angeles, California

Rosenberg, Joseph
39 West 38th St.
New York, New York 10018

Source
1 Kansas
San Francisco, California

Walbead
38 West 37th St.
New York, New York 10018

Wepra
49 West 37th St.
New York, New York 10018

Western Trading Post
32 Broadway
Denver, Colorado 80209

Winagura Company
10606 Venice Blvd.
Culver City, Calif. 90230

Venerable Bead, The
2990 Adeline
Berkeley, Calif. 94703

Yone Inc.
478 Union St.
San Francisco, Calif.

DEALERS IN COMBS AND PURSES:

This is a partial listing and a limited one at best. If you know of dealers who carry combs and/or purses as a regular part of their stock, have outstanding collections, or are able to obtain them, such information would be greatly appreciated by writing to the publisher's address found in the front of this volume.

Beddoe, Dani
P.O. Box 480104
Los Angeles, Calif. 90048

Best of Everything
242 East 77th St.
New York, New York

Cheap Jacks
167 1st Avenue
New York, New York

Creek Hill Shop
177 Bartlett
Portsmouth, N.H. 03801

Early Halloween
180 9th Avenue
New York, New York

Heart's Desire
Central Avenue
Highland Park, Ill. 60035

Helms House Antiques
P. O. Box 5457
Carmel, Calif. 93921

Holiner, Richard
101 E. Jennings
Newburgh, Indiana 47630

Johnsons Antiques
127 East Clark Avenue
Orcutt, Calif. 93455

Kasbah
85 2nd Avenue
New York, New York

Love, Harriet
412 West Broadway
New York, New York

Nassau, Lillian
22 East 57th St.
New York, New York 10022

Starr, Jana
236 East 80th St.
New York, New York

Stitch in Time
5712 San Jose St.
Richmond, Calif. 94804

Trouve
1200 Lexington Avenue
New York, New York 10001

Venerable Bead, The
2990 Adeline
Berkeley, Calif. 94703

PURSE REPAIRS

Aaron Willet
303 East 51st St.
New York, New York

Abraham and Straus
420 Fulton St.
Brooklyn, New York 11233

Alligator on the Rug, Inc.
1057 Madison Avenue
New York, New York 10001

Continued on next page

Artbag Creations, Inc.
735 Madison Avenue
New York, New York 10001

A Stitch in Time
1712 San Jose St.
Richmond, Calif. 94804

Chambre, Kurt
8406 West 3rd St.
Los Angeles, Calif. 90020

J. and G. Shoe Repair
2079 East 4th St.
Cleveland, Ohio 44114

Kaye
10 West 32nd St.
New York, New York 10001

Lester Bags
669 Madison Avenue
New York, New York 10001

Modern Leather Goods
11 West 32nd St.
New York, New York 10001

Shoil's Handbags
1110 Avenue J
Brooklyn, New York 11230

Venerable Bead, The
(See dealers)

VINTAGE CLOTHING SHOPS

An often overlooked source, particularly for purses, is the vintage clothing shop found in larger cities, sophisticated suburbs and some resort areas. The fare is usually from the 1930–1950's but some lovely turn-of-the-century purses are frequently interspersed and the price compares favorably with those found elsewhere. The following are good prospective sources for those living in or near the San Francisco, California area. A few other areas have also been discovered.

The Best of Everything
2121 Fillmore St.
San Francisco, Calif. 94123

Bizarre Bazaar
5634 College Ave.
Oakland, Calif. 94618

DeLelio's
1739 A Union St.
San Francisco, Calif. 94123

Grand Illusions
1604 Union St.
San Francisco, Calif. 94123

Look Sharp
1431 A Castro St.
San Francisco, Calif. 94131

Masquerade
2237 Union St.
San Francisco, Calif. 94123

Matinee
1124 Polk St.
San Francisco, Calif. 94109

Nostalgia
2649 South Bayshore Dr.
Coconut Grove, Miami, Fla. 33133

Old Gold
2380 Market St.
San Francisco, Calif. 94102

Painted Lady
1838 Divisadero
San Francisco, Calif. 94115

Reincarnation
214 17th St.
Pacific Grove, Calif. 93950

Shadows of Forgotten Ancestors
503 Magnolia
Larkspur, Calif. 94939

The Snow House
Columbus, Ohio 43200

The Way We Wore
1952 Union St.
San Francisco, Calif. 94123

SELECTED BIBLIOGRAPHY

Books

Armstrong, Nancy, *Victorian Jewelry,* Macmillan Publishing Co. Inc., 1976.

Binder, Pearl, *Muffs and Morals,* Dead Soldier Press, 1954.

Blum, Stella, *Victorian Fashions and Costumes from Harper's Bazaar, 1867–1898,* Dover Publications, New York, 1974

Bradford, Ernle, *Four Centuries of European Jewelry,* Spring Books, Great Britain, 1967.

Braun and Schneider, *Historic Costume in Pictures,* 1861–1890, Munich, Germany. Reprint by Dover, 1975.

Buck, Ann M., *Victorian Costume Accessories,* Universe Books, New York, 1970.

Child, Theodore, *Wimples and Crisping Pins,* Harpers, New York, 1895.

Croson, R. *Fashions in Hair,* Peter Owen, London, 1965.

Courtais, Georginne de, *Women's Headdress and Hairstyles, A.D. 600 to the Present Day,* B.T. Batsford Ltd., London, 1974.

Cox, Warren, E., *Chinese Ivory Sculpture,* Bonanza Books, New York, 1946.

Crossman, Carl L., *The China Trade,* The Pyne Press, Princeton, New Jersey, 1973.

Cunningham, C. Willett, *English Women's Clothing in the Present Century,* Faber and Faber Ltd., 1952.

Davenport, Millia, *The Book of Costume,* Crown Publishers, New York, 1948.

Doyle, Bernard, *Combmaking in America,* Perry Walton, Boston, 1925.

Earle, Alice Morse, *Two Centuries of Costume in America 1620–1820,* Macmillan Co., New York, 1903 (Dover 1970).

Edwards, Joan, *Bead Embroidery,* Taplenger, New York, 1966.

Evans, Joan, *A History of Jewelry 1100–1870,* Faber and Faber, 1970.

Field, June, *Collecting Georgian and Victorian Crafts,* Scribner's, New York, 1973.

Flower, Margaret, *Victorian Jewelry,* A.S. Barnes, 1973.

Foster, Vanda, *Bags and Purses* The Costume Accessories Series, B.T. Batsford, London, 1982.

Fregnac, Claude, *Jewelry from the Renaissance to Art Nouveau,* Octopus Books, London, 1973.

Gayside, Ann, *Jewelry: Ancient to Modern,* Viking Press, New York, 1979.

Gere, Charlotte, *American and European Jewelry,* 1830–1914, Crown, New York, 1975.

Gere, Charlotte, *Victorian Jewelry Design,* Henry Regnery Co., Chicago, Illinois, 1972.

Gerlach, Martin, *Primitive and Folk Jewelry,* Dover Press, New York, 1971, Reprint.

Giafferri, Paul L., *Millinery in the Fashion History of the World,* The Illustrated Milliner, New York, 1928.

Gill, Anne, *Beadwork,* Watson-Guptill, 1977.

Gregorietti, Guido, *Jewelry Through the Ages,* Crescent Books, New York, 1969.

Grover, S., *A History of Needlework Tools and Accessories,* Arco, New York, 1973.

Hart, Harold, S., *Jewelry: A Pictorial Archive of Woodcuts and Engravings,* Dover Press, New York, 1977.

Heiniger, Ernest, *The Great Book of Jewels,* New York Graphic Society, Boston, 1974.

Hughes, Therle, *English Domestic Needlework,* Abbey Fine Arts, London.

Kubalova, L., *Pictorial Encyclopedia of Fashion,* Hanlyn, London, 1968.

Lester, Katherine, *Accessories of Dress,* Manual Arts Press, Illinois, 1940.

Little, Frances, *Early American Textiles,* New York, 1931.

Lord, P., and Taylor, D., *The Folk Arts and Crafts of New England,* Chilton Co., Philadelphia, 1965.

McClellan, Elizabeth, *History of American Costume,* 1607–1870, Tudor, New York, 1937.

McClinton, Katherine, *Antiques Past and Present,* Clarkson and Potter Inc., New York, 1971.

Meen, V.B. Tushingham, A.D., *Crown Jewels of Iran,* University of Toronto Press, Toronto, 1975.

Moore, Doris, *The Woman in Fashion,* B.T. Batsford, New York, 1949.

Morris, B., *Victorian Embroidery,* Universe, New York, 1970.

Mourey, Gabriel, and Allance, Aymer, *Art Nouveau and Fans,* Dover, New York, 1973. Reprint.

Payne, Blanche, *History of Costume,* Harper & Row, New York, 1965.

Revi, Albert, *The Spinning Wheel's Complete Book of Antiques,* Grosset and Dunlap, New York, 1972.

Saito, R., *Japanese Coiffure,* Board of Tourist Industry, Tourist Library, Vol. #28, 1939.

Continued on next page

Bibliography—continued

Schmitt, F., *Manuel du Fabricant de Boutons and Peignes,* Librairie J.B. Bailliere et Fils, Paris, 1923.

Shikosha, (Publishers) Kyota, Japan, *Kushi Kanzashi Ten,* 1978.

Swain, Margaret, *Historical Needlework,* Barrie and Jenkins, 1970.

Swan, Susan, *Plain and Fancy,* Holt, Rhinehart, Winston, New York, 1977.

Swanson, Robert, *Plastics Technology,* McKnight Publishing Co., Bloomington, Illinois, 1965.

Trustees of the British Museum, *Jewelry Through 7000 Years,* Barrons, New York, 1976.

Waddell, Roberta, *The Art Nouveau Style,* Librairie Centrale des Beaux Arts, Paris, 1897–1911 (Dover, 1977).

White, Mary, *How To Do Bead Work,* Doubleday Page Co., 1904 (Dover, 1974).

Whiteford, Andrew Hunter, *North American Indian Arts,* Golden Press, New York, 1973.

Whiting, Gertrude, *Old-Time Tools and Toys of Needlework,* Columbia University Press, New York, 1928.

Wilcox, Ruth, *The Mode in Hats and Headdress,* Scribners, New York, 1959.

Willet, C., *Handbook of English Costume in the 18th Century,* London, 1957.

Wilson, Henry, *Silverwork and Jewelry,* Pitman Publishing, 1902 (1978 Reprint).

Winter, Ferdinand, *The Combs of All Times to the Present Day,* Leipiz, 1907.

Magazines and Catalogs

From the Lands of the Scythians, The Metropolitan Museum of Art Bulletin, No. 5., 1973–74.

Hair, Cooper Hewitt Hair Exhibition, The Smithsonian Institution's National Museum of Design Show, June 10–August 17, 1980.

Hazens Panorama of Professions and Trades, 1863.

Japanese Art Lacquers, Kushi Kogai, Sophia University, Tokyo, 1961.

Le Chapeau Parisien, April, 1912.

Marshall Field, 1899.

Montgomery Ward, 1895.

Priscilla Beadwork Book, 1911.

Richter and Phillips Wholesale Jewelry Catalogue, 1929.

Sears and Roebuck, 1899, 1925.

Sotheby's Antique and Period Jewelry, February 10, 1982.

Unger Brothers Sterling, 1904.

Manuscripts

Durant, William H., *The Comb Industry,* Leominster Daily Enterprise, August 24, 1923.

Field, Caleb, *Statistics of Comb Making in Leominster,* 1852. Rice Press, Worcester, Massachusetts.

Harris, Rendell J., *The Comb in Human History,* Cambridge University, 1927.

Little, Arthur D., *On the Making of Silk Purses from Sow's Ears,* Cambridge, Massachusetts, 1921.

INDEX